Information Age Economy

Information Age Economy

K. Sandbiller
Dezentralität und Markt in Banken
1998. ISBN 3-7908-1101-7

M. Roemer
Direktvertrieb kundenindividueller
Finanzdienstleistungen
1998. ISBN 3-7908-1102-5

F. Rose
The Economics, Concept, and Design
of Information Intermediaries
1999. ISBN 3-7908-1168-8

Sascha Weber

Information Technology in Supplier Networks

A Theoretical Approach to Decisions about Information Technology and Supplier Relationships

With 75 Figures
and 5 Tables

Springer-Verlag Berlin Heidelberg GmbH

Dr. Sascha Weber
SAP AG
IBS Discrete Industries
Neurottstraße 16
69189 Walldorf
Germany

ISBN 978-3-7908-1395-1

Cataloging-in-Publication Data applied for
Die Deutsche Bibliothek – CIP-Einheitsaufnahme
Weber, Sascha: Information Technology in Supplier Networks: A Theoretical Approach to Decisions about Information Technology and Supplier Relationship; with 5 tables / Sascha Weber. – Heidelberg; New York: Physica-Verl., 2001
(Information Age Economy)

ISBN 978-3-7908-1395-1   ISBN 978-3-642-57574-7 (eBook)
DOI 10.1007/978-3-642-57574-7

© Springer-Verlag Berlin Heidelberg 2001
Originally published by Physica-Verlag Heidelberg New York in 2001

Softcover Design: Erich Kirchner, Heidelberg

SPIN 10831160   88/2202-5 4 3 2 1 0 – Printed on acid-free paper

To my wife Niran and to my parents.

Preface

The present work by Sascha Weber addresses procurement which deals with business partners beyond the boundaries of one's organization. Procurement refers to the function of purchasing goods and services from suppliers, whether raw material used to manufacture an organization's final products, maintenance and repair supplies, or capital goods such as machinery and buildings. Major decisions in procurement concern the selection of the right suppliers with whom to establish a business relationship, the design of purchasing contracts, and the selection of information technology used to support the procurement process. In recent years the progress in information technology not only provided opportunities to rationalize the existing way of organizing procurement, but also opened up new ways of conducting business as the emergence of virtual enterprises and electronic markets may indicate.

The objective of Sascha Weber's research is to analyze and answer the question of how the use of information technology and expected progress influences procurement decisions of an organization. The analysis is conducted identifying important parameters which describe the relevant properties of information technology and supplier relationships. Information technology is distinguished firstly in terms of the task which is supported between information technology used to support the evaluation of potential suppliers and information technology for the support of the execution of a supplier relationship. Secondly, for each of these categories it is distinguished to what extent it affects the efficiency of information exchange and to what extent it is disseminated among potential suppliers, whereas supplier relationships are distinguished in respect of the duration and price of the underlying contracts. A formal model is used to represent the compound decisions concerning the selection of suppliers and the use of information technology. The model follows a microeconomic approach, i.e. its scope is a single organization and its supplier relationships.

The research disciplines of information systems and economics profit from this research by new insights gained through the integration of the concepts of search theory and transaction cost theory. These insights contribute to an improved understanding of the interdependence between the selection of and progress in information technology and the coordination of economic activities, which is still a topic of lively debate in the literature (see e.g. (Malone, Yates et al. 1987; Clemons, Reddi et al. 1993; Brynjolfsson, Malone et al. 1994)). The wider benefits to industry are primarily related to better methodological support of decisions on investments in information technology and supplier relationships. Moreover, software companies can profit in their pricing decisions and diffusion strategies for their products.

February 2001

Wolfgang König

Acknowledgements

This thesis originated from the research on the standardization of information systems at the Institute of Information Systems at the Johann Wolfgang Goethe University in Frankfurt. During discussions about the coordination of economic activities and the use of information technology, questions about the interdependences of decisions about the use of information technology and the design of supplier relationships arose. This was the starting point for the development of a theoretical approach to analyse these decisions.

I feel it necessary to offer heartfelt thanks to those people who contributed to the quality and the success this work has achieved:

Professor Dr. Wolfgang König who gave me the chance to work on this thesis with much freedom as well as time and resources for my ideas.

Professor Dr. Gerriet Müller for his review of my work and to Professor Dr. Eberhard Feess and Professor Dr. Heinz Isermann for their participation in the disputation.

Professor Dr. Peter Buxmann who contributed to the initial idea of this thesis as well as Markus Fricke, Markus Konstroffer, Frank Rose, and Falk von Westarp for invaluable discussions.

I am especially indebted to Professor Paul Swatman for making it possible to do parts of my research at Deakin University in Geelong, Australia, and to Phil Joyce and Professor Ross Smith for their excellent support in organizing the structure of this thesis.

Many thanks go to Bill Mc Cann for carefully reading the manuscript.

My deep appreciation to my wife Niran for her continuous and affectionate aid.

Finally, I am very grateful to my parents for their excellent support in all stages of my education.

Sascha Weber

Table of Contents

1 Introduction 1
  1.1 Research motivation 1
  1.2 Research objectives 6
  1.3 Research benefits 7
  1.4 Structure of the thesis 7
2 Supplier Relationships 9
  2.1 Basic aspects of supplier relationships 9
    2.1.1 Supplier relationships and procurement 9
    2.1.2 Procurement in the value chain of an organization 12
    2.1.3 Institutionalizing the management of supplier relationships 16
    2.1.4 Contracts in supplier relationships 18
      2.1.4.1 Purchasing contracts in theory 19
      2.1.4.2 Purchasing contracts in practice 21
    2.1.5 Phases of supplier relationships 24
      2.1.5.1 Evaluation phase 25
      2.1.5.2 Settlement phase 42
  2.2 Assessment of supplier relationships 43
    2.2.1 Transaction costs 44
      2.2.1.1 Asset specificity 47
      2.2.1.2 Uncertainty in terms of transaction and behavior 48
      2.2.1.3 Complexity of transaction and good 48
      2.2.1.4 Frequency of a transaction 49
      2.2.1.5 Fundamental transformation 50
    2.2.2 Production costs 50
      2.2.2.1 Economies of scale 51
      2.2.2.2 Capacity utilization 51
      2.2.2.3 Efficiency gains by specialization 51
      2.2.2.4 Arbitrage between industrial sectors and/or
              geographical locations 52
      2.2.2.5 Opportunity costs of suboptimal capital allocation 52
    2.2.3 Optimal governance structure 52

3   Information Technology **59**

  3.1   Basic aspects of information technology 59

    3.1.1   Theory of network effects 63

    3.1.2   Standards 70

      3.1.2.1   Compatibility standards 71

      3.1.2.2   Quality standards 72

      3.1.2.3   De jure standards 73

      3.1.2.4   De facto standards 74

  3.2   Information technology for the support of supplier relationships **75**

    3.2.1   Procurement applications 78

    3.2.2   Supplier search and electronic catalogs 81

    3.2.3   Information technology in the negotiation phase 88

      3.2.3.1   Electronic auctions 89

      3.2.3.2   Negotiation support systems 93

    3.2.4   Standards for structuring the communication process in the
settlement phase 98

      3.2.4.1   Open-EDI 101

      3.2.4.2   Interorganizational Procedures (InterProcs) 102

      3.2.4.3   Open Applications Group Integration Specifications
(OAGIS) 104

      3.2.4.4   Open Trading Protocol (OTP) 107

      3.2.4.5   Open Buying on the Internet (OBI) 111

    3.2.5   Standards for structuring communication objects 115

      3.2.5.1   The syntactic level: languages for the specification of
standards 118

      3.2.5.2   Standards on the semantic level 131

    3.2.6   Information technology and transaction costs 136

      3.2.6.1   Evaluation cost reductions 136

      3.2.6.2   Settlement cost reductions 138

  3.3   Information technology and changing supplier relationships **142**

    3.3.1   The move to the market hypothesis 143

    3.3.2   The move to the middle hypothesis 146

    3.3.3   Provisional results 148

**4   Decisions about Supplier Relationships and Information
Technology** **150**

  **4.1   The progress of information technology and the state preference
approach** **150**

  4.2   The basic model of supplier selection decisions **154**

    4.2.1   Acquisition and evaluation costs 157

    4.2.2   Settlement costs 162

    4.2.3   Costs of keeping the current transaction partner 162

4.2.4   Properties of the basic model...164
  4.2.4.1   Marginal evaluation costs.................................164
  4.2.4.2   Transaction volume 165
  4.2.4.3   Riskiness of the price distribution 166
  4.2.4.4   Mean value of the price distribution...............169
  4.2.4.5   Initialization costs..173
  4.2.4.6   Adaptation costs 173
  4.2.4.7   Frequency of a transaction...............................173
  4.2.4.8   Costs of exchanging the goods 174

4.2.5   Decisions in the basic model 174
  4.2.5.1   Transaction partner selection...........................174
  4.2.5.2   Outsourcing 186
  4.2.5.3   Determining the optimal contract duration.................190

4.3   Extending the basic model: the selection of information technology...200

4.3.1   Modeling the selection of information technology....................200

4.3.2   Properties of the extended model 204

4.3.3   Decisions in the extended model................................206
  4.3.3.1   The duration of supplier contracts under the condition of changing technology diffusion.............................206
  4.3.3.2   The selection of information technology under the condition of newly emerging solutions 221

5   Conclusion 232

5.1   Summary 232

5.1.1   Information technology and transaction costs 236

5.1.2   Reduced transaction costs and the design of supplier contracts 236

5.1.3   Growing dissemination of information technology and the duration of supplier contracts 237

5.1.4   The adoption of new information technology............................238

5.2   Implications for the management of supplier relationships............239

5.3   Outlook 242

6   References.. 244

7   Appendices.. 257

7.1   Appendix A: proof of (eq. 35) 257

7.2   Appendix B: proof of non-negative values of (eq. 63).....................258

7.3   Appendix C: proof of (eq. 80) 258

7.4   Appendix D: proof of (eq. 108) 259

7.5   Appendix E: proof of (eq. 130)...259

8   List of Figures 261

9 List of Tables.. 265
10 List of Used Symbols 266
11 List of Abbreviations 271

1 Introduction

This thesis concerns the impact of advances in information technology on procurement decisions in organizations. The analysis focuses on the optimal selection of transaction partners, the design of supplier contracts, and the choice of information technology solutions to support supplier search, supplier evaluation, and the settlement of a business relationship.

1.1 Research motivation

During recent years the environment in which decisions are taken in business has dramatically changed. Customers' demands for products to be developed and delivered ever more quickly and growing competitive pressures lead to the continual revision and rationalization of business processes in all functional areas. This dynamic development has been accompanied by reduced data processing and communication costs. Thus there is considerable potential for the rationalization of business processes in the increased use of information technology. Accordingly, information technology[1] not only provides opportunities for rationalizing existing business processes, but also opens up new ways of conducting business, as the recent emergence of virtual enterprises and electronic markets may indicate. These new possibilities are important for the competitiveness of an organization. In fulfilling the complex task of selecting the right information technology to be used in an organization the decision-maker must consider the effect of these technologies on an organization's business relationships.

---

[1] Certain authors in their terminology distinguish explicitly between information technology and communication technology which is necessary to integrate information technology components (e.g. (Picot, Reichwald et al. 1996)). The definition of information technology underlying this thesis does not make this distinction, i.e. whenever information technology is mentioned, this also implies communication technology.

In this thesis we focus on procurement, which deals with business partners beyond the boundaries of one's organization and which is a business process well suited to the use of information technology. Procurement refers to the function of purchasing goods and services from suppliers (Porter 1985, p. 40; Zenz 1994). Its functions include the purchase of a variety of goods and services, whether raw material used to manufacture an organization's final products, maintenance and repair supplies or capital goods such as machinery and buildings. Hence, procurement is an important function which usually accounts for at least one third of an organization's revenues or budget (Killen and Kamauff 1995).

A major decision in the procurement processes concerns the selection of the right suppliers with whom to establish a business relationship. Assuming that for given goods or services a relationship with a supplier already exists, this decision deals with the question of whether the current supplier should be changed. A well-founded decision requires the consideration of a number of aspects (Zenz 1994, p. 119). These are:

- The establishment of a relationship with a new supplier induces search activities to find the right supplier. These search activities are not free of cost;

- A new contract must be negotiated and an optimal contract must be agreed. A particular problem here is that of whether the new supplier can be trusted or not. A trustworthy supplier requires fewer resources to be spent on supervisory activities during the fulfillment of a contract. Moreover, if the purchasing organization can trust the reliability of a supplier, then there will be less need to adapt a supplier contract prior to its expiry;

- When a new supplier is chosen and a contract signed possible costs are incurred in actually initializing the new relationship. Once a contract with a new supplier is signed this often implies organizational and technical measures, e.g. the right employees in the buying organization must be informed about the relevant contact persons in the supplier organization and computer software must be adapted; and

- Changing a supplier can be expected to produce benefits in terms of the goods traded as well as the costs of exchanging these goods between the purchasing and supplying organizations. While the former finds expression in potentially better goods or services in terms of price and/or quality, the latter manifests itself in the more efficient way these goods are exchanged between the purchasing and selling organizations.

To establish a methodological basis for a decision on supplier relationships which takes these aspects into account, the well developed principles of transaction cost economy (Williamson and Masten 1995) and search theory (Hey 1981) can contribute valuable insights.

In transaction cost theory the notion of a transaction refers to the transfer of titles (Williamson 1975). In the case of a supplier relationship this infers the transfer of ownership of goods or services from the supplier to the customer and, in return, the transfer of an agreed amount of compensation from the customer to the supplier. The term transaction cost describes the costs of using, securing and transferring these titles (Coase 1937; Arrow 1969; Tietzel 1981). Transaction cost economists focus on a particular business relationship and assume that transaction costs are critical for the optimal design of that relationship. The demand that the examination of efficiency and cost structures should play an important role in the analysis of business relations (Reekers and Smithson 1994, p. 3) is supported by empirical surveys which indicate that cost and time are the most important measures for successful procurement (Perlman 1990; Zenz 1994; Fearon and Bales 1997; Segev, Gebauer et al. 1998; Buxmann and Gebauer 1999). Hence, transaction cost theory can serve as a terminological framework for a detailed examination of supplier relationships and their design determinants. However, transaction cost theory does not discuss the search process which takes place before a transfer of titles can be initiated. To fill this gap the concepts of search theory can be used.

Until the advent of search theory, economists assumed that in markets with large numbers of buyers and sellers, there would be a (known) unique price. Therefore, search problems were assumed to be non-existent. However, the real world shows that this is not the case. The same product can be available at different prices in different places. Indeed, a trade-off exists. The longer one searches, the higher the probability of finding low prices and/or better quality, but the longer one searches, the more costly it is. The purpose of search theory is to develop optimal search strategies which describe how a rational decision-maker should react when the same product is available at different prices and/or qualities at different locations in a market (Hey and Lambert 1987, p. viii). In this way, search theory can help one to determine the rules used in decisions as to how the search for suppliers should be conducted, which price and/or quality levels should be searched for, and when it is profitable to accept an offer from a supplier.

Another important decision which affects procurement concerns the use of the right information technology to support a supplier relationship. In making this decision, the prospective cost of information technology use must be compared with the prospective benefits.

On the prospective cost side, there are setup costs for purchasing new hardware and software, and cost of adapting existing systems to integrate the new technology into the current system environment. Moreover, there are current costs, e.g. the costs incurred by administration, ongoing system support, maintenance, and leasing fees (Buxmann and Gebauer 1999, p. 3). At the business level there may be additional costs incurred by necessary adaptations to the organizational structure and/or workflow organization.

On the prospective benefit side information technology provides direct advantages in terms of cost reductions, time, and quality of information flow. Eventually there may be additional indirect benefits. For example, the introduction or improvement of an order processing system may result in less of the format mismatch which can occur when data is exchanged between separate systems. Thus, orders can be more quickly processed, leading to increased customer satisfaction.

While the costs of using information technology are relatively straightforward to estimate, the benefits are more difficult to ascertain. These difficulties derive from the fact that in order to enable the support of a supplier relationship by information technology, the participating systems on the supplier and customer side must be integrated. Since organizations often own hardware and software from a variety of vendors this can be a difficult and expensive task. The need for connectivity and interoperability, i.e. the ability of heterogeneous components to work together, has generated the demand for open systems. Open systems use clearly described nonproprietary industry standards available to anyone (Alter 1996, p. 24; Picot, Reichwald et al. 1996, p. 156). Thus, open systems make it easier and cheaper to switch hardware or software brands without significant change to the participating systems.

Integration occurs in terms of basic communication on the technical level, as well as communication on the business process level. While basic communication standards (e.g. TCP/IP which forms the Internet) are widely supported, there is still no generally accepted standard for the exchange of business information. Even standards in Electronic Data Interchange (EDI), the most prominent approach in the standardization of business data exchange, have not been universally adopted to date (Buxmann and Gebauer 1999, p. 1).

The benefit of using information technology in supplier relationships depends on whether the participating systems can be successfully integrated, so that business documents can be efficiently exchanged between the purchasing organization and the supplier without format mismatch. Success is uncertain if the decisions on the respective standards used in the participating organizations are made independently. For example, when organization A decides to implement a standard for the exchange information with organization B, with the expectation that the cost per unit of information transferred will be reduced, then this benefit can only be realized when organization B supports this standard as well. In economics, this phenomenon is examined under the concept of network externalities (Katz and Shapiro 1985, p. 424).

Whether network externalities can be successfully considered when taking decisions about information technology depends on whether one succeeds in estimating the diffusion of the relevant technology among (potential) business partners. Attempts to predict the success of newly emerging information technology often fail because of the complexity of the subject. Therefore, reports on the expected diffusion of information technology are littered with unforeseen failures as well as success stories. For example, prognoses anticipated high growth rates in the use of teletex for the 1990's. These growth rates have actually never been achieved. An example of an unexpected success is fax usage, where the estimates of its diffusion were far below the real trend. As a consequence of these difficulties, decisions concerning the use of information technology between organizations are frequently described as being strategic. Often these decisions are also taken "by gut feeling", i.e. without theoretical foundation (Buxmann and Gebauer 1999, p. 1).

Decisions on supplier relationships and the selection of information technology are frequently taken independently of each other. The reason for this often lies in the organizational separation of the decision-makers. While decisions on supplier relationships are normally taken by a dedicated purchasing or operating department, the responsibility for the selection of information technology often lies in the hands of an IT department. Consequently, in supplier selection decisions the portfolio of currently used information technology is assumed to be given, and conversely decisions on information technology are derived from the current supplier relationships.

Indeed, it can be shown that decisions on supplier relationships are influenced by decisions on the information technology used to support these relationships (Malone, Yates et al. 1987; Clemons, Reddi et al. 1993; Brynjolfsson, Malone et al. 1994). For example, information technology makes it easier and cheaper to find and evaluate potential suppliers. Using the concepts of search theory the benefit of using information technology to support the search for and negotiations with suppliers can be quantified. Under the assumption that continual progress in information technology leads to lower costs in finding potential suppliers it will be profitable to sign contracts of limited duration, just to keep open the possibility of changing suppliers whenever it becomes advantageous. However, the opposite effect can also be assumed: high investment in technologies which supports the execution of a supplier relationship and which is of little use in relationships to alternative suppliers make it useful to sign long-term contracts. In the case of short-term contracts one faces the risk that these investments will not pay off, e.g. because the supplier takes advantage of his strong position when the contract is extended. The existence of a relationship between supplier selection and information technology decisions is confirmed by an empirical survey conducted by Segev et al. in 1998. In this survey purchasing managers state that:

- the number of suppliers has been reduced in the past and that this trend is expected to continue (Segev, Gebauer et al. 1998, p. 41);

- they expect the use of new information technology to influence their procurement behavior (Segev, Gebauer et al. 1998, p. 50); and

- they would become closer to their suppliers (Segev, Gebauer et al. 1998, p. 44).

The dependence between these two decisions holds conversely, as well: the decision on information technology to support supplier relationships is influenced by the features of current supplier relations. For example, the profitableness of investment in information technology to support the evaluation of potential suppliers depends on the terms of the existing contract between the purchasing organization and its current supplier. If the existing contract contains very advantageous conditions for the purchaser (e.g. an exceptionally low price), then the potential improvements attainable by supplier change are small. Thus, the potential profit from the use of information technology supporting a supplier change is also small. Analogously, the duration of a contract determines whether investments in the integration of the supplier's and customer's information technology will be paid off.

In the remainder of this chapter a more formal statement of the research objectives will be given in the form of a research question, with associated sub-questions (section 1.2). The wider benefits of this research are addressed in section 1.3. Finally, the structure of the remainder of this thesis is presented in section 1.4.

1.2 Research objectives

The objective of this thesis is to analyze and answer the question of how the use of and expected progress in information technology influences the supplier relationships of an organization. As shown in section 1.1 transaction cost theory is an appropriate instrument for analyzing supplier relationships. Therefore the influence of information technology on the design of these relationships is analyzed answering the questions:

- How does information technology influence transaction costs?

- How does a change in transaction costs influence the design of supplier contracts?

- How does progress in information technology, interpreted as a change in the costs and benefits of using information technology as well as the increasing diffusion of a particular information technology, affect the design of supplier relationships?

- How does the availability of new information technology solutions influence decisions on the adoption of information technology and the design of supplier relationships?

To refine the analysis it is useful to identify important parameters which describe the relevant properties of information technology and supplier relationships. Information technology is distinguished firstly in terms of the task which is supported between information technology used to support the evaluation of potential transaction partners and information technology for the support of the execution of a supplier relationship. Secondly, for each of these categories we distinguish to what extent it affects the efficiency of information exchange and to what extent it is disseminated among potential suppliers, whereas supplier relationships are distinguished with respect to the duration and price of the underlying contracts.

The analysis is conducted using a formal model to represent the compound decisions concerning the selection of suppliers and the use of information technology. The model follows a microeconomic approach, i.e. its scope is a single organization and its supplier relationships.

1.3   Research benefits

The research disciplines of information systems and economics profit from this research by new insights gained through the integration of the concepts of search theory and transaction cost theory. These insights contribute to an improved understanding of the interdependence between the selection of and progress in information technology and the coordination of economic activities, which is still a topic of lively debate in the literature (see e.g. (Malone, Yates et al. 1987; Clemons, Reddi et al. 1993; Brynjolfsson, Malone et al. 1994)).

The wider benefits to industry are primarily related to better methodological support of decisions on investments in information technology and supplier relationships. Moreover, software companies can profit in their pricing decisions and diffusion strategies for their products.

1.4   Structure of the thesis

In chapter 2, the basic aspects of supplier relationships are presented. It is shown how the task of managing supplier relationships is a part of procurement activities in an organization, which objectives are connected with the management of supplier relationships, how these objectives interfere with other activities in an organization, and how the management of supplier relationships is assigned to organizational units. A systematization of supplier contracts and the phases of supplier relationships is provided as well. Furthermore, it is shown how supplier relationships can be assessed using the concept of transaction cost economics and how different transaction costs due to different characteristics of supplier relationships lead to different choices of contracts.

In chapter 3, the basic aspects of information technology are described and the state of the art in information technology support of the management of supplier relationships is outlined. In this context new information technology standards, usable in supplier selection decisions as well as the organization of procurement processes, are introduced and discussed with a special focus on the question of how these standards are likely to influence transaction costs.

In chapter 4 a formal model representing decisions on supplier selection is developed and discussed in terms of our research questions. It is shown that the formal model in its basic form confirms the predictions of transaction cost theory in terms of the design of supplier contracts. In the light of this knowledge the model is used to conduct a more thorough analysis of decisions on transaction partner selection, outsourcing, and the optimal duration of supplier contracts. The basic model does not include parameters representing alternative information technology solutions used to support a supplier relationship. Therefore, proceeding from the basic model, extensions are introduced with respect to the impact of the use of alternative information technology in a supplier relationship. These extensions comprise, as well as the consideration of implementation costs and prospective transaction cost savings, dynamic aspects such as the diffusion of information technology and the growth rate of this diffusion. The dynamic character of the extended model helps with the analysis of the research questions dealing with decisions concerning the adoption of technology, progress in information technology, and the design of supplier contracts.

Finally, in chapter 5, the major results of the this thesis are reviewed and the options for future research are outlined.

2 Supplier Relationships

To analyze the impact of information technology on supplier relationships the underlying terms of supplier relationship and information technology have to be clearly defined. The present chapter gives an introduction to the basic aspects of supplier relationships (section 2.1) and describes how transaction cost theory is used to assess different possibilities of organizing these relationships (section 2.2).

2.1 Basic aspects of supplier relationships

As every organization receives goods and services[2] from other organizations, i.e. their suppliers, the task of maintaining relationships with these suppliers is faced in every industry. In this section a definition of such relations is provided (section 2.1.1). We describe how the task of managing supplier relationships is institutionalized (section 2.1.3) and integrated into an organization (section 2.1.2). Finally, we describe what contracts in supplier relationships look like (section 2.1.4) and what phases are run through during the life cycle of such relationships (section 2.1.5).

2.1.1 Supplier relationships and procurement

Relations between organizations are established for different purposes. One purpose may be to open up synergies in different functional areas, such as the procurement, manufacturing and distribution of products. In the case of procurement activities, for example, manufacturers can bundle their demands, act jointly in negotiations with suppliers and consequently achieve better conditions when signing a contract. In the case of manufacturing, production capacities can be shared in order to achieve a constant capacity utilization. Finally, in the case of

---

2   For the purpose of simplification, in what follows only the term "good" or "product" will be used. However, it will always include services as well.

distributing the goods joint route scheduling can provide a more efficient use of transportation capacities.

Another reason for establishing a relationship is to purchase goods (Porter 1985, pp. 50-52), resulting in a supplier relationship. A supplier relationship has at least two participants, a buyer and a seller of goods. These two parties sign a contract to regulate the exchange of products and payments. On the basis of this contract, goods are transferred from the supplier to the customer, while payments are made from the customer to the supplier. The purchasing organization uses the purchased goods as inputs to its production process in order to form outputs, which are sold to other organizations or to the final consumer. In respect of the kind of goods purchased, the two basic categories of direct and indirect goods are distinguished (Hough and Ashley 1992; Zenz 1994; Gebauer, Beam et al. 1998, p. 5):

- Direct goods comprise raw material and production goods, which will be part of the final product of the purchasing organization. Here, large quantities are usually bought. The goods can be standardized or they can be subject to unique specifications between the purchasing organization and the supplier. For example, a car manufacturer purchases tires from a supplier, which then go into the assembly process of an automobile. An example from the service sector is a bank which purchases services from a call center which eventually become part of the service bundle sold to the bank's customers.

- Indirect goods comprise maintenance, repair, organizational/operating supplies, and capital goods. "Indirect" means that these goods will not be part of the final product. Examples are services such as the maintenance of machines, office supplies like pencils and paper clips, and capital goods like buildings or software for planning the production process.[3]

Sometimes third parties participate in a supplier relationship. For example financial institutions may be involved in the payment process, or the services of information intermediaries may be used to find business partners.

It is important to realize that the underlying semantics of a supplier relationship implies a flow of goods from the supplier to the customer along with an accompanying exchange of information. This exchange contains, for example, the amount and quality of goods ordered and the confirmation of delivery, inducing a flow of information from the customer to the supplier. Eventually there is an exchange of invoices, which leads to information being handed from the supplier to the customer.

---

[3] According to a study conducted by Killen & Associates in American enterprises the average expenses for indirect goods comprise the biggest share of the total costs. In the average, the expenses for indirect goods comprised 33% of all expenses, followed by expenses for direct goods (25%), and personnel costs (16%) (Killen&Associates 1997, p. 2; Dolmetsch, Fleisch et al. 1999, p. 79).

The management of supplier relationships includes the tasks of selecting vendors, negotiating contracts with them, and issuing purchase orders (Lee and Dobler 1971, p. 13). The fulfillment of these tasks implies decisions about the selection of the "right" supplier with whom a relationship should be established, as well as about the design of the contract on which the relationship is based. These tasks and decisions are discussed in section 2.1.5.

The management of supplier relationships occurs in the broader scope of procurement. Zenz defines procurement as the process of purchasing goods and services and managing their inflow into the organization (Zenz 1994). Hence, procurement contains additional responsibilities such as inventory control, traffic, storekeeping, receiving, and inspection. The management of supplier relationships must concur with the objectives of procurement. These objectives are to purchase goods with the proper quality, in the proper quantities, at the proper times, from the proper suppliers, with the proper deliveries, and at proper prices (Hodges 1961, p. 8; Lee and Dobler 1971, p. 11; Zenz 1994, p. 9).

Proper quality means that the purchased good should be of the quality which is necessary to accomplish the purpose for which the item is bought. The quality should be neither unnecessarily superior nor inferior. If the quality bought is unnecessarily superior, i.e. higher than required, this will probably lead to high prices for the final product and eventually to a loss of competitiveness. If the quality is inferior, this results in waste and rejects so that the final costs are greater than it would have been if more expensive materials were used (Hodges 1961, pp. 8-9).

The proper quantity and timing of delivery are closely connected to each other. A shortage of goods due to too small a quantity being delivered or a delay in delivery possibly results in a costly interruption to the production process. On the other hand, an oversupply due to too high a quantity being delivered or a delivery being made too early can be costly because of unnecessary storage and insurance charges, interest on investment, and the possibility of deterioration and obsolescence (Hodges 1961, p. 9).

The proper delivery refers to the destination requirements of the buyer (Hodges 1961, p. 10). The ordered goods must be delivered to the place specified in the underlying contract. Here, a failure not only results in additional transportation costs, but also in follow-up costs due to a delay in delivery.

A proper supplier is one on whom the buyer can rely to fulfill the commitments which have been agreed, i.e. the purchasing organization can be confident that the supplier will deliver the quality and quantity ordered, to the proper place at the proper time, and at the agreed-upon price. These duties are part of the supplier's service (Hodges 1961, pp. 9-10).

Finally, the proper price is the lowest that the buyer can find for a given quality level of the goods purchased and a given supplier service (Hodges 1961, p. 10).

The importance of procurement objectives is not weighted equally. A recent empirical survey about procurement in the industrial and services sector conducted in the U.S. in 1998 contained a question about the most important measures of purchasing success. According to the answers, the most important procurement objectives in the participating organizations are the total cost of purchasing items, including inventory and usage costs, followed by the timely delivery of items and fast order processing (Segev, Gebauer et al. 1998, p. 20). The respondents were also asked how well they met their purchasing goals. Here, an interesting result is that the most important issues of cost and time are only ranked 7th and 8th (of 10 named) in terms of success and achievement (Segev, Gebauer et al. 1998, p. 21). These results indicate that an improvement in procurement processes has the potential to produce major benefits.

It is obvious that decisions made in the management of supplier relationships have an immediate impact on the achievement of procurement objectives. Connected with the selection of a supplier and the negotiation of a contract is a commitment to a certain level of quality with respect to the good purchased, supplier service, and price. However, when managing supplier relationships not only procurement objectives are concerned, but the achievement of objectives in other organizational areas as well. On the other hand, activities taking place in other areas of an organization influence the achievement of procurement goals. To analyze the relationship between procurement and other functional areas of an organization Porter's conceptualization of an organization as a value chain can provide valuable insights (Porter 1985, p. 33).

2.1.2 Procurement in the value chain of an organization

According to Porter, every firm's value chain is composed of nine generic categories of activity which are linked together (Porter 1985, p. 34). These activities are performed to design, produce, market, deliver, and support its product and can be represented using a value chain as it is shown in Figure 1 (Porter 1985, p. 36).

Porter defines the term "value" as the amount buyers are willing to pay for a good. Value is measured by total revenue, which is a reflection of the price of a product and the amount that can be sold. A firm is profitable if the value it commands exceeds the costs incurred by the activities necessary to create the product (Porter 1985, p. 38).

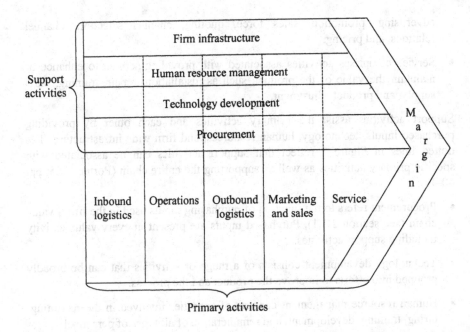

Figure 1:   The value chain of an organization. Source: (Porter 1985, p. 37)

The value chain consists of value activities and margin. While value activities are the physically and technologically distinct activities a firm performs, margin is the difference between total value and the cost of performing the value activities. With regard to value activities, Porter distinguishes between primary and support activities. Primary activities are the activities involved in the physical creation of the product, its sale, its transfer to the buyer as well as aftersale service, and comprise inbound logistics, operations, outbound logistics, marketing and sales, and service (Porter 1985, pp. 39-40):

- Inbound logistics include activities associated with receiving, storing, and disseminating inputs to the product, such as material handling, warehousing, inventory control, vehicle scheduling, and returns to suppliers.

- Operations include activities associated with transforming inputs into the final product, such as machining, packaging, assembly, equipment maintenance, testing, printing, and facility operations.

- Outbound logistics comprise activities associated with collecting, storing, and physically distributing the product to buyers, such as the warehousing of finished goods, material handling, delivery vehicle operation, order processing, and scheduling.

- Marketing and sales includes activities associated with providing means by which buyers can purchase the product and which get them to do so, such as advertising, promotion, sales force, quoting, channel selection, channel relations, and pricing.

- Service comprises activities associated with providing service to enhance or maintain the value of the product, such as installation, repair, training, parts supply, and product adjustment.

Support activities assist the primary activities and each other by providing purchased inputs, technology, human resources, and firm wide infrastructure. The dotted lines in Figure 1 reflect that support activities can be associated with specific primary activities as well as supporting the entire chain (Porter 1985, pp. 40-43):

- Procurement refers to the function of purchasing inputs used in the firm's value chain (see section 2.1.1). Purchased inputs are present in every value activity including support activities.

- Technology development consists of a range of activities that can be broadly grouped into efforts to improve the product and the process.

- Human resource management consists of activities involved in the recruiting, hiring, training, development, and remuneration of all types of personnel.

- Firm infrastructure usually supports the entire chain and consists of a number of activities including general management, planning, finance, accounting, legal, government affairs, and quality management.

Since procurement tends to be spread throughout the organization, interdependencies exist between procurement and virtually all other activities. Major interdependencies, however, are between purchasing activities and processes taking place in technology development, operations, and marketing and sales (Hodges 1961, pp. 10-13; Lee and Dobler 1971, pp. 23-27).

Activities in technology development usually imply responsibility for the technical specification of input goods going into the final product of an organization and the equipment used in the production process. Prices paid for these input goods are related to their specifications. For example, the specification of items based on common standards can enlarge the number of suppliers willing to provide these items. A larger basis of potential suppliers leads to competitive prices, so that the good can be purchased cheaply. Hence, the success of an organization in its procurement objectives depends, among other things, on whether the purchased goods are oriented according to common standards (Lee and Dobler 1971, pp. 23-24).

An important task in operations activities is to draw up a production schedule, which specifies at what time and in which place input goods must be available. This schedule is eventually transmitted to the purchasing department where it is used for drawing up a procurement schedule. A serious problem may occur when production does not allow sufficient time to purchase the required goods. If the time between the actual use of a good in the production process and the submission of the information about this demand to the purchaser is small, then possibly additional costs are incurred, e. g. premium prices, special production runs, or premium transportation costs (Lee and Dobler 1971, pp. 24-25). Therefore, whether procurement objectives are reached depends on the timely submission of information about the demand from production to the purchaser.

Sales and marketing activities influence procurement in a similar way to operations activities. The purchasing-production-sales cycle starts with a sales forecast. The sales forecast is the basis for the production schedule, which is in turn the basis for the purchasing schedule. Hence changes in the sales forecast must be communicated to production and purchasing quickly to permit these departments to change their schedules as painlessly and economically as possible. On the other hand, purchasing must immediately transmit information about changes in prices of the input goods to sales. Thus, sales will be able to evaluate the effect of these price changes on price estimates given for future sales quotations, on current selling prices, and on plans for future product lines (Lee and Dobler 1971, pp. 25-26).

Besides relationships between procurement and other activities within a value chain, an organization is embedded in a larger stream of activities which is termed the "value system" (Porter 1985, p. 34). In a value system preceding an organization's value chain are the value chains of suppliers which create and deliver the purchased inputs used in the buyer's chain, whereas an organization's output products flow into the value chains of their customers. As regards the vertical linkage between an organization and its suppliers, the way supplier activities are performed affects the costs of performance of the buyer's activities (et vice versa). For example, procurement and inbound logistics activities interact with a supplier's order entry system, while a supplier's application engineering staff works with a firm's technology development and manufacturing activities (Porter 1985, p. 50).

An important decision concerns the definition of an organization's border within the value system. Procurement activities comprise the investigation of potential suppliers for the provision of input goods. Basically, among the suppliers that can be considered is the buyer's own firm (Lee and Dobler 1971, 341). The decision on whether a good should be purchased from an external supplier or produced in-house is known as make-or-buy decision or outsourcing[4] decision. Hence, the

---

[4] Although the term outsourcing is often used for the tasks of information processing, e.g. Knolmayer defines outsourcing as the complete or partial transfer of previously internally fulfilled tasks in information processing to economically independent service businesses (Knolmayer 1993), it can be understood more generally as the purchasing of goods and services from outside (see e.g. (Kreis 1993, pp. 216 and 474; Vogelmann 1997, p. 9)). In this thesis, outsourcing is interpreted in the latter way.

border of an organization within a value system is usually determined by outsourcing decisions which are made in procurement.

To describe the range in a value system covered by an organization the term vertical integration is often used. If a large share of necessary inputs are produced in-house, then an organization is vertically highly integrated. In contrast, a large share of the customer's inputs purchased from external suppliers causes the organization to be vertically low integrated[5] (Baligh 1986, p. 1481; Johnston and Lawrence 1988, p. 98). In chapter 4 we show how decisions on supplier selection and the vertical integration of an organization can be treated in a common approach.

When considering the importance of procurement activities in the value chain of an organization, and the complexity of these activities due to their interrelation with other functional areas of an organization, it is clear that procurement tasks are often assigned to specialized departments. In the next section we discuss, how the management of supplier relationships is implemented by forming organizational units and to what extent purchasing activities are decentralized in practice.

2.1.3 Institutionalizing the management of supplier relationships

In organizations beyond a certain size, all or some of the tasks of procurement are usually assigned to dedicated organizational units. Lee and Dobler distinguish between materials management and purchasing departments as institutions in an organization which cover the procurement function with different scopes (Lee and Dobler 1971, pp. 13-15). While the purchasing department is usually responsible only for the tasks of managing supplier relationships, the materials management department follows the idea of an integrated management approach to planning, acquisition, conversion, flow, and distribution of production materials from the state of input goods to the final products. Thus it covers all functions of procurement (Lee and Dobler 1971, p. 13).

When the management of supplier relationships is organized, a fundamental decision is made about the degree to which the purchase function is to be centralized, i.e. whether purchase activities are carried out centrally by a dedicated department or in a decentralized way by personnel from other functional areas of an organization (Hodges 1961, p. 159; Lee and Dobler 1971, p. 19; Heinritz, Farrell et al. 1986, p. 72; Zenz 1994, p. 83).

---

[5] Porter distinguishes forward and backward integration. Forward integration denotes the extension of an organization's value chain in the direction of its customers, which happens, for example, when the customer's organization is bought. Backward integration means that the value chain is extended in the direction of an organization's suppliers, i.e. input goods previously purchased from suppliers are now produced in-house (Porter 1980).

The benefits of a centralized organization of purchasing activities come primarily from advantages due to specialized competencies of the employees involved in purchasing, the bundling of demands, and a better position in negotiations with suppliers.

When the purchasing function is fulfilled by specialists in a purchasing department, negotiations and contracting are based on broad experiences in this field. Employees specializing in purchasing buy more efficiently than less skilled persons for whom purchasing is a secondary responsibility (Lee and Dobler 1971, p. 20).

The bundling of demands occurring in different organizational units leads to a more efficient use of resources. Operational costs are cut, because efforts are less duplicated, fewer orders are processed for the same quantity of goods purchased, and the number of order records kept is reduced. Moreover, cost savings with respect to the transportation of the goods purchased may be realized because of a better utilization of transportation capacities. More effective inventory control is possible because of a better knowledge of stock levels, material usage, lead times, and prices. Finally, possibly suppliers are able to offer better prices and better service because their expenses are reduced. Their sales staff have fewer persons to contact, fewer orders to prepare, fewer shipments to make, fewer invoices to prepare, and fewer financial records to keep (Lee and Dobler 1971, p. 20).

Closely connected with the bundling of demands are advantages resulting from a better position in negotiations with suppliers. For example, quantity discounts are made possible by consolidating all orders for the same or similar goods (Lee and Dobler 1971, p. 20).

In practice, however, one may also observe that purchasing is organized in a decentralized manner. Decentralization of the purchasing function occurs either by dividing the purchasing department into subdivisions or by splitting up the purchasing tasks between the purchasing department and the other functional units of an organization (Heinritz, Farrell et al. 1986, p. 71). Which of these methods is followed depends on the characteristics of the underlying purchasing processes.

A division of the purchasing function between subdivisions of a purchasing department is carried out in cases where an organization is geographically highly distributed. For example, in multiplant organizations where the production sites are situated in different countries and/or different continents, local purchasing departments usually have a better knowledge of local legal conditions or local practices in supplier relationships (Hodges 1961, pp. 168-170; Heinritz, Farrell et al. 1986, p. 71).

The splitting of purchasing tasks between the purchasing department and other units of an organizations is useful in cases where a closer communication between the receiver of the purchased goods and the supplier is necessary. For example, in research or product development the designer building a prototype of a new product often does not know exactly what he or she wants. Consequently, concepts must frequently be discussed with the supplier before it is possible to select specific products to be used in the prototype. After specifications become firm, however, the purchasing department usually takes responsibility for the procurement of the necessary input goods (Lee and Dobler 1971, p. 22).

Another reason for splitting up purchasing tasks results from overhead costs caused by dedicated purchasing departments. Overhead costs are fixed in character and comprise, e.g., wages for purchasers and costs incurred by providing workplaces. These costs must be covered by cost savings in the purchasing process realized through the greater specialization of the purchasing personnel. The costs incurred during the purchasing process, e.g. information processing costs when a purchase order is generated and transmitted to the supplier, are variable in character. The sum of potential cost savings is the higher the more purchase orders are processed. Hence, the overhead costs of a purchasing department are only covered if a critical volume of purchased goods is reached. This is often not the case with the occasional procurement of goods. To reduce overhead costs, purchasing activities are sometimes split up in terms of operational and managerial tasks (Heinritz, Farrell et al. 1986, p. 71). The purchasing department selects suppliers and negotiates outline agreements (for details on purchasing contracts see section 2.1.4), while the ordering is done in the departments where the demand for the purchased goods occurs.

The management of supplier relationships also comprises the design of appropriate purchasing contracts. Since contracts form the legal basis on which supplier relationships are founded, the task of designing these contracts is of exceptional importance, no matter whether it is fulfilled by a dedicated purchasing department or by employees in other functional units of an organization. Subsequently we introduce into the basic features of supplier contracts inasmuch as they can be identified from a theoretical as well as from a practical viewpoint.

2.1.4 Contracts in supplier relationships

A purchasing contract in the economic sense is an explicit or implicit declaration about the exchange of goods and/or services between humans (who can act individually or as part of an organization) who agree on that declaration, because they expect an improvement in their utility (Milgrom and Roberts 1992, p. 127; Wolff 1994, p. 42; Picot, Reichwald et al. 1996, p. 51). In theory, contracts are distinguished with respect to their completeness and explicitness (Williamson 1975; Wagner 1994).

2.1.4.1 Purchasing contracts in theory

In complete contracts all possible states of the world which are relevant to the relationship between the contracting parties are anticipated in its declarations. Especially in case of long-term contracts, this requires high capabilities in terms of information processing and prognosis (Picot, Reichwald et al. 1996, p. 53). Since complete contracts are costly or even unfeasible, renegotiations may be necessary (Williamson 1975). Once the purchasing organization has committed itself to a particular supplier, changing the trading partner is costly and the supplier has the incentive to behave opportunistically when renegotiating the contract. Hence there is a trade-off between the costs of considering all possible states in the conditions of a contract and the costs caused by possible losses due to opportunistic behavior of the contracting partner when renegotiations of the agreement become necessary.

Explicit contracts are exactly specified in a written form, while implicit contracts are based on the fulfillment of implicit norms which are known to both contracting parties. Implicit contracts cannot or may not be specified in a written form. An example of an implicit norm is a reputation mechanism implemented indirectly in a contract (Wagner 1994, p. 13). The supplier receives an additional premium from the customer, which serves as a reward for not behaving opportunistically. If the supplier behaves opportunistically, then it will lose the premium.

Depending on the completeness and explicitness of contracts, in (Macneil 1978) and (Picot, Reichwald et al. 1996) the authors distinguish between classical, neoclassical, and relational contracts.

In classical contracts the exchange of the goods and the payment occur at the same time or, if not occurring at the same time, they are defined taking all possible states into consideration in the contract. The identity of the contracting partner does not play a role, i.e. relationships to a particular contracting partner which have existed before or which may exist afterwards have no influence on the current contract with this contracting partner. Differences between the contracting parties are settled on the basis of formal criteria, looking neither at the personality of the contracting parties, nor at their future interests. An example is spot market-contracts, e.g. the purchase of screws and bolts in a hardware store. Classical contracts are usually complete and explicit.

In comparison with classical contracts, neoclassical contracts are related to a period of time. Not all possible contingencies can be anticipated in the contract conditions, i.e. neoclassical contracts are partially incomplete. In case of differences between the contracting partners a third party, e.g. an arbitration court or an expert, can be called on to solve the dispute. Examples are long-term contracts with suppliers and leasing contracts.

Relational contracts are focused on long-term relationships. They are usually incomplete and contain mainly implicit declarations, which are based on trust.

Thus the identity of the contracting parties plays a dominant role. Disputes can only be solved by the contracting parties themselves. Mediation by third parties is impossible, because certain variables of the contract are not describable and thus not verifiable by a court or an arbitrator. Nevertheless these variables can be observed by the parties involved in the relationship (Grossman and Hart 1986; Hart and Moore 1990). The difference between neoclassical and relational contracts with respect to completeness is that neoclassical contracts can theoretically be made complete. However, the number of possible states is too large, so that completeness can only be reached by prohibitively high costs, whereas in the case of relational contracts, the incompleteness is more a result of the impossibility of verifying the conditions of an agreement by a third party.

In (Williamson 1985, pp. 75-78) the author distinguishes two types of relational contracts: bilateral and unified governance. While in bilateral governance the autonomy of the contracting parties is maintained, in unified governance the transaction is organized within the organization. Employment contracts are an example of unified relational contracts (Picot, Reichwald et al. 1996, p. 53). The distinction between relationships regarding ownership and control is also followed by Grossman, Hart, and Moore. In (Grossman and Hart 1986, p. 693) and (Hart and Moore 1990) the authors separate internal and external relationships and describe an organization as consisting of assets that it owns or over which it has control. Following these approaches, unified governance can also be interpreted as the hierarchical coordination of production (Williamson 1975, pp. 20-40; Picot and Dietl 1990, p. 178).

The issue of making contracts with suppliers using markets vs. hierarchical coordination of production has been widely debated in the literature under the notion of vertical integration. In this discussion some authors see the concepts of market and hierarchy as something completely different, while others place particular emphasis on the similarities of relationships in markets and hierarchies. In (Baligh 1986, p. 1481), for example, the author describes an organization as a set of relations between persons. In these relations persons define decision rules for other persons to use in making decisions. In other words, this concept of a relation contains one person, the superior, who has the authority to tell another person, the subordinate, how to decide and what to do. If the subordinate does not follow the decision rules provided by the superior, then the latter has the right to impose sanctions. From relationships based on decision rules Baligh distinguishes relationships between persons (or organizations) based on the exchange of goods. Here, each participating party loses and gains control over specific elements (e.g. values and goods) of its environment. A set of these exchanges concerning one kind of good or service is identified as a market. Therefore, vertical integration is interpreted as the replacement of the exchange of goods by decision rules, which leads to a change of the size of an organization.

Compared to Baligh, in (Alchian and Demsetz 1972) the authors do not see a significant difference between relationships within and relationships between organizations. They call it a delusion to define an organization by the power to settle issues by authority or disciplinary action superior to that available in the conventional market. They argue that, with respect to authority and disciplinary action, the relationship between employee and employer is indistinguishable from ordinary market contracting between any two people. Like an employer who can define decision rules for his or her employees and discharge them if an employee performs poorly or does not comply, a customer can stop purchasing from a supplier, punish a supplier by withholding future business, or sue a supplier for delivering faulty products (Alchian and Demsetz 1972, p. 777).

The contributions by Baligh and Alchian and Demsetz provide only an excerpt of the market vs. hierarchy debate and are therefore simply one example. A comprehensive discussion of this issue would go beyond the scope of this work[6]. However, the important conclusion derived from this brief discussion is that markets and hierarchies have in common the fact that they are based on contracts (Picot, Reichwald et al. 1996, p. 54). Therefore, one can distinguish between different forms of organizing the production of a good by different kinds of contracts, where the alternative of internal relationships does not conceptually make a big difference to the case of contracting with external suppliers. From this follows the important fact that decisions on supplier relationships and outsourcing decisions can be treated in a single, integrative model. This approach is followed in chapter 4.

The theoretical concepts of classical, neoclassical, and relational contracts are an idealization and can be faced in practice in a number of different designs.

2.1.4.2 Purchasing contracts in practice

The agreement, which comes nearest to the concept of a classical contract, is the single-item, fixed-price order (Zenz 1994, pp. 55) or the spot market contract (Milgrom and Roberts 1992, p. 131). These basic constructs can be extended with respect to the price and the amount of goods traded. Both of these extensions become necessary as the duration of a contract increases, i.e. the contract becomes neoclassical.

In practice, a fixed-price purchasing contract is the one most preferred by purchasing organizations, because it combines low administration costs with high incentives for suppliers to produce efficiently. Moreover, all financial risks are borne by the supplier (Lee and Dobler 1971, p. 126). In cases where a fixed price is undesirable, for instance because of the risk of inflation when the contract increases in duration, a rule of price determination can be used. For example, using an escalator clause the price of the purchased good can be tied to a price

---

[6]   For a comprehensive summary of this debate cf. (Michaelis 1985, pp. 176-190).

index so that the price of the purchased good changes with a change in this index (Lee and Dobler 1971, p. 127; Zenz 1994, p. 55).

Another kind of agreements observable in practice is cost-type contracts. In cost-type contracts the price of a good is determined by the costs actually incurred on the supplier's side in producing the good. In consequence, the buyer assumes almost all the financial risks. Generally, the supplier is guaranteed all their costs up to a predetermined figure, and the supplier is usually also guaranteed a fee in addition to the costs. Therefore, the supplier has no effective incentive to keep the costs, and thus the price, low. Moreover, cost-type contracts are expensive to administrate, as the allowable costs must be agreed upon in advance and continually audited as the relationship lasts (Lee and Dobler 1971, p. 129).

With regard to the amount of goods traded on basis of a purchase contract instead of making a contract on a single item, an agreement can be reached to provide a designated quantity of items over a period of time. This kind of contract is referred to as blanket contract (Zenz 1994, p. 55). A variant of a blanket contract is an agreement to furnish all the buyer's needs for particular items over a designated period of time. Here the total quantity is not fixed, but is calculated at the end of the period covered by the contract. Estimates of demand are usually provided during the bidding stage (Zenz 1994, p. 56). There are variations of the basic construction of a blanket contract such as national contracts (Zenz 1994, p. 61) or systems contracts (Zenz 1994, p. 63).

National contracts are used in multiplant companies with the aim of bundling the demand for the purchased goods, thus gaining a volume-bargaining advantage. National contracts are usually negotiated by the purchasing department. Once the national agreement has been signed, the individual plant purchasing managers are notified of its existence and of how they can proceed to place orders against the master contract, for example by using preprinted release forms (Zenz 1994, p. 61).

A similar approach is followed with systems contracts. Systems contracts involve a master contract negotiated with suppliers to cover large groups of products. In the master contract an exclusive supply arrangement for specified products for a period of time with set prices is established. The essential difference between systems and blanket contracts is that the systems contract involves additional services from the supplier side, such as stocking and warehousing, i.e. systems contracts merge the organization's ordering and inventory functions (Zenz 1994, p. 65).

In (Noordewier 1989, p. 39) the author provides a detailed comparison of blanket and systems contracts from an empirical point of view. According to this comparison, systems contracts in practice are much more likely to

1. be informal in nature,

2. rely on periodic billing procedures rather than on individual order invoicing procedures,

3. allow nonpurchasing personnel to issue order releases,

4. use special catalogs,

5. require vendors to maintain minimum inventory levels, and

6. not specify the volume of contract items a buyer must purchase.

Going a step further, the entire financial responsibility for the inventory of purchased goods can be handed to the supplier. When the supplier of a good owns the inventory, then this is also referred to as "stockless purchasing" (Zenz 1994, p. 62). A variation of stockless purchasing is just-in-time purchasing (Zenz 1994, p. 63). The purpose of just-in-time purchasing is to eliminate inventories of finished goods, raw materials, and parts. It is crucial that all materials shipped "just-in-time" must be of high quality since there are no extras to substitute for rejects.

Special purchase procedures are often established for items which cost insignificant amounts of money, are demanded in unforeseeable periods, and/or are needed promptly (Zenz 1994, p. 70). To be able to provide these items quickly and in an unbureaucratic manner a number of specialized small-order techniques have been developed to bypass the usual receiving, inspection, and storage functions.

While classical and neoclassical contracts can be approximated by spot market contracts and its extensions, relational contracts are based rather on implicit agreements due to the fact that a complete specification of all contract conditions is impossible. Relational contracts are of particular importance concerning investments in the relationship from the supplier's side. The purchasing organization has the interest that its supplier invests in the quality of the exchanged goods, information sharing, innovation, and responsiveness (Bakos and Brynjolfsson 1993, p. 42). If it is possible to make a complete contract, then the required level of investment by each party can be explicitly specified. However, these investments may not be verifiable by a third party, such as a court or an arbitrator, even though they may be observed by the parties of the relationship (Grossman and Hart 1986; Hart 1988; Hart and Moore 1990). If these investments are observable but nonverifiable, then the contracting parties cannot specify conditions based on the outcome of these investments. Hence, Bakos and Brynjolfsson refer to these investments as being non-contractible (Bakos and Brynjolfsson 1993). For example, when judging a supplier's effort to innovate in developing a specific part, the purchasing organization and the supplier may be able to observe whether adequate innovation has been undertaken compared with industry norms and technological developments, but it may be impossible to demonstrate this to the satisfaction of a court (Bakos and Brynjolfsson 1993, p. 44).

To make the supplier willing to make non-contractible investments, the buying organization must provide incentives. This can happen by implicit declarations such as the buyer's commitment to sign a long-term contract. Moreover, the gains from the investments must be shared with the supplier. In this way the supplier can expect that the investments will be paid off. The resulting relationship is of a symbiotic character (Picot, Reichwald et al. 1996, p. 263) and is also referred to as strategic partnering (Zenz 1994, p. 74).

In strategic partnerships mutual trust is of exceptional importance (Zenz 1994, p. 74; Picot, Reichwald et al. 1996, p. 263), since once the buying organization has made a commitment for a long-term contract, it must be confident that the supplier will actually make the investment as it is expected to do. However, implicit declarations based on trust are the major features of relational contracts. Thus, relational contracts under bilateral governance can be approximated by strategic partnerships.

In summary it may be said that the theoretic concepts of classical, neoclassical, and relational contracts can be approximated in practice by purchasing contracts as shown in Table 1.

Table 1: Practical examples of classical, neoclassical, and relational contracts.

theoretical concept	practical example
classical contract	spot-market contract
neoclassical contract	blanket contract
bilateral contract	
• bilateral governance	strategic partnership
• unified governance	in-house production

Purchasing contracts provide a legal framework in which business relations take place and thus are more representative of the static aspects of a supplier relationship, whereas the dynamic aspects can be represented using a phase concept to describe the activities taking place during the life cycle of a supplier relationship.

2.1.5 Phases of supplier relationships

The activities taking place in a supplier relationship can be divided into phases according to their functions and their approximate order, as shown in Figure 2. The phases are the evaluation phase in which information on potential suppliers and their products is collected and contracts are negotiated and the settlement phase in which the goods are exchanged and payments are made[7].

---

[7] Different authors name these phases differently (cf. e.g. (Lee 1998) or (Schmid 1993)). However, the semantics and order of these phases is roughly the same.

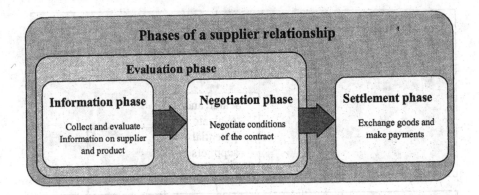

Figure 2:   Phases of a supplier relationship.

When a customer makes a decision whether to maintain the relationship with the current supplier or to establish a relationship with a new supplier, then the profitableness of both alternatives must be evaluated. Activities for the evaluation of potential suppliers have to be taken into consideration as well as changes that may emerge during the execution of the relationship in the settlement phase.

The decisions and activities taking place during the evaluation and transaction phase are subsequently discussed in more detail.

2.1.5.1   Evaluation phase

The evaluation phase contains two major tasks, as illustrated in the upper box of Figure 3:

- search for a potential supplier;

- evaluate the potential supplier previously found in the search. This contains activities for negotiating a price and other features of the good traded, as well as judging the potential supplier with respect to its trustworthiness.

How the activities in the evaluation phase are organized in detail depends on how difficult it is to find the right trading partner and whether the features of the traded good and/or the contract are the subject of negotiations between the trading parties. Next search theory is introduced to describe how the search for suppliers can be formalized. Then the economic aspects of negotiations are discussed.

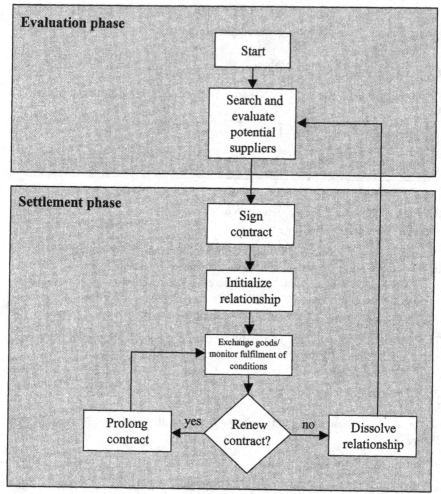

Figure 3:   Phases of a supplier relationship – detailed view.

2.1.5.1.1   Search theory

Until the advent of search theory, economists assumed that in markets with large numbers of buyers and sellers, there would be a (known) unique price. Therefore, search problems were assumed to be nonexistent. However, the real world shows that the same product can be available from different sellers at different prices in different places. When conducting search activities a trade-off must be considered: The longer one searches, the more likely it is that low prices can be found, but the longer one searches the more costly it is. The purpose of search theory is to develop optimal search strategies which describe how a rational decision-maker should react when the same product is available at different prices at different locations in a market (Hey and Lambert 1987, p. viii).

As a first step the simplest form of a search model is introduced as described and analyzed in (Hey 1981, pp. 57-66). In this basic model a risk-neutral decision-maker observes a random variable X as often as desired. One observation is obtained through one search step and incurs constant costs of c (>0), which we further refer to as marginal search costs. All observations are taken from a known constant distribution function $F(.)$. The reward of the search is the maximum value of X observed (Hey 1981, p. 56). This setting describes a sequential, single-stage, static, and non-adaptive search problem with perfect recall for which an optimal strategy for the searcher can be derived and analyzed (Hey 1981; Hey and Lambert 1987). It is sequential because in each search step only one observation is drawn from the set of possible observations. It is single-stage because the searcher looks only for the value of one single variable. It is static because time restrictions in the search process do not apply. It is non-adaptive because the distribution function of X is known to the searcher. Finally, perfect recall means that all search results can be equally recalled during the search process. Removing the simplifications the search model can be extended and thus used to represent activities in supplier search better[8].

2.1.5.1.1.1   The basic search model

In the basic model as outlined above it is the searcher's problem to apply a search strategy which maximizes the reward net of all search costs incurred. An optimal strategy involves deciding on an optimal stopping rule, or, in other words, on an optimal acceptance set of stopping values of X (Hey 1981, p. 57).

In each stage of the search process the searcher faces the problem of deciding whether it is worthwhile to take another observation or to stop the search. If the searcher decides to stop, the reward will be the maximum value of X observed so far, which is z. If the searcher decides to take another observation and then to stop, the net reward will be either z or the newer observation, depending on which of these two is greater minus the marginal search costs incurred by the last observation. Thus, the expected gain $G(z)$ of the next search step is given by

(eq. 1) $$G(z) = [zF(z) + \int_{z}^{\infty} x\, dF(x) - c] - z .$$

The term in square brackets represents the expected net reward after searching once more. The new observation incurs costs of c and is either less than, equal to, or greater than the up to now maximal observation z. The first term in square

---

[8]   For a survey of literature on search theory see (Hey 1979a, pp. 90-92).

brackets describes the case that the new observation leads to a value of x less than z. In this case the best observation z so far is selected, which happens with the probability of $F(z)$. The second term in the square brackets represents the case of an observation greater than z, which leads to an expected value of x multiplied by the probability of finding this value. (eq. 1) can be simplified using integration by parts, leading to

(eq. 2) $$G(z) = \int_{z}^{\infty}[1 - F(x)]dx - c.$$

The first derivation of the expected gain leads to

(eq. 3) $$G'(z) = -[1 - F(z)].$$

Since $F(z) \in [0;1]$ increases monotonically, $G(\infty) = -c$, and $G(-\infty) > 0$ it is clear that a unique value exists at which the expected gain from search reaches zero. Denote this value by x^*, then

(eq. 4) $$G(x^*) = \int_{x^*}^{\infty}[1 - F(x)]dx - c = 0.$$

This means that if a value observed up to now is less than x^* then the expected gain from the next search step will be positive. But if the maximum value observed so far is greater than x^* then the expected gain from the next search step is negative. Hence, x^* is a critical value, which is also referred to as optimal reservation value. The optimal search strategy can be derived as follows (see Figure 4):

"Keep on searching until a value of X greater than or equal to x^* is observed (where x^* is given by (eq. 4)); then stop searching and take the reward." (Hey 1981, p. 58)

Figure 5 illustrates the graphic determination of the optimal reservation value as it is described by (eq. 3) and (eq. 4) for a normally distributed random variable X. The hatched area in Figure 5 equals the marginal search costs c.

29

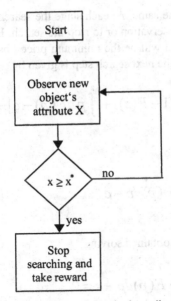

Figure 4:   Search strategy when observing the single attribute X.

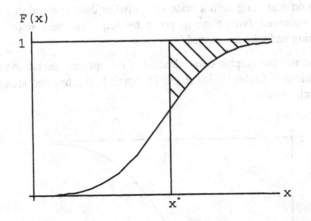

Figure 5:   Graphic determination of the optimal reservation value, following (Hey 1981, p. 63, Figure 5.1).

The basic search model describes the search for as large as possible a value of X. This formulation is used, for example, to analyze the search for goods on a market when information about the quality of products is sought (Hey 1979a, p. 93). A different criterion in the search for goods on a market can be the price of the products offered. Stigler was among the first economists to examine this problem in his pioneering paper of 1961 (Stigler 1961). The basic decision in this altered search problem remains the same. At each stage the searcher faces the problem of whether to take another observation or to stop the search. However, if the searcher decides to stop, the reward will be the minimum price observed so far. Therefore the expected gain $G(z)$ of the next search step is given by

$$(eq. 5) \quad G(z) = [z(1 - F(z)) + \int_{-\infty}^{z} p \, dF(p) - c] - z.$$

Integration by parts leads to

$$(eq. 6) \quad G(z) = \int_{-\infty}^{z} F(p) dp - c.$$

The reservation price p^* is obtained solving

$$(eq. 7) \quad G(p^*) = \int_{-\infty}^{p^*} F(p) dp - c = 0$$

and the optimal strategy is therefore:

> "Keep on searching until a price of P smaller than or equal to p^* is observed (where p^* is given by (eq. 7)); then stop searching and take the reward."

Figure 6 illustrates the graphic determination of the optimal reservation price for a normally distributed random price P. As in Figure 5, the hatched area equals the marginal search costs c.

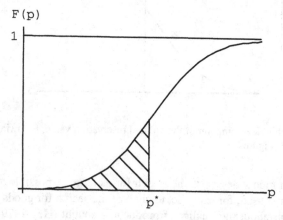

Figure 6: Graphic determination of the optimal reservation price, following (Hey 1981, p. 114, Figure 7.1).

The figure shows that (Hey 1981, p. 114):

- the reservation price is an increasing function of the marginal search costs;
- a shift of the price distribution to the right causes p^* to increase by the same amount, i.e. search intensity will be unchanged; and
- an increase in risk causes a decrease in p^*.

To determine the total costs of a search one has to sum up the marginal search costs incurred during the search process. The total costs of search depend on the expected number of observations until the reservation price is found which can be obtained as follows. Let the random variable N denote the number of search steps taken before stopping. Then the probability that a price smaller than the reservation value is found in the nth search step, $P(N=n)$, is the product of the probability to find $n-1$ times a price greater then p^* and the probability of finding a price less than p^* in the nth search step (Hey 1981, p. 62):

$$(eq. 8) \quad P(N = n) = [1 - F(p^*)]^{n-1} F(p^*) \quad n = 1, 2, ...$$

Hence, the number of search steps follows a geometric distribution[9], and the expected number of search steps $E(N)$ results from the mean value of this distribution (Mendenhall, Schaeffer et al. 1981, p. 632), which is defined by

$$(eq. 9) \quad E(N) = \frac{1}{F(p^*)}.$$

From (eq. 9) it is clear that the lower the reservation price, the larger the expected number of observations.

The basic search model so far assumes that a sequential search takes place, i.e. the searcher makes exactly one observation at each stage and depending on the expected gain decides whether another search step should be undertaken (McCall 1965). Consequently, the resulting price is fixed with respect to its upper limit (the reservation value), while the number of samples drawn to find out the supplier providing this price is uncertain. Alternatively one can make a predefined number of observations ("fixed sample-size") and select the best price offer from these samples (Stigler 1961). Here, the resulting price is uncertain, while the number of conducted search steps is fixed. Nelson compared sequential and fixed sample-size search strategies (Nelson 1970). Under what conditions which of these strategies promises the better results is the subject of the next section.

---

[9] For more on geometric distributions see (Mendenhall, Schaeffer et al. 1981, pp. 85-86).

2.1.5.1.1.2   The optimal sample size

The question of the optimal sample size can be posed by asking: "what is the optimal number of suppliers that the decision maker should contact before purchasing the goods?"

Let p_n be the price charged by the nth supplier contacted in the search, and let $p_{(N)}$ be the minimum price charged by the first N suppliers contacted. Furthermore, assume that only one unit of the good is purchased. Then the question posed above can be answered by finding N so that the sum of the expected price resulting from the search $E(p_{(N)})$ and the total search costs cN is minimized (Hey 1979a, p. 84):

$$(eq. 10) \quad E(p_{(N)}) + cN \rightarrow min!$$

A trade-off exists: since one expects to get lower prices the longer one searches it is intuitively clear that the first term decreases as N increases. Whereas the second term increases with N. Treating N as continuous, differentiating (eq. 10) with respect to N, and setting the result equal to zero yields the first-order condition

$$(eq. 11) \quad \int_{m}^{u} [1 - F(p)]^N \log[1 - F(p)]dp + c = 0,$$

where m and u are the lower and the upper bound of the price for the good searched for which are defined by $max[x; F(x)=0]$ and $min[x; F(x)=1]$ respectively (Hey 1979a, p. 85). The optimal sample size N^* is then one of the two integers nearest to the N that solves (eq. 11) (Hey 1979a, p. 86).

The resulting optimal strategy is therefore:

"Keep on searching until N^* suppliers are found (where N^* is given by (eq. 11)); then stop searching and take the reward."

A search strategy based on a fixed sample size may in some cases not be optimal. For example, it implies that even if the first sample leads to a price equaling the lowest possible price of the underlying distribution, the search will not be stopped until N^* samples are drawn. It can be formally shown that under the assumption that the marginal search costs are independent from the form of the searching procedure a sequential search is always optimal (Degroot 1970; Hey 1979a, p. 87; Hey 1981, p. 57).

In practice, however, the assumption that marginal search costs will be independent of the search strategy is often not fulfilled. For example, opportunity costs due to time restrictions may exist. The longer the search takes, the longer one renounces possible price reduction when changing supplier. Since a search for a fixed number of samples can be conducted in parallel it is faster than a sequential strategy and opportunity costs are lower. That is why mixtures of sequential and parallel search strategies have been proposed, such as "keep on searching till either a price less than p^* is found or until N^* searches have been made" (Hey 1979a, p. 90). The treatment of time restriction in search models is discussed in the next section.

2.1.5.1.1.3 Dynamic optimization and recall

In the case of an infinite horizon in every step of the search process the expected total reward of the search is constant. This changes as soon as the horizon becomes finite. Using backward induction Hey shows that with every step towards the search horizon the possible total reward of the search decreases (Hey 1981, p. 70). Consequently, the willingness to accept bad search results increases, i.e. the searcher becomes less choosy. This means that the reservation value decreases over time and from the searcher's point of view the optimization becomes dynamic[10].

Closely connected to the finite-horizon search problem is the question of recall. In the infinite horizon model the reservation value is constant and a once unacceptable observation will always remain unacceptable. Hence, it makes no difference if previous observations can be remembered, whereas in case of a finite horizon the reservation value decreases as the search horizon is approached. Here, the question of recall is crucial since it may happen that previously rejected observations become acceptable as time passes by (Hey 1981, p. 74).

The qualitative properties of the model without recall are similar to those of the model with recall, i.e. as the horizon is approached, the reservation value decreases. Moreover, Hey shows that since recall makes the searcher better off, all reservation values of the model without recall are (except in the final period) lower than their counterparts in the recall model (Hey 1981, p. 75). Between the polar cases of total recall and no recall are models considering partial recall (see, for example, (Landsberger and Peled 1977) and (Karni and Schwartz 1977)).

2.1.5.1.1.4 Multi-stage-search

So far only search models which consider the searcher's evaluation of one attribute have been discussed. In reality it can be observed that more than one dimension of an entity is of interest. For example, when evaluating potential suppliers for a good, a purchasing organization is possibly interested not only in the price, but also in different qualitative attributes of the good or the supplier. In these cases sampling takes place from multivariate distributions (Hey 1981, p. 76). A difference in the analysis of multi-stage-searches evolves from the way in which

---

[10] For a mathematical derivation of these statements and its proofs by mathematical induction see (McKenna 1987, pp. 93-96) and (Hey 1981, pp. 66-76).

the search is being conducted and whether the observed attributes are statistically dependent on each other.

The search in several dimensions can take place simultaneously or sequentially. In a simultaneous search, observations of all attributes are made at the same time. Hence, information about the value of one attribute of an observation cannot be used in order to judge the expected value of the other attributes. Consequently, the resulting search strategy would be basically unchanged compared to the one-dimensional case, except for the higher degree of complexity of the analysis (Hey 1981, p. 76).

On the other hand, in a sequential revelation of the attribute values several stages are run through. In each of these stages one attribute is observed, and depending on the value of this attribute it is decided whether the values of the other attributes should be revealed as well. In case of correlated search dimensions information about the degree of correlation can be used to decide whether the revelation of further dimensions is profitable. This question is, for example, analyzed by McKenna under the notion of residual uncertainty. He distinguishes between an observable attribute value of an entity and the true value of this attribute, which can only be discovered by experience, e.g. by testing the entity. He further assumes that the observable and true values of the attribute are positively correlated (McKenna 1987, pp. 101-104). The search strategies derived may be of use in the search for suppliers. For example, a searcher may intend to evaluate different suppliers of a good which are represented by two correlated dimensions of interest, the price and the quality. Figure 7 describes the search process[11]. If the values of these two attributes are uncertain, then they can be represented by random variables, say P and X. In a sequential search, the searcher first obtains observations on just one dimension, e.g. the price. As soon as an acceptable price is found, the searcher either obtains an observation on the second dimension depending on this value (when $p \leq p_1^*$), i.e. the quality, or accepts the observation without further investigation (when $p \leq p_2^*$, while $p_2^* < p_1^*$). When deciding to observe the second dimension, the result can either be acceptance or rejection of the sample. In the latter case the search is begun again, i.e. selecting a different supplier and observing the price. When the search terminates, the reward is the value for the finally accepted pair of p and x. The general search strategy is not changed in principle when the search sequence is reversed, i.e. if quality is looked for first, and then the price.

---

[11]. The search strategy described here is also discussed in (MacQueen 1964).

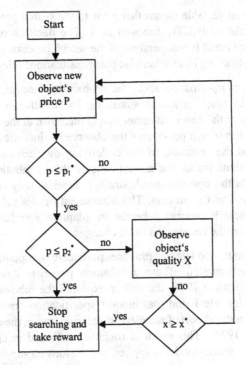

Figure 7:   Sampling in a two-stage search process for quality and price, following (Rose 1999, p. 93, Figure 12).

The search models discussed so far are based on the crucial assumption that the searcher is perfectly informed about the probability distribution of the variables he or she is looking at. But why should information about price distribution be known, when the identity of potential suppliers providing these prices is unknown? To solve this contradiction and to make search models more realistic adaptive search strategies have been developed.

2.1.5.1.1.5   *Adaptive search*

Adaptive search strategies are applied when the distribution from which the searcher takes observations is unknown (McKenna 1987, p. 104). As in the basic search model it is assumed that the searcher observes a continuous random variable X whose distribution is represented by a probability function. If this probability function is unknown, there are two possible sources of information (Hey 1981, p. 93):

- observations on some external variable; or

- observations on X itself.

Observing an external variable means that prior to the search process information is collected about the probability function of X. The decision on the amount of information to be collected is independent of the search process. Hence Hey refers to this problem as "learning in an otherwise passive situation" (Hey 1981, p. 87).

The second source of information about the probability function, the observation of X itself, leads to adaptive search strategies. In adaptive search models the probability function of the observed dimension is unknown at the beginning of the search process. As the search progresses the observed values are used to estimate the mean value and the precision of the underlying distribution. The larger the number of observations made, the more precisely the distribution is known. In static search models the optimal search strategy depends only on the maximum value so far observed in the process. The assessment of this value is unchanged during the whole search process, whereas in adaptive search, this assessment changes over time, i.e. the reservation value changes.

When applying search models in practice particular scrupulousness must be devoted to the determination of the distribution parameters and the marginal search costs. In (Gastwirth 1976) the author explored the robustness of optimal-reservation-price rules. He found that modest specification errors could lead to dramatic increases in the expected numbers of searches and in the expected cost of buying (Rothschild 1974). This result is roughly confirmed in chapter 4 of this work where the basic search model is applied to decisions on supplier search.

Search theory focuses on the derivation of an optimal strategy for the searcher. Here the search costs are usually treated in an aggregated form and not further discussed. However, when search theory is used to support the management of supplier relationships, then the composition of search costs may be of interest. Often it is not sufficient just to find a potential supplier, but additional negotiations are necessary in order to specify a contract. Only then can a decision on a supplier be taken. The way search and negotiation activities can be brought together in an integrated approach is examined in the following section.

2.1.5.1.2 Negotiations

"Negotiation is a form of decision-making where two or more parties jointly search a space of possible solutions with the goal of reaching consensus." (Guttman, Moukas et al. 1998) In game theory negotiations are formalized as bargaining games (Nash 1950; Nash 1953). In two-person bargaining games, for example, it is assumed that both negotiating parties have a known utility function representing the parties' interests. Every potential contract is represented by a combination of utilities for each side. If the utility functions are known, the total utility for all possible contracts can be calculated, resulting in an efficient frontier as shown in Figure 8. A contract is efficient when no contract exists which both of the negotiating parties would prefer at the same time, i.e. one side can only improve its position to the disadvantage of the other side (Jelassi and Jones 1988, p. 77).

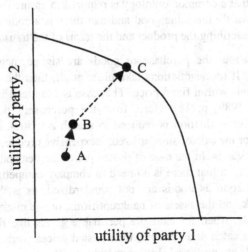

Figure 8:   Efficient frontier of contracts between two parties, following (Jelassi and Jones 1988).

A bargaining game comprises a protocol (Guttman, Moukas et al. 1998), i.e. the rules of the game which determine how one can get from one combination of utilities to another, thus approaching the efficient frontier. A possible sequence of utility combinations is given in Figure 8, where the parties start from combination *A*, reach combination *B* through negotiations and finally end up at combination *C* through further negotiations. Furthermore, a bargaining game is determined by the parties' strategies. A strategy is a plan of action undertaken by the negotiator which conforms to the rules of the game (Guttman, Moukas et al. 1998).

The point reached on the efficient frontier is determined by the relative power of the negotiating parties. A difference in the power of negotiation manifests itself in the choice of the rules and, once the rules are given, in the gradient of the path towards the efficient frontier. In terms of our example, if party 2 is more powerful than party 1, then a point on the efficient frontier will be reached which is nearer to the axis of ordinates (and vice versa).

Activities in negotiation involve the basic steps of preparing and conducting the negotiation (Jelassi and Jones 1988, p. 78). During the preparation the situation is studied, the participants are identified, and an understanding of the issues and interests involved is developed. In particular, the parties have to learn about the relevant properties of the transaction (e.g. delivery time, delivery quantity, and financing terms) and the good they intend to exchange (e.g. when software is purchased the issues of compatibility, warranty, maintenance, etc.). Moreover, the relative importance of these properties with respect to the parties' utilities must be discovered. After the preparations the negotiations are conducted. Here, the parties exchange a series of messages and offers until an agreement is reached. One important fact is that a common ontology is required to ensure that the participants are referring to exactly the same good and that there is a common understanding of the attributes describing the product and the terms of the transaction.

When contracts about the purchase of goods are signed, negotiations are not always necessary. If no negotiations take place at all, then the purchaser faces a fixed offer of goods with a fixed price. This case is examined in terms of posted prices (Milgrom 1989, p. 18). Here, from the purchaser's point of view, the problem of supplier evaluation is reduced to search activities. Posted prices are commonly used for the sale of standardized, inexpensive products, primarily in the field of consumer goods. In the case of posted prices the demand of all buyers can usually be satisfied, so that there is no need to compare competing bids (Milgrom 1989, p. 19). As soon as goods are not standardized, as is the case with, for example, livestock and the assets of bankrupt firms, or the market clearing prices are highly unstable, when for example perishable goods like fish are sold with daily variations in catch and demand, then posted prices work poorly and other institutions of trade are preferred (Milgrom 1989, p. 19).

If negotiations take place, then the resulting bargaining game can take place on the basis of different rules. With respect to the rules, in (Milgrom 1989, p. 18) the author distinguishes between centralized and decentralized markets. In a centralized market demand and supply of a particular good meet in the same location, and all trade takes place simultaneously (Blouin and Serrano 1998, p. 1). Centralized markets are represented in practice by auctions which are market institutions with an explicit set of rules determining resource allocation and prices on the basis of bids from the market participants (McAfee and McMillan 1987, p. 701).

In the case of bidding and pricing, many different sets of rules have been developed for auctions. We will not discuss and evaluate all possible kinds of auctions but rather restrict the discussion to the four basic types of auctions. These are (McAfee and McMillan 1987, p. 702):

- Oral, open, ascending-bid auction (English auction);

- Oral, open, descending-bid auction (Dutch auction);

- First-price sealed-bid auction; and

- Second-price sealed-bid auction (Vickrey auction).

The English auction is the most commonly used form. The price is successively raised until one bidder remains. This can happen by having an auctioneer announce prices, the bidders call the bids themselves, or the bids are sent electronically with the current best bid posted. An essential feature of an English auction is that at any time, each bidder knows the currently best bid. English auctions can be found, for example, when antiques and works of art are sold (McAfee and McMillan 1987, p. 702; Milgrom 1989, pp. 7-8).

The Dutch auction is the converse of the English auction. The auctioneer calls an initial high price, and then lowers the price until one bidder accepts the current price. The Dutch auction is used in practice, for example, for selling cut flowers in the Netherlands, fish in Israel, and tobacco in Canada (McAfee and McMillan 1987, p. 702; Milgrom 1989, p. 6).

In a first-price sealed-bid auction, potential buyers submit sealed bids. The highest bidder is awarded the item for the price he or she bid. The basic difference to the English auction is that in the English auction the bidders are able to observe their rivals' bids while in the sealed-bid auction they are not. Accordingly, in the English auction bidders can revise their bids depending on the bids of the competing bidders. Sealed-bid auctions are used, for example, in the tendering of U.S. government procurement contracts (McAfee and McMillan 1987, p. 702; Milgrom 1989, p. 6).

In a Vickrey auction the bidders submit bids being aware that the highest bidder wins the item but pays a price equal to the second-highest bid. Although this auction has theoretical advantages because the bidder reveals his or her true willingness to pay for the auctioned good, it is seldom used in practice (McAfee and McMillan 1987, p. 702; Milgrom 1989, p. 8).

In respect of the total profit, first-price auctions like the Dutch and the first-price sealed-bid auction lead to identical results, i.e. the identity of the winner and the price the winner pays are always the same (Milgrom 1989, p. 7). The same holds for second-price auctions like the English and the Vickrey auction (Vickrey 1961; Milgrom 1989, p. 8). A difference between first-price and second-price auctions can occur concerning the division of the total profit between the bidder and the seller of the auctioned good. What the division of profit looks like in detail is not obvious. Since the bidder in a first-price auction pays the price of the highest bid for the auctioned good, it seems that the achieved price will be higher in a first-price than in a second-price auction. Therefore one may assume, that the seller prefers a first-price auction to a second-price auction. It is observable too, however, that the bidder in the first-bid auction optimally shades the bid down to allow a margin for profit, whereas the bidder in a second-bid auction finds it optimal to bid the full amount of his or her valuation (Milgrom 1989, p. 9). Examining this question, Milgrom derived the Revenue Equivalence Theorem (McAfee and McMillan 1987, p. 707; Milgrom 1989, p. 10). According to the Revenue Equivalence Theorem first-price and second-price auctions yield exactly the same expected profit for every bidder valuation and the same expected revenue for the seller. The proof of the theorem holds under the following assumptions (McAfee and McMillan 1987, p. 706):

- The bidders are risk neutral;

- The independent-private-values assumption applies, i.e. any bidder's valuation of the auctioned good is statistically independent from any other bidder's valuation;

- The bidders are symmetrical, i.e. all bidders are drawing their valuation from the same probability function; and

- Payment is a function of the bids alone.

However in practice it can be observed that one auction rule performs better in some cases than another auction rule. For example, English auctions are the most prevalent auctions in the world, yet industrial procurement auctions are almost always sealed-bid auctions (Milgrom 1989, pp. 10-11). This phenomenon can be explained by dropping some of the assumptions behind the derivation of the Revenue Equivalence Theorem.

Dropping the independent-private-values assumption, Mc Afee, Mc Milland and Milgrom examined to what extent the expected profit is influenced if the bidders' valuations depend on a common random factor. In this way the bidders' estimates are positively correlated. This is often the case, for example, in auctions for oil and gas drilling rights, where the rights being acquired are based on uncertainties which are determined by common factors such as future world energy prices (Milgrom 1989, p. 13). While under these conditions the expected total surplus is still the same in first-price and second-price auctions, for every bidder's valuation of the good the bidder's expected profit is smaller in the second-price auction and the seller's expected revenue is correspondingly higher (McAfee and McMillan 1987, pp. 720-723; Milgrom 1989, pp. 13-17).

The prevalence of first-price auctions for industrial procurement can be explained relaxing the assumption about the payment function. In industrial procurement bidders are potential suppliers and the bid-taker is a buyer. Often the buyer's decision on the quantity being purchased depends on the price achieved in the auction. Under this condition it can be shown that for every level of cost of the winning bidder, the first-price auction leads to a lower average price than the second-price auction (McAfee and McMillan 1987, pp. 716-718; Hansen 1988; Milgrom 1989, pp. 11-13). Hence, in this setting purchasers are likely to choose first-price auctions for the acquisition of goods.

Auctions are suitable for trading some, but not for all kinds of goods. Since all buyers and suppliers meet in a central market place the buying organization faces, apart from finding the auction, no search problem. The item for sale is displayed, and the bidders may usually inspect it to gather information about its specifications. Moreover, items sold by auction are usually sold "as is", eliminating the need to negotiate different variables characterizing the good, i.e. auctions restrict the negotiation to the single dimension of price. These attributes make auctions primarily suitable for products whose features, except the price, are not negotiable.

Auctions are not practicable if it is too expensive to gather the competing buyers together, if the item is storable and the timing of the buyer demands varies (Milgrom 1989, p. 19), or when product features are subject to negotiations and complex contractual arrangements are necessary.

In cases where no auctions are available supply and demand are brought together using decentralized markets. In a decentralized market trade takes place in pairwise meetings of buyers and suppliers (Blouin and Serrano 1998, p. 2). The pairwise meetings may include negotiations about the features of a product, its price, and contract conditions. In decentralized markets the costs of contacting potential trading partners become particularly important when the participating parties are geographically distributed. Moreover, there are no generally accepted rules for negotiations taking place in pairwise meetings. By way of comparison, auctions have the advantage of being connected with a commonly known set of rules, a geographically or logically central location, and a predetermined trading time known to all participants. In this way, prices can usually be determined faster and the conduct of auctions can be delegated more easily to an unsupervised agent (Milgrom 1989, pp. 18-20).

To mitigate the disadvantage of high contact costs in decentralized markets pairwise meetings can be organized in a geographically or virtually centralized form. Typical examples comprise trading gateways provided by intermediaries. Traditionally, these gateways are trade fairs, which have been used for a long time to enable the efficient organization of negotiations. Recently the Internet has been used to provide virtualized gateways for decentralized markets (see also chapter 3.2), so that the aspect of contact costs is of diminishing importance.

In the evaluation phase of a supplier relationship, negotiation activities can be integrated with search models. In the case of pairwise meetings the evaluation of potential trading partners takes place in two stages. The first stage includes activities to find and contact a potential supplier. In the second stage either all conditions of the purchasing contract are clear and no negotiations are necessary, or negotiations take place. No negotiations are necessary when purchasing standardized goods, for example standard office software. Otherwise the conditions of the contract, such as quality, quantity, and/or price of the purchased good, have to be worked out. Once the negotiations are completed and the conditions of the contract are clear, the customer decides whether to accept the current offer or to continue searching. This decision can be made on basis of the rules evolving from the search models discussed in the previous section.

When the good sought is suitable for auctions then search activities are restricted to the problem of finding an auction where the desired good is offered. One search step in the evaluation phase then comprises activities of finding an auction, inspecting the offered good, and bidding. If the purchaser does not succeed, then the activities of the evaluation phase are repeated.

2.1.5.2   Settlement phase

When an offer is accepted or the purchaser succeeds in an auction, then the settlement phase starts (see Figure 3). First the contract is signed. Then the relationship is initialized. An important distinction evolves from whether the trade relationship is newly formed or whether the participating parties already have an established relationship. This difference is discussed in the literature under the notion of "open" and "closed contracting" (Lee 1998, p. 3). In case of a newly formed relationship the transaction partner may have to make technical and/or organizational adaptations.

On the technical side, the supplier's and customer's software must be connected. This requires a common communication standard, which must possibly be implemented first[12]. Furthermore, in order to enable an automated exchange of business data, the participants must agree upon a common format for the structure of the exchanged data. This implies the synchronization of the formats of the underlying databases.

On the organizational side, the establishment of a relationship to a new supplier might imply the adaptation of business processes. This may be the case, e.g., with warehousing. If the new supplier takes control of warehouse management functions, then the department of the purchasing organization which previously fulfilled this task will be reorganized, i.e. it will be cut back or assigned alternative tasks.

Moreover, the customer must learn how to handle the new supplier's product (Klemperer 1987b, p. 375). The knowledge required to use a product is often not transferable to products delivered by other suppliers. This can even be the case if the different products are functionally identical. A number of software companies, for example, offer spreadsheet programs that are functionally nearly identical, but if a customer has learned to use one of the products, there is a strong incentive to continue to buy software from the same manufacturer.

Once the relationship is initialized the goods are exchanged and payments are made. When the purchase is complete, the customer has the option of keeping the relationship by prolonging the contract or dissolving the relationship and looking for an alternative supplier. If the latter happens, the process restarts with the evaluation phase.

The execution of a supplier relationship is associated with operations risk as well as opportunism risk (Clemons, Reddi et al. 1993, pp. 15-16). Operations risk involves the possibility that a supplier will not fulfill the agreed conditions of the contract. Here, monitoring activities can be conducted to reduce this risk. Whereas opportunism risk becomes relevant when a contract is renegotiated, e.g. because it

---

[12]   The issue of standards and standardization is further discussed in section 3.1.2.

has expired and the purchasing organization wishes a prolongation. The risk that a supplier may act opportunistically is especially high if the purchasing organization has made high investments in the current relationship which are of little use in relationships with alternative business partners. Opportunism risk is also high if there are only few or difficult to identify alternative suppliers for the purchased good.

2.2 Assessment of supplier relationships

When making decisions on business relations the question of how different alternatives of acting can be assessed arises. There is a broad range of theories which are appropriate for the analysis of business relationships, ranging from the economic approaches (e.g. game theory, agency theory, and strategy-oriented approaches), through political approaches, to interorganizational theories (Sydow 1992). In (Reekers and Smithson 1994, p. 2) the authors identify three major approaches which are particularly appropriate in the context of business relationships and information technology standards: transaction cost theory, resource dependence theory, and the network approach.

Transaction cost theory assumes that the cost of transactions is critical for the choice of an optimal governance structure. The unit of analysis is a particular business relationship which is analyzed in terms of the economic costs of setting up, operating, and maintenance. Thus the focus lies on the examination of efficiency and cost structures (Williamson 1975; Reekers and Smithson 1994, p. 3), whereas the resource dependence theory assumes that organizations try to gain control over necessary external resources. The focus of analysis is placed on dependence relations, and political motives are emphasized (Pfeffer and Salincik 1978; Reekers and Smithson 1994, p. 4). Finally, the network approach focuses on the network of interdependent relationships (Fulk and Boyd 1991; Reekers and Smithson 1994, pp. 4-5). Whereas the scope of transaction cost theory and resource dependence theory is mainly the analysis of separate relationships[13], the network approach takes into consideration the fact that organizations interact within a wider network.

In this work the efficiency and cost structures of a single supplier relationship are emphasized. Thus a closer view of transaction costs is necessary. In the following

---

[13] The basic features of transaction cost economy (focus on single relationships, no consideration of dependence relations and political motives, its static nature, etc.) are also the major subjects of criticism. The purpose of this work, however, is not the comprehensive discussion of the pros and cons of transaction cost theory. An overview of the criticism of transaction cost theory and a comprehensive comparison of other theoretic approaches on the explanation of business relationships is provided in (Sydow 1992, pp. 145-165).

sub-sections a definition and refinement of transaction costs as well as a discussion of transaction cost determinants is initially provided. Secondly, since the choice of a governance structure has an influence on production costs, the latter are analyzed as well. Thirdly, an overview of how transaction cost economists derive the optimal governance structure for business relationships under different conditions on basis of a minimization of transaction and production costs is provided.

2.2.1 Transaction costs

The term transaction costs is often used in the analysis of trade relations in markets, and in this context are described as the costs of using, securing and transferring titles (Tietzel 1981, p. 221). Transaction costs are also referred to as the "costs of running the economic system" (Arrow 1969, p. 48) or as the costs of using the market (Coase 1937, p. 390). For a detailed analysis, further refinement of transaction costs is necessary.

According to (Gurbaxani and Whang 1991, p. 64) (market) transaction costs are synonymous with the external coordination costs involved in using an outside market. These are subdivided into operational costs due to the loss of operational efficiencies and contractual costs. While operational costs consist of costs of searching, transportation, inventory holding, and communication (for communicating with geographically separated vendors), contractual costs involve the costs of writing and enforcing contracts.

In (Brynjolfsson, Malone et al. 1994, p. 1631) the authors divide the costs of producing a good into production costs and coordination costs. Production costs are defined as the costs of the physical production process, whereas coordination costs are caused by managing the dependencies between the production tasks, i.e. "making sure that the right things and the right people are in the right places at the right times" (Brynjolfsson, Malone et al. 1994, p. 1632). Coordination costs are further divided into the subcategories "internal coordination costs" and "external coordination costs". Internal coordination costs include the costs of deciding when, where, and how a good is to be produced in-house. On the other hand, external coordination costs have to be paid as soon as the product is purchased from an outside supplier and include the supplier's costs for marketing, sales and billing, as well as the costs of finding this supplier, negotiating contracts and paying bills. In addition to production and coordination costs, in (Malone, Yates et al. 1987, p. 1319) the author analyses vulnerability costs, the "unavoidable costs of a changed situation that are incurred before the organization can adapt to a new situation".

In (Clemons, Reddi et al. 1993, p. 14) the authors not only analyze coordination costs as part of the transaction costs, but also indirect costs caused by transaction risk. The authors distinguish between costs induced by operations risk and those resulting from opportunism risk. Operations risk becomes an issue when the other party in a transaction willfully misrepresents or withholds information, or underperforms its agreed responsibilities. Sources of operations risk are information asymmetries, differences in bargaining power, or incomplete as well as unenforceable contracts. Opportunism risk, on the other hand, is the risk "associated with a lack of bargaining power or the loss of bargaining power directly resulting from the execution of a relationship, that is, a difference between ex ante and ex post bargaining power" (Clemons, Reddi et al. 1993, p. 16). Sources of opportunism risk are relationship-specific investments, small numbers bargaining or a loss of resource control (e.g. the supplier uses the relationship to "steal" know-how and consequently becomes a competitor).

Since in this work the use of information technology in different phases of a supplier relationship (see 2.1.5) is analyzed, a distinction of transaction cost components according to the phase of the transaction in which they are incurred is appropriate. Phase-oriented approaches to classify transaction cost components are widespread in literature (see e.g. (Picot 1982, p. 270; Picot 1991, p. 344; Rennings, Fonger et al. 1992; Schmid 1993, p. 467; Isermann and Kaupp 1996, p. 61; Windsperger 1996, pp. 13-19)). Moreover, in (Wegehenkel 1981, p. 21) the author distinguishes between sunk and running transaction costs depending on the phase in which the current transaction is when a decision on this transaction takes place.

Following phase-oriented approaches and considering our systematization of the life cycle of a supplier relationship we distinguish between the evaluation costs of a transaction which are incurred during the evaluation phase, and the settlement costs of a transaction which are caused during the settlement phase.

The evaluation costs of a transaction consist of:

- contact costs to find a potential transaction partner and to establish initial contact;

- costs of gathering further information about the potential transaction partner;

- negotiation costs, incurred through negotiations, contractual arrangements, and agreements between partners; and

- decision costs when deciding whether to continue searching or to accept an offer.

On the other hand, the settlement costs of a transaction consist of:

- costs of signing the contract;

- costs of initializing the relationship[14];

- costs of exchanging goods and payments;

- adjustment costs, incurred by supervising agreements[15] and planned or unplanned changes of the original provisions of the contract;

- decision costs when deciding whether to prolong a contract or to change to an alternative supplier; and

- in the case of a change of transaction partner the costs of resolving the relationship withto the previous supplier. These costs also comprise penalties, which can be contractual, e.g. when resolving a contract before its maturity, or can be indirect[16]. Indirect costs are caused by losing non-transferable cost advantages due to a repeated use of a certain supplier. Airlines, for example, enroll passengers in "frequent-flyer" programs that reward them for repeated travel on the same carrier (Klemperer 1987b, p. 376).

The costs connected with the change of a transaction partner, i.e. costs of signing the new contract, initialization costs, decision costs, and costs of resolving the relationship to the previous supplier, are defined in the literature as switching costs (Klemperer 1987b, p. 376)[17] or setup costs (Thum 1995, p. 85).

In respect of the participants in a transaction two behavioral assumptions are employed: bounded rationality and opportunism (Williamson 1991, p. 92). The first behavioral assumption is discussed in (Simon 1976). According to Simon, though humans intend to act rationally they sometimes fail in this (Simon 1976, p. XXVIII). The reasons are the limited information processing capacity of the human brain and problems of communication. The latter arises when abilities or knowledge can only partially be described in words. The assumption of bounded rationality excludes the possibility of complete contracts (Williamson 1991, p. 92).

The second assumption describes the phenomenon that humans tend to pursue their personal interests even by accepting disadvantages for others and disregarding social norms. In consequence, "promises to behave responsibly that are unsupported by credible commitments will not, therefore, be reliably discharged." (Williamson 1991, p. 92) The prospect of opportunistic behavior makes the issue of trust particularly important.

---

[14] Initialization costs comprise also learning costs for acquiring the ability to work together with the new supplier and to handle the product delivered by the new supplier.

[15] These costs are also referred to as agency costs.

[16] Klemperer refers to the indirect costs also as "artificial switching costs" (Klemperer 1987b, p. 376).

[17] For the fundamental contribution to the theory of switching cost cf. (Weizsäcker 1984).

To make transactions accessible to a systematic analysis transaction cost economists have introduced different dimensions in respect of the properties of a transaction and also concerning environmental conditions in which transactions take place. These are the conditions of asset specificity, the degree and type of uncertainty to which transactions are subject, and the frequency in which transactions occur (Williamson 1991, p. 93). These dimensions are seen as the principal determinants of transactions. The condition of asset specificity is judged to be the most important determinant in decisions on governance structures (Williamson 1985, p. 52). Nonetheless other authors have extended these dimensions by additional factors. Of these additional dimensions the complexity of a transaction and the traded goods was given the most attention (see, e.g., (Picot and Dietl 1990, p. 179)).

2.2.1.1 Asset specificity

The notion of specificity can be interpreted in two ways. On the one hand, specificity can be understood as a feature of the traded product. A highly specific good is usually custom-made and available from only a few suppliers. On the other hand, specificity can be related to investments made to support the transaction or the production of the good. If these investments cannot be used for alternative purposes, then they are specific to the relationship. Relationship specific investments are also referred to as idiosyncratic investments, i.e. investments specialized on particular transactions (Williamson 1985, pp. 52-53). Moreover, transactions inducing nonspecific investments are also characterized as standardized transactions (Williamson 1985, pp. 72-73). In (Williamson 1985, p. 55), the author distinguishes between four types of specificity: site specificity, physical asset specificity, human asset specificity, and specificity due to dedicated assets[18].

In case of site specificity the buyer and seller are situated geographically closely to each other. This happens with the aim of minimizing inventory and transportation costs. An example of site specificity is the steel producer choosing to locate its steel works near large deposits of iron-ore or coal.

Physical asset specificity is present when one or both parties to a transaction make investments in equipment and machinery which is only usable in the current transaction and which has lower value in alternative uses. This kind of investment is done, for example, when the supplier of a car manufacturer invests in special machines in order to produce an intermediate product that only fits the automobile of its customer.

---

[18]   According to (Picot and Dietl 1990, p. 179) the distinction of these four sources of asset specificity is neither disjunctive nor absolute. There might be other sources of specificity, e.g. time-specific investments.

Human asset specificity is present when investments in relationship-specific human capital arise, i.e. when employees gain specific knowledge about a transaction partner. Moreover, it may happen that special skills are acquired when a relationship requires the application of a specific production technology.

Finally, dedicated assets are investments by a supplier which are made only in order to sell a significant amount of a (standard or non-standard) product to a particular customer. If the contract were terminated prematurely it would leave the supplier with excess capacity.

Relationship specific investments are particularly a problem when the transaction partner behaves opportunistically (Williamson 1975, p. 27; Picot and Dietl 1990, p. 179). In renegotiations of a contract, e.g. with the purpose to prolong the current contract or to make adaptations, the party that has made relationship-specific investments is particularly vulnerable, primarily because they cannot reliably threaten a change of transaction partner. Opportunistic behavior in this context means that the other party takes advantage of this vulnerability and uses its power to secure a greater share of the net benefit expected from the relationship.

2.2.1.2 Uncertainty in terms of transaction and behavior

Contracts as a basis of relations only reflect the knowledge existing at the moment of their signing. As these are based on bounded rationality, it is impossible to develop a detailed strategy to anticipate all possible changes in advance (Picot and Dietl 1990, p. 179). Hence a transaction can be subject to uncertainty in terms of the (unforeseen) necessity of changing the contract once it is signed (Picot, Reichwald et al. 1996). Unforeseen changes in a contract can occur with different frequency and extent. Frequent changes in the conditions of a contract, e.g. prices, scheduled times, and amounts, lead to renegotiations and thus to higher transaction costs (Picot, Reichwald et al. 1996, p. 43).

An additional source of uncertainty derives from the behavior of the contracting parties. Behavioral uncertainty is primarily relevant when adaptations of a contract become necessary (Williamson 1985, p. 58). As we have seen in the previous section in the context of asset specificity, as soon as relationship-specific investments have been made, the investor faces the problem that the transaction partner might behave in an opportunistic way. Behavioral uncertainty emerges when the investor is not sure about the transaction partner's inclination to opportunistic behavior.

2.2.1.3 Complexity of transaction and good

In contrast to uncertainty, complexity refers to a situation which is fixed, but can only, or only partly be managed in terms of dependent factors (Picot and Dietl 1990, p. 179). The transaction as well as the traded good can differ in terms of complexity. The complexity of a good increases with the number of attributes necessary to describe it sufficiently in a certain context. The complexity of a transaction changes with the number of possible states considered in the underlying (complete) contract.

2.2.1.4 Frequency of a transaction

The concept of frequency can be applied to transactions in different ways. Frequency in its original sense relates to time, so that it denotes the number of exchanges of the traded good in a given period of time. Alternatively, detached from the time dimension, it can be interpreted simply as the amount of goods exchanged on basis of a single supplier contract, which can also be called the transaction volume of a contract (Williamson 1985, pp. 60-61; Picot and Dietl 1990, p. 180). Finally, frequency can be used to describe the number of contracts signed within a given period of time. These three measurements are correlated to each other as illustrated in Figure 9.

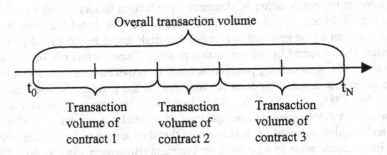

Figure 9:   Different notions of "frequency".

Given a reference period in which a particular number of goods is traded and given that the transaction volume is a multiple integer of this amount. Furthermore, if the overall transaction volume of a sequence of business relationships is given, e.g. determined by the duration of the life-cycle of the traded good, then ceteris paribus the greater the number of contracts the lower the volume of goods exchanged per contract (et vice versa). Moreover, if the transaction volume per contract is given, then the greater the frequency in the first sense, the greater the number of contracts necessary to exchange the overall transaction volume.

Unfortunately, in the literature it is often not clear what kind of measurement the authors are referring to when speaking of "frequency". Otherwise they usually follow the second interpretation, while it is additionally assumed that a single contract is signed for the total expected demand for a particular good.

2.2.1.5   Fundamental transformation

If a good is purchased from an external supplier for the first time, then the transaction partner who offers the best conditions for the purchase is selected. The contract partner is chosen under the conditions of competition and equal opportunities for every supplier. As soon as a contract is signed and specific investments are made, the current trading partner has an advantage compared to alternative potential transaction partners when negotiations about the prolongation of the contract take place. This change in character of a business relation is denoted in (Williamson 1985, pp. 61-63) as the fundamental transformation of a large numbers bidding condition at the outset into one of bilateral supply thereafter. In (Picot and Dietl 1990, pp. 179-180) the authors refer to the fundamental transformation as ex ante and ex post specificity. An ex ante unspecific market-like relationship changes into a specific monopoly-like relationship when a transaction has been established.

2.2.2   Production costs

Production is the combination of elementary production factors in order to obtain an output (Michaelis 1985, p. 84). Production factors can be human work, aggregates used in the production process, materials going into the final product, and materials consumed by the production process. These factors can be provided either internally, thus causing production costs, or provided by external suppliers. In the latter case acquisition costs are incurred on the purchaser's side (see also (Michaelis 1985, pp. 83-85)). When analyzing governance structures for transactions, a ceteris paribus assumption is often made in respect of production costs and acquisition costs, i.e. it is assumed that they are equal for all alternatives taken into consideration in a decision on contracts (Bössmann 1982, p. 665; Picot 1982, p. 271; Windsperger 1983, p. 899; Michaelis 1985, p. 89). However, in respect of an external supplier's production costs, in (Bretzke 1994, pp. 321-327) the author identifies five advantages which are likely to lead to reduced acquisition costs for the purchasing organization. The five advantages are:

- realization of economies of scale;

- cost degression by optimizing capacity utilization;

- increasing efficiency by specialization;

- decreasing labor cost by arbitrage between industrial sectors and/or geographical locations[19]; and

---

[19]   Bretzke refers only to branche arbitrage (Bretzke 1994). However, this aspect can be extended to arbitrage between different geographical locations as well.

- opportunity costs caused by a suboptimal allocation of capital in the customer's organization.

2.2.2.1 Economies of scale

Economies of scale describe the aspect of declining average costs per unit of goods produced when the amount of production increases. Let the total production costs C be the sum of the fix costs c_f and the variable costs c_v, weighted by the amount produced x, so that

(eq. 12) $C = c_f + c_v x$.

Then the average costs

(eq. 13) $C_a = \dfrac{c_f}{x} + c_v$

decrease in x. Neglecting profits and assuming that a supplier has more than one customer for a given good and that the cost structures, i.e. the fixed and variable costs, are the same for the supplier and its customers, then the supplier's price, which forms customer's acquisition costs, is lower than the customer's production costs. Moreover, the supplier which produces large amounts of goods has a stronger position in negotiations with the suppliers which deliver the inputs for the production of these goods, thus leading to lower variable and fixed costs.

2.2.2.2 Capacity utilization

The utilization of capacity can vary randomly over time. This leads, on the one hand, to opportunity costs incurred by insufficient production capacity, which become manifest in a loss of sales orders. On the other hand, idle capacity costs are caused by excess production capacity. These costs are reduced on the supplier's side, when a particular good is jointly produced for a number of customers, because the variations in customers' demands compensate each other to some extent. The compensating effect, however, is reduced or even completely vanishes in the case of systematic variations in capacity utilization, caused, for example, by seasonal fluctuations in demand.

2.2.2.3 Efficiency gains by specialization

Efficiency gains can be realized on the supplier's side for two reasons: experience and effort. Experience in the production process increases with the amount of goods produced, thus leading to reduced variable unit cost. Moreover, assuming that there is more than one supplier available for a particular good, then the efforts in optimizing and executing the production process are the greater the more intensive the competition between the suppliers. On the other hand, producing a good in-house often means no pressure of competition because there is no risk of the producing department's losing the "customer". Consequently efforts are less intense and production costs are comparatively high.

2.2.2.4 Arbitrage between industrial sectors and/or geographical locations

If supplier and customer are embedded in different industrial sectors, it may be that a supplier's labor costs are lower than the labor costs borne by its customer, e.g. those caused by the different power of trade unions in the respective sectors. The same argument holds for lower costs on the supplier's side caused by its geographical location, e.g. in countries with lower labor costs or better access to resources.

2.2.2.5 Opportunity costs of suboptimal capital allocation

Opportunity costs are incurred when limited capital is not used in the business area where it promises the highest return. If the decision criterion for capital allocation is the maximization of the return on investment, then only those business areas which promise the highest returns on investment should be kept in-house. As a result of the factors discussed in sections 2.2.2.1 to 2.2.2.4, the supplier's return on investment is comparatively higher for a good on which it is specialized than the customer's, since the latter concentrates on the production of other products, i.e. the supplier has an advantage in terms of opportunity costs.

The discussion of transaction costs and production costs so far reveals a trade-off: although the relationship with external suppliers is subject to increased transaction costs as the behavioral assumptions of bounded rationality and opportunistic behavior become relevant, these additional costs are compensated by acquisition cost reductions because of production cost advantages on the supplier's side. Consequently, when the customer decides on the governance structure, transaction costs as well as production costs must be taken into consideration.

2.2.3 Optimal governance structure

The principal dimensions in terms of which transactions differ influence the structure and value of transaction costs (Williamson 1985). Different structures and values of transaction costs lead to different choices of governance. In order to analyze how the dimensions of specificity, uncertainty, complexity, and frequency influence contracting, we discuss as a first step the way these dimensions influence the evaluation and the settlement costs of a supplier relationship. As a second step we show how an optimal governance structure is derived from the ascertained dependencies.

Increasing asset specificity leads to an increasing interest of the transaction partners that the relation continues, due to the fact that otherwise relationship specific investments would not be paid off. In terms of transaction costs, high asset specificity means that the purchasing organization must expend extensive resources to evaluate potential transaction partners in terms of their prospective behavior in a transaction. Moreover, asset specificity leads to increased settlement costs. It is not usually possible to preclude the behavioral uncertainty in the evaluation phase completely. Therefore one may still expect losses in the settlement phase due to opportunistic behavior when contracts are renegotiated. These losses are greater the higher the behavioral uncertainty.

A similar argumentation holds when specificity relates to the purchased goods. If the traded goods are specific, then it will be harder to find transaction partners, and negotiations will be more costly, because no standard contracts can be used. Moreover, the expected loss caused by opportunistic behavior of a transaction partner grows as well, because the transaction partner cannot easily be changed. Hence the settlement costs will also be high.

In terms of transaction costs the presence of uncertainty results in greater evaluation and settlement costs compared to a situation without uncertainty. Behavioral uncertainty can be reduced by extending activities to evaluate potential transaction partners in the evaluation phase of a business relationship. Thus for a given amount of accepted risk growing uncertainty in terms of transaction partner behavior leads to increasing evaluation costs incurred during the search process. In the settlement phase, on the other hand, behavioral uncertainty becomes apparent when a contract is adjusted. The higher the risk that the transaction partner may behave opportunistically during renegotiations of a contract, the greater the expected loss from this opportunistic behavior.

Uncertainty in terms of environmental changes influences the number of possible states which must be considered when a contract is negotiated. The evaluation costs are greater the more states are taken into account, i.e. the higher the uncertainty. In the settlement phase, on the other hand, uncertainty in terms of environmental changes works rather through the number of necessary renegotiations of a contract over the course of a transaction. The higher the uncertainty, the more often renegotiations are necessary and the greater the settlement costs.

The degree of complexity of transactions and goods has a similar effect to uncertainty. A high complexity of the traded goods results in more product attributes to be evaluated in the search process. Hence evaluation costs will be high. As the efforts in case of transaction partner change grow, this makes the buyer more vulnerable to opportunistic behavior, so that the settlement costs will also be high.

On the other hand, complexity in terms of the conditions of a transaction leads to more complex contracts, so that negotiation costs are raised when establishing a relationship for the first time as well as when adaptations of an existing contract become necessary.

It is obvious that the frequency of a transaction, understood as the amount of goods purchased on basis of a contract, influences the total transaction costs through its volume dependent components, e.g. the costs of exchanging the traded good. The volume independent parts of the transaction costs are more interesting. As a transaction becomes less frequent, the unit evaluation costs increase and the volume independent investments in the evaluation of transaction partners are less likely to be paid off. In particular, efforts made in the negotiation of transaction-specific governance structures are no longer profitable. The same holds for the components of the settlement costs which are independent of the transaction volume, e.g. the initialization cost.

A synopsis of the transaction determinants and their influence on the evaluation and settlement costs is provided in Table 2.

Table 2: Synopsis of transaction determinants and their influence on transaction costs.

Transaction determinant		Evaluation costs	Settlement costs
Specificity	of the traded good	Increase with growing specificity because potential transaction partners can hardly be found.	Increase with growing specificity because alternative transaction partners are difficult to find, so that the risk of opportunistic behavior increases.
	of assets used to support the transaction	Increase with growing specificity because purchaser must cover himself against the risk of opportunistic behavior.	Increase with growing specificity because of the risk of opportunistic behavior in case of contract adaptations.
Uncertainty	in terms of the behavior of transaction partners	Increase with growing uncertainty because more efforts must be made to evaluate potential transaction partners.	Increase with growing uncertainty because of the risk of opportunistic behavior in case of contract adaptations.
	in terms of environmental changes	Increase with growing uncertainty because more possible states must be considered in a contract.	Increase with growing uncertainty because more contract adaptations are expected.

Table 2: Continued.

Transaction determinant		Evaluation costs	Settlement costs
Complexity	of the traded good	Increase with growing complexity because more product attributes must be evaluated.	Increase with growing complexity because greater evaluation costs makes the buyer more vulnerable to opportunistic behavior.
Complexity	of the transaction	Increase with growing complexity because contracts are more complex.	Increase with growing complexity because renegotiations of contracts are more expensive.
Frequency	in the interpretation of the number of purchased goods per contract	Increasing frequency leads to lower unit evaluation cost because the evaluation costs are independent from the transaction volume.	Increasing frequency leads to lower unit settlement cost because the initialization costs are independent from the transaction volume.

On taking a closer look at the determinants influencing the settlement costs of a transaction, we notice that some transaction determinants have a direct impact on cost parameters. This is the case for both kinds of uncertainty and the complexity of a transaction, whereas all transaction determinants (except the frequency of a transaction) have an indirect influence on the settlement costs through increased evaluation costs: as evaluation costs grow, the costs of changing transaction partner grows, too, so that the expected loss caused by opportunistic behavior of the transaction partner is increasingly imminent.

Williamson derives the optimal governance structure in dependence from investment characteristics which range from nonspecific, i.e. standard transactions, to idiosyncratic, and frequency of the transaction, which can be recurrent or occasional. It is assumed that uncertainty and opportunistic behavior are present. Moreover, four assumptions are made (Williamson 1985, p. 72):

1. Suppliers and buyers intend to be in business on a continuing basis.

2. Potential suppliers for any given requirement are numerous, i.e. ex ante monopoly in ownership of specialized resources is assumed away.

3. The frequency dimension refers strictly to buyer activity in the market.

4. The investment dimension refers to the characteristics of investments made by suppliers.

Varying the dimensions of specificity and frequency, the different contract types induce different transaction costs. Depending on the variations considered, this leads to an optimal selection of contracts as described in Figure 10.

Classical contracting is the main governance structure for nonspecific transactions of an occasional, e.g. purchasing standard equipment, and recurrent kind, e.g. purchasing standard material (Williamson 1985, p. 73). Market governance[20] is superior to neoclassical or relational contracting, because being standardized, purchase and supply arrangements are easy to work out. There is no need for precautions to prevent opportunistic behavior. It is relatively cheap to change transaction partner, which leads to high incentives for suppliers not to behave opportunistically. In case of nonspecific but occasional transactions buyers and sellers are less able to rely on direct experience to safeguard transactions against opportunism. However, rating services or the experience of other buyers of the same good can often be consulted. The existence of these facilities provides incentives for parties to behave responsibly.

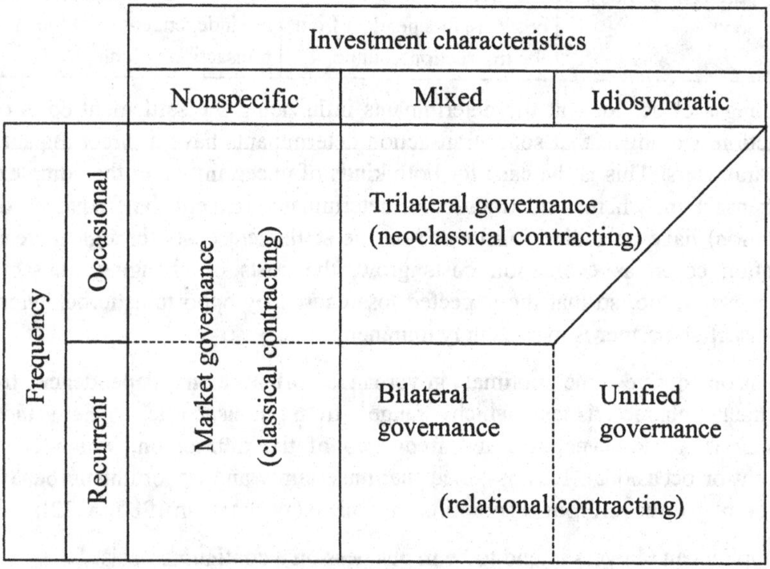

		Investment characteristics		
		Nonspecific	Mixed	Idiosyncratic
Frequency	Occasional	Market governance (classical contracting)	Trilateral governance (neoclassical contracting)	
	Recurrent		Bilateral governance	Unified governance
			(relational contracting)	

Figure 10:   Efficient governance. Source: (Williamson 1985, p. 79, Figure 3-2)

---

[20] The term of market governance used by Williamson is misleading. Neoclassical and relational contracts are negotiated and signed using markets, too. See also the discussion about market and hierarchy in chapter 2.1.4.1.

Neoclassical contracts are the best alternative for occasional transactions which are moderately to highly specific (Williamson 1985, pp. 73-74). An example of an occasional transaction of moderate specificity is the purchase of customized equipment, whereas the construction of a plant is a highly specific transaction. Once such a contract has been established, there are strong incentives for the party which has made specific investments to see the contract completed, since the transfer of specialized assets to an alternative transaction partner would be costly. Compared with classical contracting, neoclassical contracting has the advantage that in case of disputes the resolving mechanisms by using third parties assistance are not as grave for the transaction as is the case when being involved in a lawsuit with the transaction partner (Picot and Dietl 1990, p. 181).

According to Williamson, bilateral governance is the best choice for recurrent transactions which are moderately specific as is the case for example when purchasing customized material (Williamson 1985, pp. 75-77). Again, the nonstandardized nature of the transaction prompts the transaction partner to be interested in a continuing trading relationship. The recurrent nature of the transaction potentially permits the cost of specialized governance structures to be recovered. The higher contracting costs are compensated by a lower loss caused by opportunistic behavior, i.e. the higher contracting costs of a bilateral contract compared to those of a neoclassical contract are worthwhile.

Unified governance is the best alternative for recurrent and partly occasional transactions which are highly specific (Williamson 1985, p. 78). An example of this kind of transaction is the site-specific transfer of intermediate products across successive stages. When assets become more specialized to a single use and thus less transferable to other purposes, economies of scale can be as fully realized by the buyer as by an outside supplier. The choice of contract then depends only on the adaptive properties of the contracts. The advantage of in-house production compared to bilateral or neoclassical contracting is that adaptations can be made in a sequential way without the need to consult, complete, or revise interfirm agreements. Moreover, unified governance allows efficient and long-term incentive mechanisms and monitoring systems which are likely to limit opportunistic behavior (Picot and Dietl 1990, p. 181).

The approach of Williamson to explaining the occurrence of different governance structures has gained considerable popularity. The basic hypotheses, particularly with respect to the vertical integration of organizations, have been confirmed in a number of empirical works (Monteverde and Teece 1982; Walker and Weber 1984; Lazerson 1988; Sydow 1992, pp. 149-150; Fischer 1993, pp. 119-120; Kaas and Fischer 1993, pp. 691-692). However, empirical work examining governance structures making finer distinction between contractual alternatives, apart from the choice between "market" and "hierarchy", is rather rare and their results neither definitely disprove nor confirm the predictions of transaction cost theory (Sydow 1992, p. 144).

In this chapter we introduced the basic aspects of supplier relationships by describing the organization of procurement. We discussed the theoretical concepts of classical, neoclassical, and relational contracts and confronted these with supplier contracts observable in practice. To obtain a basis to evaluate different designs of a supplier relationship, we used the concept of transaction costs. We distinguished between evaluation and settlement costs according to the evaluation and the settlement phase of a supplier relationship and showed how transaction cost economists derive the optimal contract for a business relationship by minimizing transaction costs. Before addressing the question of how information technology influences the design of supplier relationships, we must be analyze, how information technology is likely to change transaction costs. The basic aspects of information technology and its impact on transaction costs are the subject of the next chapter.

3 Information Technology

The aim of the present chapter is to analyze how information technology is likely to influence transaction costs and to discuss the conclusions drawn from this by theory. First, an introduction to the basic aspects of information technology is given and we discuss, how information technology is used in information systems (section 3.1). Subsequently, a number of examples are provided to show how information technology is used to support procurement activities in organizations (section 3.2). Finally, in section 3.3 an overview of theoretical and empirical work related to the impact of information technology on relationships between organizations is given.

3.1 Basic aspects of information technology

Information technology is hardware and software that perform data processing tasks (Alter 1996, p. 715). Hardware is the devices and other physical things involved in processing information. This can be e.g. computers, physical networks, and data storage devices. Software is the computer programs that interpret user inputs and tell the hardware what to do (Alter 1996, p. 2). In (Mertens, Bodendorf et al. 1998, p. 12) the authors distinguish between system software and application software according to its nearness to the hardware or the user. The purpose of system software is to make the hardware usable. This happens independently from the application context in which the hardware is used. System software forms the interface between application software and the hardware, whereas the purpose of application software, as used in organizations, is to provide support in the fulfillment of operational tasks. The context in which application software is implemented and used can vary from simple support by a word processor in writing correspondence to complex tasks such as the automation of workflows by workflow management systems, the processing of data by database management systems, or the exchange of orders between customers and their suppliers by order processing systems.

On the technical level, computers can be interconnected to constitute a network. Components of a network are the computers with hard- and software facilities to get linked to the network (e.g. network adapter, modem, and the respective drivers), the physical links between the computers, and network protocols. A network can be used to exchange information between computers on the level of the application. The system formed in this way is also called an information system (Alter 1996, p. 2). An information system is used to capture, transmit, store, retrieve, manipulate, or display information used in one or more business processes (Alter 1996, p. 2). Indeed, information technology unfolds its benefits through its use in information systems. This assumption is implied whenever we address information technology and its influence on business processes.

We can distinguish different types of information systems depending on the application context in which they are used. One distinction is between information systems primarily used to support business processes taking place within a particular organization on the one side, and information systems used between organizations on the other side. The former serve the purpose of supporting the hierarchical form of task accomplishment and are referred to as intraorganizational information systems (Mertens 1988; Scheer 1990; Mertens and Griese 1991; Picot, Reichwald et al. 1996). The latter support primarily interorganizational information processing and electronic data exchange and are called interorganizational information systems (Picot, Reichwald et al. 1996).

Intraorganizational information systems are further classified by their function in decision making into transaction processing systems, management information systems, and decision support systems (Alter 1996, p. 214; Stair and Reynolds 1998, p. 344).

Transaction processing systems collect and store information about business transactions in an automated or manual way. Examples are systems for order entry, inventory control, payroll, accounts payable, and general ledger. The input to these systems is triggered by basic business transactions such as customer orders, purchase orders, receipts, and invoices (Stair and Reynolds 1998, p. 344). In (Picot, Reichwald et al. 1996, p. 167) concerning transaction processing systems the authors distinguish between quantitatively-oriented operative systems and value-oriented accounting systems. The task of operative systems is to steer transaction processes and to deliver information about the status and course of quantitatively-oriented value-added processes. These basic processes are overlaid by value-oriented planning functions that are accomplished by accounting systems, e.g. systems for warehouse accounting, facilities accounting, and accounts receivable. The operative systems deliver the input for accounting systems. The information collected and stored by transaction processing systems serves as the foundation for management information systems and decision support systems.

Management information systems combine transaction processing system data with data from external sources and convert it in order to provide managers with routine information for monitoring performance and managing the organization (Alter 1996, p. 214; Picot, Reichwald et al. 1996, p. 167).

While management information systems focus on the support of well-structured routine decisions, decision support systems assist in solving poorly structured decision problems (Alter 1996, p. 214; Picot, Reichwald et al. 1996, p. 167). This is achieved by providing access to suitable information, a collection of methods, decision models, and/or analysis tools. A particular form of decision support systems is executive decision systems (or synonymously executive information systems) that assist senior-level executives in their decisions (Stair and Reynolds 1998, p. 647). Another kind of decision support systems is specialized in supporting teamwork. These groupware systems help teams work together by providing access to team data, structuring work flows, structuring communication, and make it easier to schedule meetings (Alter 1996, p. 214; Picot, Reichwald et al. 1996, p. 167).

Information systems to support interorganizational information processing and electronic data exchange are classified by the phase of a business relationship (see 2.1.5) in which they are primarily used. In the settlement phase of a business relationship information systems are used to support (Picot, Reichwald et al. 1996):

- administrative tasks of interorganizational information processing with the purpose to enable the electronic exchange of accounting data and the computer-supported transmission of payment orders;

- order of items from suppliers, e.g. based on the demand at the assembly line;

- marketing and sales with the purpose to exchange purchasing data with customers;

- electronic connections to shipping agents or trading firms in the shipping logistics area; and

- cooperation between organizations in product development by enabling the exchange of information, e.g. technical specifications or construction data.

On the other hand, in the evaluation phase of a business relationship interorganizational information systems are used to support

- transaction partner search, e.g. Internet search engines help to identify products in electronic catalogs provided by suppliers; and

- negotiations of contracts, e.g. negotiation support systems assist in finding contract conditions acceptable for all contracting parties.

In both cases, inter- and intraorganizational information systems, a critical task is the bringing together of different information system elements. This task is also called integration. Integration happens in different dimensions, e.g. in terms of functions, data, and media (Picot, Reichwald et al. 1996, pp. 154-156; Mertens, Bodendorf et al. 1998, pp. 45-47)[21]. The integration of functions[22] within an organization serves the purpose of enabling integral approaches to solving operational tasks. For example, the integration of systems in procurement and manufacturing allows the integrative planning of production schedules and supplier orders. The benefit of this integration is reduced cost because there is less manual data transfer between the systems interacting in a business process. Therefore information passed between these systems runs through the business process faster.

To enable the integration of functions the data of the underlying business processes must often also be integrated. To return to the example of the integration of procurement and manufacturing systems, it is necessary for both systems to use a common database to deal with the availability of supplies and the terms of delivery. Besides the advantage of avoiding multiple data input in different systems, the consistency of data is also enhanced in this way.

Finally, different forms of media can be integrated, leading to multimedia systems. A supplier, for example, can use different types of media to present their product to potential customers. An appropriate technique for media integration is the creation of hypertext documents using the Hypertext Markup Language (HTML). In this way, as well as a textual description the multiple dimensions of a product can be described with the help of pictures, movies, and sound. The benefit of a multimedia description of goods is that more information about a particular product can be conveyed. Consequently the recipient of this information has a more realistic impression of the characteristics of a good, i.e. products of a high complexity can be described better.

A necessary condition of integration is that the components to be integrated be compatible with each other, i.e. that they be able to interoperate. Since organizations often own hardware and software from a variety of vendors the condition of compatibility is not always fulfilled. Indeed, it can be very expensive to make heterogeneous components interoperable. This problem leads to the demand for open systems. Open systems use clearly described nonproprietary industry standards available to anyone (Alter 1996, p. 24; Picot, Reichwald et al. 1996, p. 156). Thus, open systems make it easier and cheaper to switch hardware or software brands without significant change in the participating systems. Interoperability is achieved by using common standards for interconnecting the participating information systems. However, the mere existence of a standard is not sufficient to make an arbitrary interconnection of different systems possible.

---

[21] A description of the manifold dimensions of integration is provided in (Mertens, Bodendorf et al. 1998, pp. 45-47).

[22] We use the terms "function" and "process" synonymously (cf. (Mertens, Bodendorf et al. 1998, p. 45)).

Often there are competing standards among which users can choose and the decision for one standard prevents the user easily connecting with systems using other standards. Famous examples are ANSI X12 and EDIFACT for the exchange of business documents[23]. Hitherto, due to the cost of changing technology, the decision to use one of the two standards for the exchange of business documents has been a barrier to doing business with users of the other standard. Hence when a decision on the use of a particular information technology is made, as well as the support of standards, the diffusion of these standards among (potential) business partners is crucial.

In the remainder of this section the theory of network effects is used to analyze the determinants of decisions on the use of technology in general (section 3.1.1). Then we examine the issue of standards and standardization in section 3.1.2.

3.1.1 Theory of network effects

The benefit of using a particular good originates from two sources, the stand-alone utility of a good and the utility due to network effects (Thum 1995; Westarp and Wendt 2000). While the stand-alone utility of a good exists independently from its interfaces with other goods, the utility due to network effects depends on whether a good can be (easily) combined with other goods. Hence, the notion of "network" refers to the set of users consuming[24] the same (compatible) goods (Katz and Shapiro 1985, p. 424). The theory of network effects provides a number of approaches that serve in the analysis of individual buying decisions, marketing strategies, supply and demand equilibria, and welfare implications (Westarp and Wendt 2000). In the following, we only go into the question of how network effects influence the individual buying decisions of consumers.

Network effects are further subdivided into direct and indirect network effects (Katz and Shapiro 1985, p. 424). A good is subject to direct network effects if the benefit of its use increases with the number of consumers using that good. All media serving direct communication between its users underlie strong direct network effects. Electronic mail is an example of a communication medium that provides little benefit if nobody else uses this tool. However, the more potential communication partners use electronic mail, the higher the expected benefit of changing to that medium.

Indirect network effects can have different sources (Thum 1995, pp. 8-12): the consumption of complementary goods, learn effects, uncertainty, and

---

[23] For a detailed description of ANSI X12 and EDIFACT see chapter 3.2

[24] Literature about network effects follows the convention of using the terms "consumer" and "consumption" when talking about the users and use of a good. This does not mean that institutional users are excluded from the analysis. We adopt this terminology.

technological similarity. If the demand for a good rises, then the incentive to provide complementary goods increases as well. The more complementary goods are available for a product, however, the greater the incentives for new customers to purchase this product. An example of these interdependencies between users through the consumption of complementary goods is post purchase service (Katz and Shapiro 1985, p. 424). The decision on the purchase of a good may be influenced by the expectation of whether maintenance or consultancy services will be provided for this product afterwards. Another example is computer software provided to run on the basis of a particular hardware (Thum 1995, p. 8). The programming of software causes high fixed costs, while the variable costs of duplicating software are almost zero. Therefore, the incentive to develop software for this platform increases with the number of its users and the amount of available software for particular hardware grows with the diffusion of this hardware[25].

Furthermore, indirect network effects emerge when consumers of a product come to learn about the possible applications of a good upon using it. This sounds unusual at first. Still, even the manufacturer of a good sometimes is not sure about the possible application of its own product, as a statement of Masaru Ibuka, the founder of Sony, about the introduction of video recorders illustrates: "You can't research a market for a product that doesn't exist." (Thum 1995, p. 9). As was the case with video recorders, the consumers find out about the possible use of a product as they use it. Potential new consumers learn about the new applications that make it possibly worthwhile for them to buy this product. The effect of diffusion of knowledge from current owners to new potential consumers is also referred to as "informational spillover" (Thum 1995, p. 10). The more consumers adopt a new technology, the greater these informational spillovers.

Uncertainty causes interdependencies between consumers particularly in case of durable goods. When a good is used over a long period of time, then this usually involves a demand for spare parts and after sales service. If there are a number of competing technologies from which the purchaser can choose, then he or she can't be certain whether the selected technology will survive over the whole period in which it is used. The more consumers decide to buy a particular technology, the more certain a potential purchaser can be that spare parts and complementary product for this good will be available in the future.

Finally, network externalities emerge if there are a number of competing technologies which are technologically similar. To make products technologically similar the manufacturers usually have to accept a change in their production technology, which leads to rising production costs. Nevertheless the manufacturers are encouraged to accept this change, since technological similarity

---

[25] For a formal analysis of indirect network effects induced by complementary goods cf. (Chou and Shy 1990; Church and Gandal 1992; Church and Gandal 1993).

can possibly lead to increasing compatibility, so that the consumers' willingness to pay for these goods increases. Here, network effects emerge, because the manufacturer's decision on compatibility is usually made without considering the impact of this decision on the competitor's customers.

Empirical work indicates that the existence of network effects influences the decisions on the use of information technology. In an empirical survey conducted with the Fortune1000 companies in Germany and the US, MIS managers had been asked for their estimation of the importance of a number of selected factors for decisions on software (Westarp and Wendt 2000). These factors included features indicating network effects and stand-alone utility. For example, the respondents were asked to rate the importance of whether their business partners predominantly use the same solution. The respondents could choose among five categories from "very important" to "unimportant" and the question was posed for three categories of software: enterprise resource planning (ERP, e.g. SAP and Baan), office communication software (e.g. MS Office and Lotus Smart Suite), and EDI-systems (i.e. software to support the exchange of documents using EDI-standards). An important result of this survey is that the relative importance of utilities due to network effects and stand-alone utility in decisions on the selection of software is different for the three software categories. As shown in Figure 11, EDI-systems have a low stand-alone and high network effect utility, while ERP-systems traditionally have a high stand-alone and a low network effect utility. An example of software for which both of the dimensions are typically rated as being important is office communication software (e.g. MS Office and Lotus Smart Suite).

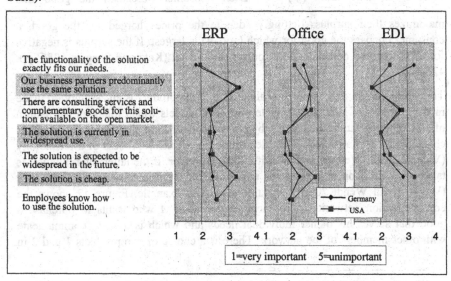

Figure 11:   The importance of selected factors for decisions on software.
Source: (Westarp and Wendt 2000, Figure 2)

Apart from the stand-alone utility of a good and the benefits caused by network externalities there is a third factor when making decisions on the use of information technology: the switching costs. Switching costs are caused by implementing the purchased technology in the existing environment, e.g. the cost of making the new technology compatible with other technologies with which it will interact[26]. Once a decision in favor of a particular technology is made and the relevant switching costs are borne, the purchaser loses flexibility in the future choice of alternative solutions, i.e. the user is "locked in" to this technology. Klemperer refers to this phenomenon as a change of products from ex ante homogeneity to ex post heterogeneity after the purchase (Klemperer 1987b, p. 376).

There are a number of approaches to decision models considering network effects[27]. Among the first were Katz and Shapiro. In (Katz and Shapiro 1985) they develop a model in which the consumers' willingness to pay is split up on the two terms: r, denoting the consumer's basic willingness to pay for the good i, and the externality function $v(y_i^e)$ as the value the customer attaches to the network effect when the installed base (i.e. the expected number of users of the good) is y^e (eq. 14). Consumers are assumed to be heterogeneous in their basic willingness to pay for the product, but homogeneous in their valuations of the network externality.

$$(eq. 14) \quad r + v(y_i^e) - p_i$$

The externality function is taken to be twice continuously differentiable, with $v'>0$, $v''<0$, and $\lim_{y \to \infty} v'(y) = 0$. Each consumer purchases the good that maximizes their surplus. Letting p_i denote the price charged for the good, a consumer chooses the good for which (eq. 14) is largest. If the surplus is negative for all i, then the consumer stays out of the market (Katz and Shapiro 1985, pp. 426-427).

The interpretation of y_i^e as the installed base of the product is an assumption made in the tradition of structural diffusion network models which focus on the pattern of all existing relations between subjects in a network and show how the structural characteristics of a social system determine the diffusion process of a technology (Valente 1995; Westarp and Wendt 2000). However, if the latter interpretation is taken as a decision parameter for the consumer wrong decisions may occur. In (Westarp and Wendt 2000) the authors give an example: Figure 12 shows the communication network environment of consumer A who wants to purchase a good that serves his or her individual needs and which is used to communicate with other members of the network. There is a choice of two products 1 and 2 in

---

[26] For the detailed discussion of switching costs before the background of supplier relationships see section 2.2.1.

[27] For a brief overview cf. (Westarp and Wendt 2000).

the market. Under the assumption that both products are free and have identical functionality the buying decision depends only on the network effects. Applying traditional models that base the decision whether to adopt a particular technology on the size of the installed base, consumer A would buy product 2 since the installed base with 4 existing adopters is greater than the installed base of product 1.

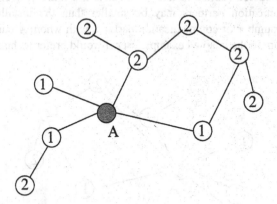

Figure 12:   Static communication network environment of consumer A, following (Westarp and Wendt 2000, Figure 3).

The solution to this problem is simple. If the decision maker focuses on their communication partners instead of the installed base, the consumer will decide correctly to buy product 1 since the majority of the direct communication partners uses this solution. This assumption is made in relational diffusion network models which serve the purpose of analyzing how direct contacts between participants in networks influence the decision to adopt a technology (Valente 1995; Westarp and Wendt 2000). However, though in the case of static networks this interpretation leads to better decisions, when considering the dynamics of a network, the decision may still be wrong. Indeed, as Farrell and Saloner point out, much discussion of the adoption of innovation has been conducted in terms of whether to adopt, and if so, which innovation to adopt. The important problem of when a new technology should be adopted has received much less attention (Farrell and Saloner 1987, p. 15). To illustrate the effect of network dynamics, let us extend the example by two additional factors: network growth and fluctuation.

Consider that the number of users of each technology grows with different rates over time. Then the communication links to communication partners who use neither technology 1 nor technology 2 (and who are thus not included in Figure 12 as members of the network) have to be considered in a decision as well. If the number of users for technology 2 grows faster than the number of users of technology 1, then the decision to implement product 2 may be correct.

68

The second extension of the example takes into account that A possibly has changing communication partners over time. If it is assumed that the underlying business is not changed when changing communication partners and that with each communication partner this business is done over the same period of time, then besides the currently active links to communication partners (non-dotted lines adjacent to A in Figure 13), possible links to potential communication partners must also be considered (dotted lines adjacent to A in Figure 13). The number of potential communication partners may be smaller than the installed base and greater than the number of communication partners with whom A currently keeps up communication. In the adapted example user A would prefer technology 2.

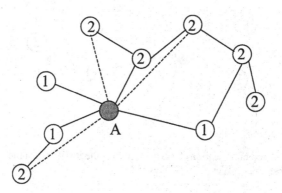

Figure 13:   Dynamic communication network environment of consumer A.

However, as is true of the application of every decision-supporting model, the decision-maker faces the problem of collecting the relevant input data. Although the quality of the decision improves with the amount of relevant data collected and the precision of this data, the task of data collection can be so expensive that the benefit of getting close to the optimal decision is compensated for by high information costs. Hence, in technology adoption decisions simple heuristic approaches, e.g. taking the installed base as approximation for the relevant network, extended by estimated growth rates of technology diffusion, may be justified in some cases.

A problem of uncoordinated decisions on the adoption of innovative technologies is that, as long as the installed base of the new technology is sufficiently small in comparison to the established technology, nobody wants to be the first to give up the advantages of the greater network effects of the established technology. Therefore, even if the new technology were superior as compared to the old technology, i.e. it would be desirable from an overall economic point of view to change, the change does not happen. This effect is also called "excess inertia" of technology adoption (Thum 1995, p. 19).

The installed base plays an important role also in the strategy of technology providers, who are particularly interested in reaching a larger market share for their products. Hence, there is an interaction between the consumers' adoption decisions and the manufacturers' price and product strategies. These price and product strategies usually aim at overcoming the effect of excess inertia by extending the installed base of their product. There follow a few examples of possible strategies.

The seller of a technology can exploit the lock-in effect when introducing a new technology into the market by subsidizing the price of the offered product, i.e. selling it at (or even lower than) cost price. As soon as enough users are locked in to this technology, further developed versions of the good or complementary products can be sold with a higher margin. This strategy of intertemporal price discrimination is also known as the sponsoring of technology (Thum 1995, p. 46)[28]. The limits of this strategy emerge as soon as there are many suppliers of a particular technology so that the consumer can, though not change technology, change the supplier with relatively low switching costs, i.e. competition prevents sellers from exploiting lock-in effects.

Alternative strategies are based on special forms of purchasing contracts, e.g. update and service contracts. Update contracts are particularly common on the software market. This is a form of price discrimination in which a relatively high price is demanded from buyers who purchase the good for the first time, while the consumers of the installed base are offered update versions for a special rate, i.e. the consumers who already own an older version of the product are paying only for the technological progress (Thum 1995, p. 89). Whereas in case of service contracts the consumer buys a technology together with all future improvements of this technology, i.e. the manufacturer provides all further versions of the product for no additional remuneration. Examples from the software market are anti-virus programs and accounting software. However, service contracts are connected with a moral hazard problem. There is a lack of incentives for the seller to actually develop the software further once the version upgrades have already been sold in advance. Therefore, service contracts are only observable in cases where the need for further development of the technology is given exogenously (Thum 1995, p. 96).

Finally, there are strategies that do not aim at price discrimination but rather at the elimination of uncertainties. One such uncertainty may be the purchasers' fear that a technology provider, insofar as there are no competitors providing the same technology, exercises monopoly power, setting high prices for the good. In this case, the seller can extend the production from one to at least two competing

---

[28] An analysis of the impact of lock-in effects caused by the presence of switching costs on the competition between suppliers can be found in (Klemperer 1987a; Klemperer 1989; Klemperer 1992).

manufacturers. By doing this, the manufacturer voluntarily abandons monopoly power and provides a signal that in the future the consumers can expect competitive prices (Thum 1995, p. 112).[29] The strategy of second sourcing can be observed in the information technology market quite often when granting licenses to original equipment manufacturers (OEM's), though there may be other motives for such behavior, such as a short-term increase of production capacity.

However, from an overall economic point of view, some manufacturer strategies, though preventing the case of excess inertia, overshoot the mark and result in technological change which is too fast. This case of an "excess momentum" of a technology adoption possibly emerges, for example, if the seller announces the introduction of a new product that will be incompatible with the technology currently used[30]. In effect, new consumers delay their purchase. Therefore, as soon as the new product is introduced into the market, there is an installed base large enough to induce sufficient network effects between the new users. Since the effect on the users of the old technology is not considered, this change might be undesirable (Thum 1995, p. 20).

Network effects occur if different users combine technologies to support interaction. To enable this interaction a common basis must be obtained, i.e. the manufacturers of the technologies must coordinate themselves in their product designs, e.g. by agreeing upon certain common properties of their products. This common basis is obtained by the specification of standards. The notion of standards and standardization in the context of information systems is the subject of the next section.

3.1.2 Standards

According to Buxmann we generally define a standard as the specification of the structure and the behavior of system elements (Buxmann 1996, p. 10)[31]. In case of information technology standards these system elements comprise soft- and hardware components. Depending on the objective followed by standardization and the way that standardization is achieved we distinguish between compatibility and quality standards in one dimension and de jure and de facto standards in the other dimension.

---

[29] For a further analysis of how this seemingly paradoxical behavior occurs, and empirical results cf. (Shepard 1987; Swann 1987; Farrell and Gallini 1988).

[30] The strategy of preannouncement was first analyzed in (Farrell and Saloner 1986a).

[31] Definitions of the term "standard" are manifold in literature and change with the aims of the author. We omit an extensive discussion of different notions of standards. For readers interested in the discussion of different approaches to the definition of standards cf. (Vries 1996).

3.1.2.1 Compatibility standards

Products are compatible when their design is coordinated in some way, enabling them to work together. In (Farrell and Saloner 1987, pp. 1-2) the authors distinguish three classes of compatibility: physical compatibility, communication compatibility, and compatibility by convention.

Farrell and Saloner refer to physical compatibility if physical objects are designed to fit together physically or electromagnetically. Examples are computer hardware components like CPU and motherboard or nut and bolt, whereas communication compatibility denotes the ability of two physical devices to communicate with one another. While physical compatibility is obtained by standardizing physical product properties, communication compatibility is usually reached by the specification of communication standards. We will deal with communication standards in the context of supplier relationships in section 3.2. Finally, in the case of compatibility by convention the benefits from coordinated product design are not physically embodied. Examples include standard time and currency.

Compatibility is not always a matter of "yes" or "no". There can be degrees of compatibility (Farrell and Saloner 1987, p. 2). Two word processors, for example, may be compatible because both support rich text format for the exchange of documents. However, since the specific formats of the word processors and rich text format may have different strengths in describing particular text or layout formats (e.g. footnotes, tables, graphics, etc.), some of the original layout information possibly gets lost when documents are exchanged. Therefore, the compatibility is only partial.

Technologies that were originally incompatible with each other can be made compatible by the use of converters ("ex post compatibility") (Thum 1995, p. 30). Taking the example from the previous paragraph, the interchangeability of documents can also be obtained by converters, instead of using a common format. In our example a converter would be a piece of software plugged into the word processor which makes it possible to save the document in the format of the target software. The advantage of converters is that network effects can be realized without limiting the variety of products. Still, a problem is that often the result of the conversion is of poor quality[32].

Compatibility leads to a number of general advantages (Farrell and Saloner 1987, pp. 5-6). Clearly the major reason for using compatibility standards is to enable network effects among the users of different technologies. Moreover, there are competitive effects. When two functionally identical products are compatible, then the competition between sellers is based on price rather than design. In addition, the existence of compatibility standards encourages competitors to enter the market, because they need not to build up an installed base for their products.

---

[32]   A systematic analysis of converters is provided in (Farrell and Saloner 1992).

Compatibility has an influence on the variety of products. Compatibility requirements limit the variety of products (Farrell and Saloner 1986b), because the sellers' latitude with respect to the design of their products is restricted. On the other hand, variety can be increased by possible mix-and-match purchases. For example, the buyer of a personal computer has a wide choice in combining hardware components from different manufacturers like network and graphics adapters, because there is a broad range of products that commonly support the local bus standard of PCI[33].

Another advantage of compatibility is possible cost savings by allowing greater economies of scale. Since compatibility standards allow the use of interchangeable parts in the production of a good, different manufacturers can use common suppliers. These suppliers can exploit economies of scale in a better way by bundling different orders and will thus be able to provide low prices. Cost savings can also be realized when purchasing complementary product that are more readily or more cheaply available, as many people own the original product. Finally, compatibility lowers the costs of learning how to use the good when changing to a competing product. This is because knowledge about using a technology can possibly be more easily transferred from one compatible product to another.

3.1.2.2 Quality standards

While consumers use compatibility standards with the aim of combining different technologies, be it for communication purposes or to facilitate the assembly of different products, quality standards have the function of supporting the exchange of goods between transaction partners. Quality standards initially became manifest in defined quality grades of products, and go back to the beginning of international trade where they were primarily used to describe properties of raw materials, e.g. middling cotton, No. 2 medium-grain rice, or Santos No. 4 coffee (Kindleberger 1983, p. 378). Hence quality standards provide a standardized description of product properties.

Because of moral hazard problems, the fulfillment of quality standards is often confirmed by an independent third party in the form of certificates. These certificates can concern not only particular properties of a product, but also apply to conditions that must be fulfilled by the production process (e.g. with respect to the existence of quality control procedures) or the machines and employees participating in the production process (e.g. confirming that the personnel has particular abilities in the application of software). A prominent example is the ISO 9000 certification, which includes a family of standards defining a quality assurance program approved by the International Standards Organization (ISO).

---

[33] PCI stands for Peripheral Component Interconnect.

Companies that conform to these standards can receive an ISO 9000 certification. This doesn't necessarily mean that the company's products are of high quality, but that the company follows well-defined procedures for ensuring quality products. Increasingly, software buyers insist that their (software) suppliers have an ISO 9000 certification (Webopaedia 1996c). Finally, certificates can be used to signal the fulfillment of compatibility requirements, i.e. a quality standard is used to confirm the use of compatibility standards.

The benefit of quality standards is that buyer and seller are supported in coming to an agreement about the purchase of a product, since the properties of the good can more efficiently be communicated between the transaction parties. Furthermore, quality standards have a signaling effect (Kleinemeyer 1998, p. 63). If the quality of a good is not observable by the consumer until it is purchased, then it may happen that the consumers will anticipate the risk of receiving bad quality by demanding price reductions from the supplier. Consequently it is no longer profitable for the suppliers to offer high quality products. This adverse selection of supply leads to a failure of the market mechanism when trading a product (Akerlof 1970). The conformity of a product with quality standards reduces the information asymmetry between seller and customer by signaling the fulfillment of minimum quality requirements. Furthermore, the role of other signals such as reputation and advertising is reduced (Shapiro 1983; Farrell and Saloner 1987; Grant 1987). In this way, as in the case of compatibility standards, quality standards influence the competition between sellers. Since the role of advertising and reputation is reduced, competition is based on price instead (Farrell and Saloner 1987).

3.1.2.3   De jure standards

An alternative way of classifying standards is according to the way that standardization is achieved into de jure and de facto standards (Kleinemeyer 1998, pp. 52-54). The specification of de jure standards happens in institutions that are dedicated to this task. These can be governmental institutions that possibly have the power to enforce the adoption of standards by law (mandatory standards) or committees. Standardization committees are groups voluntarily formed by organizations and/or individuals with the aim of negotiating the specification of a standard that will subsequently be accepted at least by all the committee members. In the area of information technology committees are often formed by a variety of organizations and individuals like software vendors, researchers and representatives of governmental institutions[34].

---

[34]   An example is the Object Management Group (OMG), which was founded to develop vendor independent specifications for the software industry. The OMG now includes over 800 members from different industrial sectors and science (see http://www.omg.com).

A problem of standardization by committees is that they are slow. Often many months pass between meetings of the relevant committees. Therefore technologies are sometimes prototyped by organizations before a standard is officially set, thus producing sunk costs. Once costs are sunk, however, these organizations fight hard for "their" standard to be adopted. This may lead to inferior solutions or the standardization may be delayed (Farrell and Saloner 1987, p. 4).

3.1.2.4 De facto standards

In comparison to de jure standards, de facto standards are the result of purchasing decisions made by adopters on a market and/or by decisions on product design by individual sellers. Basically, there are two major ways in which de facto standardization can happen, by leadership and by competition (Farrell and Saloner 1987, p. 3).

In case of standardization by leadership the decision of a seller (or a customer) with a high market share on the design (purchase) of a new product often stands at the beginning. In anticipation of a high market share for the new product due to the market power of the seller (buyer), other market participants follow and orient their decisions according to the market leader (Farrell and Saloner 1987, p. 3). A good example is the microprocessor market. As the market leader Intel extended the instruction set of its Pentium-microprocessor by particular instructions to accelerate vector operations, the competitors AMD and Cyrix quickly followed integrating this new functionality into their products. If there is no dominant player on a market, then a de facto standard emerges as one of a number of functionally similar goods prevails over competing products, as was the case in the microprocessor market in the 1980's (Swann 1987).

In summary it may be said that standards are specified and used with different economic aims. Major aims comprise the reduction of transaction costs and the realization of economies of scale (Kindleberger 1983, p. 387)[35]. While economies of scale can be realized by the use of compatibility standards, transaction cost reductions can be achieved by the use of compatibility as well as quality standards. In the next section we describe and discuss a number of selected examples of information technology and standardization approaches that are of importance in the management of supplier relationships. In this connection the focus is on possible transaction cost reductions attainable by the use of communication standards.

---

[35] As it is pointed out by Oberlack, there is the additional economic aim of limiting (negative) external effects (Oberlack 1989, pp. 22 and 40). Pollution is an external effect of production. This effect can be limited by specifying environmental standards like threshold values for toxic substances emitted in the production process.

3.2 Information technology for the support of supplier relationships

The shape of a supplier relationship is influenced by the availability of information technology (or standards[36]) supporting the exchange of goods and information between the transaction parties. If we have a closer look at the details of such a relationship then we discover that the interaction between supplier and customer is manifested in a number of message exchanges. The purpose of these message exchanges varies according to the phase of the supplier relationship. While in the evaluation phase messages are exchanged to gain information about products offered and offering suppliers, in negotiations the transaction parties communicate about possible contract conditions, whereas in the transaction phase of a supplier relationship messages are exchanged about the delivery of goods and payments.

The exchange of messages over the course of a transaction is usually controlled by application software. Here the determination of messages and the sequence of the messages is either encoded in the application software or the application software is based on other software components where these rules are implemented. For example, application software can provide the facilities for electronic data exchange as part of its functionality or it can rely on dedicated EDI systems (see Figure 14).

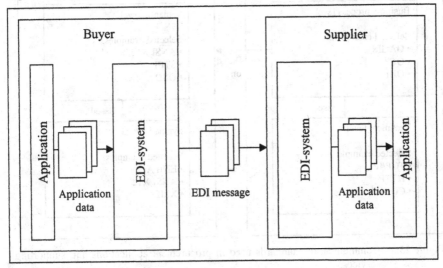

Figure 14:   Application software based on EDI-system, following (Mattes 1999, p. 98).

---

[36]   Since we examine information technology primarily in the sphere of network effects, we further use the terms "information technology", "standard", and "information technology standard" synonymously.

76

To enable the exchange of messages, the participating information technology used on both sides must be compatible[37]. Compatibility can be achieved by using the same software solution (i.e. from the same software company) or by using different software solutions that both support a common communication standard. Depending on the entities standardized we distinguish between communication standards that focus on the information objects transferred between the transaction partners (these are also referred to as EDI standards) and standards that concentrate rather on structuring the communication process. Within each of these two classes we further make a distinction between standards on a more generic level and standards with a stronger focus on contents. While the former can be used independently of a particular application in a supplier relationship, the latter are applied primarily in the context of a certain business process in a supplier relationship. An overview of these types with selected examples and the relationships between these types is given in Figure 15:

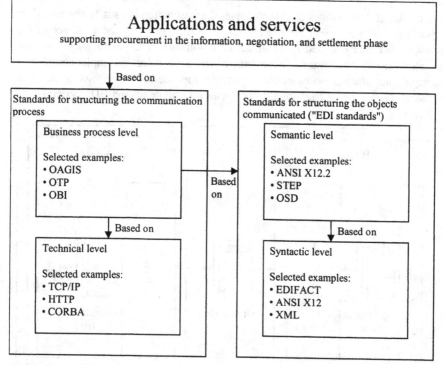

Figure 15: Communication standards used in procurement applications and supporting services.

---

[37] To express this more precisely, we mean communication compatibility as defined in (Farrell and Saloner 1987, p. 2). For the different kinds of compatibility see section 3.1.2.1.

Standards for structuring the communication process on the technical level are of an enabling character for information technology based communication. These comprise, e.g., basic communication protocols like TCP/IP and HTTP, but also middleware standards controlling the interaction of applications such as the Common Object Request Broker Architecture (CORBA).

Standards for structuring the communication process on the business process level use generic services provided by standards on the technical level. In particular, these standards specify the sequence in which business documents are exchanged between transaction partners. The Open Trading Protocol (OTP), for example, defines the conditions under which certain kinds of messages are exchanged between business partners in electronic purchase transactions. A similar function is fulfilled by Open Buying on the Internet (OBI), but with a focus on the purchase of non-strategic, indirect materials by large, distributed organizations. A broader approach is followed by the Open Applications Group, which designed the Open Applications Group Integration Specifications (OAGIS). OAGIS describes data and process sharing by the specification of scenarios for typical business processes and explains how application program methods can exchange data with other compliant business applications.

Standards for structuring communication objects on the syntactic level have the character of metalanguages with the purpose of providing generic elements and a grammar with rules about the combination of these elements that can be used to define communication objects on the semantic level. Widespread examples in the business area are X12 from the American National Standards Institute (ANSI X12) and the United Nations Electronic Data Interchange for Administration, Commerce and Transport (EDIFACT[38]), which are used to derive standard business documents like purchase orders or invoices. A recent approach that can be used for the same purpose is the Extensible Markup Language (XML).

On the semantic level the metalanguages of the syntactic level are used to specify communication objects that are exchanged in a transaction. ANSI X12.2, for example, is the ANSI X12-based standard designation of an invoice. An internationally established standard for the description of physical product data is the Standard for the Exchange of Product Model Data (STEP), whereas the Open Software Description (OSD) provides an XML-based vocabulary for describing software packages and their interdependencies. Another approach, the Web Interface Definition Language (WIDL), uses XML grammar to provide a general method of representing request/ response interactions over standard web protocols. Thus automated interaction with HTML/XML documents and forms becomes possible.

---

[38]   Sometimes EDIFACT is also referred to as UN/EDIFACT. There is no difference between EDIFACT and UN/EDIFACT. The prefix "UN" simply means that EDIFACT is recommended by the United Nations Economic Commissions for Europe.

Standards for structuring the communication process use specific or standardized specifications of the objects communicated. OTP, for example, includes an XML-based definition of OTP messages exchanged over the course of an electronic transaction that is specific to OTP, whereas OBI on the other hand works with standard messages based on ANSI X12 such as ANSI X12 850 for order transmissions.

In the following sub-sections we provide a number of selected examples of information technology that can be used to support transactions. This selection comprises established solutions as well as a number of innovative approaches. Since the classical procurement applications usually focus on the settlement phase of a supplier relationship, apart from these systems a number of solutions and services have emerged which aim at the support of transaction partner search and negotiations. The aim is to show how transaction costs can possibly be reduced by the use of information technology in all phases of a supplier relationship. We examine major solutions which support the procurement of direct and indirect goods in section 3.2.1. Subsequently, we show how transaction partner search (in 3.2.2) and negotiations (in 3.2.3) can be supported by information technology. Procurement applications are often based on standards concerned with the procurement process and the information passed between the business partners. A selection of standards which structure the communication process, particularly in terms of the settlement phase, is presented in section 3.2.4, whereas standards for structuring communication objects are examined in section 3.2.5. Finally, in section 3.2.6 we discuss what transaction costs are likely to be influenced by the given approaches.

3.2.1 Procurement applications

There are a number of commercial products sold under the label of procurement or electronic commerce systems that due to the lack of generally accepted standards often use their own definitions of business scenarios and are thus incompatible to each other[39]. The general aim connected with the use of procurement software is to make the procurement process more efficient, i.e. to lower the cost of ordering goods and to accelerate the process thus shortening the time from order to delivery. The way in which these aims are reached differs depending on the type of goods purchased. In section 2.1.1 we distinguished between the procurement of direct and indirect goods. Software supporting activities in the procurement of these goods is subject to different requirements.

---

[39] A list of selected solutions is provided in (Kerridge, Slade et al. 1998, p. 30). For a case study describing the issues and problems of implementing such a system in the McKesson Corp. cf. (Segev, Porra et al. 1999).

For applications which support the procurement of direct goods a close integration with production planning software is crucial. The idea is that the process from customer order to the procurement of the required input goods runs automatically without changing data and media formats and with minimal manual intervention. Traditionally, the suppliers delivering direct goods rarely change so that there is a predefined set of suppliers with whom the procuring organization collaborates. Initial attempts to improve the procurement process by means of information technology have focused primarily on the acquisition of direct goods. These attempts relied on enterprise resource planning (ERP[40]) systems to automate and track production purchases. In SAP R/3, for example, the functionality supporting the procurement of goods is part of the material management module. In this way it guarantees that the procurement process is fully integrated with other administrative functions, such as production planning, sales, and controlling. However, focusing on the integration of internal processes other issues have been neglected. One of the resulting problems is that ERP systems offer little support for sharing business information with external trading partners (AberdeenGroup 1999). Another problem is that the user interfaces of ERP systems are often not user-friendly, i.e. casual users cannot find their way through the masks intuitively (Dolmetsch, Fleisch et al. 1999, p. 79). The first problem is mitigated by the implementation of EDI facilities that allow the exchange of business data among trading partners. The second problem is less severe because the employees who are responsible for the procurement of direct goods are usually specialized professionals and experienced users of integrated ERP systems. Hence the advantage of integration usually outweighs the disadvantages.

As regards ERP software the market in Germany is dominated by SAP. According to the results of an empirical study conducted among the Fortune 1,000 in Germany and the US 77% of the respondents use R/3 and 48% use R/2. The use of competitive products is far smaller. 16% of all responding companies use Oracle-Application, 7% use Paisy, and 3% use Baan Triton, whereas in the US the market for business software is much more heterogeneous. The most common products in the sample are Peoplesoft (51%), SAP (R/3: 40%, R/2: 4%), Oracle-Application (36%), J.D. Edwards (22%), and Baan Triton (9%) (Buxmann, Westarp et al. 1998).

In comparison with direct goods, the procurement of indirect goods poses different demands on the software. Indirect goods are often cheap and the demand for those goods irregular. Moreover, the production of the final product does not immediately depend on the availability of these goods. Hence, expensive stock-keeping systems do not pay off. Another important point is that the ordering of indirect goods is triggered by employees who are not specialized in the use of

---

[40] Enterprise Resource Planning systems are business management systems that integrate different functions in an organization, e.g. planning, manufacturing, sales, and marketing.

complex ERP software. Although in principle the procurement modules of ERP systems can be used for purchasing indirect goods, most ERP systems do not address the requirements of purchases of indirect goods adequately (Dolmetsch, Fleisch et al. 1999, p. 78). Therefore the procurement of indirect goods may often be managed in the traditional way using paper-based order forms, so that the process takes time and employees tend to off-contract ("maverick") spending directly from suppliers of their choice, thus bypassing the internal control and procurement procedures. The lack of automation leads to increased materials costs and reduced negotiation leverage (AberdeenGroup 1999). Recently, under the label of "electronic procurement" (Nenninger and Gerst 1999, p. 290) some attempts at solving these problems have been made. One attempt to automate the procurement of indirect goods is desktop purchasing systems (DPS). DPS have in common the fact that they are Internet-based and enable a self-service purchasing environment that moves product selection and order initiation to the desktops of frontline employees while maintaining the corporate contracts, business rules, and process workflow of the buying organization (Dolmetsch, Fleisch et al. 1999, p. 79). The aim of DPS is primarily to increase efficiency by automation, so that procurement professionals can focus on more strategic tasks.

In the area of DPS the market is dominated by new software companies like Ariba Technologies and CommerceOne (Dolmetsch, Fleisch et al. 1999, p. 80). The software of these vendors is usually provided with interfaces to major ERP systems. Established vendors of ERP software also provide new modules for their business software which aim at the procurement of indirect goods and which particularly address the issue of ergonomics by providing graphic and intuitively usable user interfaces. At the time of writing there is a close-run race between the software companies SAP and Oracle which are both trying to get a foot in the market for procurement systems. Currently research and consulting companies see Oracle's Strategic Procurement Solution as the leading product in the area of the procurement of direct and indirect goods (AberdeenGroup 1999; Orlov 1999)[41].

A critical success factor for the acceptance of a procurement system is that the product and price information is up to date and complete. There are three primary strategies for attaining and managing catalog content (AberdeenGroup 1999): content aggregation, supplier-managed content, and third-party-managed content.

Content aggregation requires the replication and integration of multiple supplier catalogs into a single, aggregated catalog that is hosted within the buying organization's firewall. The aggregated catalog is usually provided with facilities enabling searches for products and prices across multiple suppliers. Content aggregation on the buyer's side is connected with the problem of keeping

---

[41] Although Ariba Technologies, CommerceOne, SAP, and Oracle are the major players in the market of procurement systems, there are a vast number of further software companies selling software specialized in the support of procurement. A market overview is provided in (Purchasing 1999).

replicated data up to date. This is a costly task when the underlying data are highly volatile. The problem of data synchronization is avoided when the content is managed by the supplier. The buyer then accesses information about products, prices and availability directly from the suppliers' Web sites. However product and price comparisons are then costly because the buyer has to visit a number of different sites to gain the necessary information. Finally, content management can be done by a third party that develops and maintains a master catalog of suppliers and products that is remotely accessible through the Internet. The third party ensures data quality and provides a metadata layer to support cross-catalog searches. The third party often also provides custom catalogs that reflect unique contracts between buying organizations and their suppliers.

While procurement solutions usually focus on the efficient settlement of a supplier relationship, particularly assuming that there is a predefined set of suppliers with whom business is conducted, the evaluation phase is rarely supported. Therefore, apart from the classical procurement systems there are a number of solutions and services that focus on the support of transaction partner search and negotiations. To integrate these two trends recent approaches have attempted to establish Internet-based gateways for supplier selection in the form of virtual marketplaces. Examples are MySAP.com[42] from SAP and Oracle Exchange[43] from Oracle Solutions. The major aim of these approaches is to extend the automated data exchange between the respective ERP systems of the participating transaction partners to the evaluation phase.

In the following two sections we present and discuss a number of selected approaches to information technology which supports the evaluation phase of a supplier relationship. In detail, these are:

- facilities supporting the search for potential suppliers such as electronic shopping malls, search engines, electronic yellow pages, and online product catalogues;

- electronic auctions;

- negotiation support systems; and

- software agents inasmuch as they are used to carry out or support activities which take place in the evaluation phase of a supplier relationship.

3.2.2 Supplier search and electronic catalogs

The activities of finding potential transaction partners and gathering information about them and their products take place at the beginning of a supplier

---

[42] http://www.mysap.com
[43] http://www.oracleexchange.com

relationship. In recent years these activities have been subject to a number of innovations using the Internet. Buyers are supported by new search facilities which are usually made available by intermediaries like search service providers which are accommodated on the suppliers' side by new forms of presenting their products to potential customers, e.g. by electronic product catalogs containing a multimedia supported description of the goods offered or by new access points to their products through electronic shopping malls.

As regards search service providers there are a number of different solutions that allow the searcher to investigate the World Wide Web for information which matches a previously specified search criterion. These search services are usually based on retrieval systems, which in the Internet are also called search engines. Search engines work basically in the following way: at regular intervals an index is generated for the contents of virtually all information coded in Web pages in the Internet. The search then takes place by the specification of a string by the searcher, which is applied to the index. The matching results are subsequently presented in the form of a link list on a Web page. The service provided by search engines is usually free of charge. A major problem with current search engines is that the results are often not sufficiently precise. To put this in more formal terms, the recall and precision ratio of a search result may not be sufficient. Recall and precision ratio are benchmarks originally developed to evaluate the quality of information retrieval systems (Wedekind 1975, pp. 214-215; Rowley 1992, pp. 170-173; Rose 1999, pp. 14-15):

$$\text{(eq. 15)} \quad \text{Recall ratio} = \frac{\text{Number of relevant documents retrieved}}{\text{Total number of relevant documents in the system}}$$

$$\text{(eq. 16)} \quad \text{Precision ratio} = \frac{\text{Number of relevant documents retrieved}}{\text{Total number of documents retrieved}}$$

In the context of search engines in the Internet these quality measures have to be slightly modified. Instead of delivering documents, search engines retrieve hyperlinks to information sources.

The recall ratio is usually inversely proportional to the precision ratio (Rowley 1992, p. 171; Rose 1999, p. 14). If the results of a search are unsatisfactory, i.e. the number of links to relevant information is too small, then the search can be broadened. In effect, though the number of links to relevant information increases, the number of irrelevant links increases as well. If it is assumed that the number of irrelevant links grows faster than the number of relevant links, then the precision ratio decreases as the search is broadened. Hence, a greater recall ratio has been achieved at the expense of lower precision in the result. Nevertheless, if one is unsatisfied with a search result because the precision ratio is too small, then the search can be narrowed. Then, however, the number of relevant links retrieved will also decrease.

In the context of the evaluation of potential suppliers for a particular product the searcher could use the services of search engines to look for potential suppliers, e.g. by using the product name as the search string. Say the user is looking for office supplies such as transparencies, then he or she could formulate a search string "transparenc"[44] and would receive links to a number of Web sites providing information about that good. However, these links may lead to sellers of the good, but also to other Web sites that use this word in a context different from selling, i.e. the precision ratio could be low. The relatively simple search strategy as described above becomes even more problematic when a good cannot be named in a definite way. To mitigate this problem a search service provider can offer sophisticated query facilities such as the logical combination of strings or iterative searches. In the case of the transparency example, the purchaser could search for Web pages containing the strings "transparenc" and "price" at the same time, thus increasing the probability that the resulting links will lead to product offers of sellers. The same effect can be obtained by using an iterative search strategy, i.e. in case of too many and/or imprecise results the current link list can be taken to form the basis of the next query[45]. Another way to increase the precision ratio of search results is to classify the contents of Web pages. Yahoo[46] is an example of this kind of directory service. Using our example, the searcher looking for transparencies could follow the hierarchy "Business and Economy > Companies > Office Supplies and Services > Administrative Support > Presentation Services > Presentation Services and Equipment > Slides and Overhead Transparencies" down to a list of sellers offering this good.

It is not only the searcher who has an interest in finding potential suppliers of a particular product efficiently, but the suppliers also have an interest in being found easily. A simple way of reaching this goal is by actively registering oneself in directory services. Moreover, suppliers can accommodate the precision of searches by using sophisticated concepts for marking the information they provide. We show in section 3.2.5.2 by means of the Open Software Description and Web Interface Definition Language how XML can be used to provide information about the semantics of the contents of Web pages in a formalized way.

Traditionally the use of central services provided by intermediaries have been explained by a reduction of contacts, i.e. through bundling offers and making them available to inquiring firms, the number of necessary contacts between buyers and suppliers of goods can be reduced (Baligh and Richartz 1967). As we have seen,

---

[44] Since search engines usually make substring searches, by formulating "transparenc" results are received containing the string "transparency" as well as "transparencies".

[45] An example is the search engine Hotbot (http://www.hotbot.com), which provides the possibility of combining substrings in a simple way as well as iterative search facilities.

[46] http://www.yahoo.com

this is not true for search services in the Internet. Although decentralized activities of finding potential suppliers are replaced to some extent by using central search services, this does not mean that further inquiries about the suppliers' products are entirely substituted. The searcher still has the problem of only having a link to a seller's page. In order to find further information about a particular product, the searcher then has to visit each vendor's catalog separately and possibly to navigate through each of those catalogs to find the desired product. The fact that vendors organize their catalogs differently makes such navigation more difficult. The concept of bundling "smart" product catalogs from different manufacturers of a particular good and making them accessible as a uniform "virtual" catalog has been developed at Stanford University on the initiative of the Commerce Net Consortium (Keller 1997).

The primary goal of the smart catalog approach is to enable the creation of single company catalogs with search mechanisms that facilitate the transition to multi-company cross-catalog search mechanisms (Keller 1997). The benefit for the searcher is that a number of product offers can be retrieved and compared through a single access point and in a single step. The idea is that a distributor or a retailer provides a virtual catalog that dynamically retrieves information from multiple smart catalogs and presents this product data in a unified manner with its own appearance and feel. This retrieval is performed dynamically, on the user's request, based on the user's search criteria, and using the terminology of the distributor or any connected vendor. The attribute "smart" denotes the property of being searchable, machine-readable, and machine-sensible, i.e. the semantics of the product data in the catalog are understood by querying computers (Keller 1997). The issue of machine-sensibility is an especially crucial aspect of making the concept work. It is achieved by using ontologies to describe the structure and the terms of each catalog as well as the relationships among these terms formally. Keller defines four types of ontology used in the smart catalog approach (Keller 1997): base, domain, product, and translation ontology.

- *Base ontologies* are used to define common terms, such as engineering math, legal terminology, standard terms, and conditions. Base ontologies are shared among all users of this approach and are created by universities and research laboratories. For example, a common business term for payment timing is "2 10 net 30," which means that a 2% discount may be taken for payment within 10 days, and full payment must be received within 30 days. The definitions in base ontologies should be usable for all smart catalogs.

- *Domain ontologies* contain terms common to all or most vendors in an area, e.g. CPU speed, RAM size, or disk storage capacity in the area of computer hardware vendors. Typically domain ontologies are created by standards bodies and trade associations.

- *Product ontologies* contain company-specific terminology and refer to domain ontologies. Product ontologies are created by individual companies. Other companies may refer to them.

- *Translation ontologies* are used to translate specific terms used in one ontology to related terms used in another ontology. Keller expects there to be service organizations that create and maintain product ontologies and translation ontologies on behalf of other organizations.

The communication between virtual catalog and smart catalogs takes place using the Agent Communication Language (ACL). ACL consists of the Knowledge Interchange Format (KIF) which is a query and data description language capable of encoding practically any data source or query capability, the Knowledge Query and Manipulation Language (KQML)[47], which is used in order to communicate KIF among the agents in the smart catalog architecture, and a set of ontologies. In practice, several smart catalogs have been built in the domains of workstations, test and measurement equipment, and semiconductors (Keller 1997).

Although smart catalogs make information retrieval and navigation easier, the searcher still has to choose among a number of different vendors. They are currently working on the delegation of this final task using software agent technology. The first and most prominent example in this area is Andersen Consulting's BargainFinder[48], which is a shopping agent for online price comparisons. For a given product BargainFinder requests prices from different merchant Web sites and presents the merchant with the cheapest offer to the user. The problem of finding price information in different suppliers' catalogs when the structure of these catalogs is neither standardized nor described in a standardized manner is solved by using "wrappers" which transform the information from a specific Web site into a locally common format[49]. The locations of online stores selling CD's and the methods to search for a product and discover its price are hand-coded. In this way, the concept of wrappers involves high maintenance costs since wrappers must be adapted each time the vendor changes the access method or catalog presentation format (Guttman, Moukas et al. 1998).

The practical application of BargainFinder in the market of music CD's leads to interesting results for the automation of price comparison in the Internet. For example, one third of the CD merchants accessed by BargainFinder blocked its price requests. The major reason for this was that many merchants do not want to compete on price alone. As soon as they offer value-added services on their Web sites they are bypassed by BargainFinder and therefore not considered in the

---

[47] KIF and KQML were developed as part of the ARPA Knowledge Sharing Initiative. KIF is currently undergoing standardization by ANSI (Keller 1997).

[48] http://bf.cstar.ac.com

[49] For technical details about the concept of wrappers cf. (Kushmerick, Weld et al. 1997).

consumer's buying decision. However, it was also the case that Andersen Consulting received requests from a number of relatively unknown merchants who wanted to be included in BargainFinder's price comparison (Guttman, Moukas et al. 1998).

Beside the costs of finding potential transaction partners and finding information about their products, another component of evaluation costs is incurred by judging the trustworthiness of a potential transaction partner. Once an offer is found, the searcher is often uncertain whether the given data about the good corresponds with the truth or whether the supplier will be amenable should there be disputes after a contract is signed. There are different ways of mitigating this problem:

- rely on one's own experiences, i.e. make contracts only with suppliers with whom there is currently a relationship or with whom there had been a business relationship before;

- make further inquiries about potential transaction partners, e.g. using rating agencies; or

- use the experiences of other organizations.

Following these strategies leads to additional evaluation costs. In the case of the first option these costs have an indirect character and find expression in giving up the opportunity of possibly finding a transaction partner who would provide better conditions. The additional evaluation costs of options two and three are incurred directly by paying for the expertise of a third party. Rating agencies are well established in few areas. Moody's and Standards & Poor's are examples of agencies generating and selling information about the creditworthiness of organizations. The information is sold, for instance, to banks to calculate the risk when granting loans. Finally, the use of the experience of other organizations is a new concept, which is also discussed under the notion of "collaborative filtering" (Arnheim 1996).

Collaborative filtering is a technique primarily used in the consumer area. The basic idea is to help people make choices based on the opinions of other people. This takes place by building databases of user opinions of particular items. Collaborative filtering systems use these databases to find users whose opinions are similar and make predictions of user opinion about an item by combining the opinions of other likeminded individuals (Good, Schafer et al. 1999). GroupLens is an example of a collaborative filtering system for newsgroups on the Internet. The purpose is to help people find articles they will probably be interested in out of the great number of articles available. News reader clients display predicted scores and make it easy for users to rate articles after they have read them. Rating servers, called "Better Bit Bureaus", gather and distribute the ratings. The rating servers predict scores based on the heuristic that people who agreed to a proposal in the past will probably agree again (Resnick, Iacovou et al. 1994).

The concept of collaborative filtering has the potential to help in the process of supplier evaluation, e.g. when customers provide a rating of suppliers on the basis of their experience in terms of their satisfaction. The first steps in this direction took place as single customers started to publish reports about their (usually bad) experiences with certain suppliers in the Web. A step further has been taken by Kasbah[50], which provides a distributed trust and reputation mechanism called the "Better Business Bureau" (Guttman, Moukas et al. 1998). It works as follows: after the completion of a transaction both parties rate how well the other party managed their half of the deal (e.g., accuracy of product condition, completion of the transaction, etc.). These ratings can then be used to help in judging the reliability and trustworthiness of a transaction partner.

However, before the concept of collaborative filtering can be applied to support supplier selection decisions, a number of problems must be solved. In particular, the issues of start up, the provision of incentives, reliability, and privacy are considered to be important (Arnheim 1996):

- To make a collaborative filtering system work a "critical mass" of recommenders must be reached, i.e. one must find enough people who provide rating information. This is essential to be able to derive recommendations that are statistically founded.

- The provision of incentives for recommenders to participate in the system continuously is also a problem. During start up initial recommenders receive no immediate benefit from their participation, because the critical mass has not yet been reached.

- The reliability of recommendations may be restricted due to users who deliberately manipulate the ratings, e.g. suppliers who perform poorly could try to improve their reputation by rating themselves through non-existent third parties.

- Privacy in the context of collaborative filtering means that an unauthorized third party will not be able to track the recommenders' rating. In GroupLens, for example, the system only knows a user's pseudonym.

Once a potential supplier is found and evaluated the purchasing organization either faces a standard purchase contract, i.e. the price of the good is fixed and the conditions of the transaction determined, or the price and/or contract conditions are subject to negotiations. While in the first case the searcher only has to make the decision whether to accept the offer, in the second case further activities in the form of negotiations are required.

---

[50] Kasbah is a multiagent marketplace which we describe and discuss in section 3.2.3.

3.2.3 Information technology in the negotiation phase

While in the information phase the potential of automation is increasingly exploited, activities in the negotiation phase are still mainly done by hand (Beam and Segev 1997, p. 263). Depending on whether negotiation activities of none, one, or all of the participating parties are automated a distinction is made between manual, semi-automated, and automated negotiations (Beam, Segev et al. 1996, p. 2). Negotiations can be automated using software agents acting on behalf of their human principals. The automation of negotiations is difficult for two major reasons (Beam and Segev 1997, p. 264):

- An ontology is required to ensure that the participants are referring to exactly the same good and that there is a common understanding of the attributes describing the product and the terms of the transaction, e.g. delivery time, delivery quantity, and financing terms.

- Privacy concerning the negotiation strategy of the software agent's principal is required (Varian 1995). To function effectively, the computerized agent has to know about its principal's preferences, e.g. the maximum willingness to pay for a good. If the seller of a good can learn the buyer's willingness to pay, it can make a take-it-or-leave it offer extracting the buyer's entire surplus.

In case of centralized markets[51] these problems are less severe (Beam, Segev et al. 1996, p. 6). Auctions restrict the negotiations to the single dimension of price and the items for sale are usually displayed and sold "as is". Thus the need to trade-off different product attributes and the need of a common ontology to classify and describe these attributes is mitigated. The privacy problem can be reduced by selecting an appropriate auction mechanism. If a mechanism is used which causes all participants to reveal their willingness to pay truthfully as is the case for a Vickrey auction (see section 2.1.5.1), then there is no need to worry about keeping the willingness to pay private (Varian 1995). Since auctions are characterized by a well defined set of rules they are particularly suitable for the use of information technology. Auctions supported by information technology are referred to as electronic auctions. An overview and discussion of current solutions for electronic auctions is conducted in section 3.2.3.1.

In decentralized markets, on the other hand, the ontology and privacy problems are crucial. Usually more than the single dimension of "price" must be considered, and as the complexity of negotiations grows, cognitive limitations and socio-emotional problems become more significant (Anson and Jelassi 1990, p. 185). Therefore the use of information technology is concentrated more on the support of the negotiators in their decisions, while automation aspects play a minor role. Negotiation support systems and approaches based on the use of software agents are introduced in section 3.2.3.2.

---

[51]   The notion of centralized market is introduced and discussed in section 2.1.5.

3.2.3.1   Electronic auctions

Electronic auctions have existed for several years. Prominent examples are the computerized auctioning of pigs in Singapore (Neo 1992) and flowers in Holland (van Heck, van Damme et al. 1997). Auctions in the Internet started in 1995. Since the number of Web users is rising steeply a proliferation of electronic auctions can be observed (Klein 1997, p. 3). There are numerous Web sites listing hundreds of auctions for many different kinds of goods. Examples are AuctionNet[52], the Internet Auction List[53], Bid Find[54], The Auction Hunter[55], eBay[56], and Onsale[57].

Web based electronic auctions are generally organized in the way that a host site acts as a broker offering services for sellers to post their goods for sale and allow buyers to bid on those items. Most auctions open with a starting bid, which is the lowest price, the seller is willing to accept. Detailed information on every item for sale is available online. For high value items, additional information may be obtained via e-mail. Bidders look at the description and then start the bidding either by sending an e-mail or filling out an electronic form. The bids are shown on a page at the host's Web site and updated continuously to show the current highest bids. Most auctions are live, i.e. the bidders compete in real time (Turban 1997, p.7). To illustrate the functioning of this system we examine a concrete implementation of an electronic auction on the basis of Onsale.

Example of an electronic auction in Onsale

Onsale Inc. was founded in June 1995 in Mountain View, California and sells refurbished computer products, travel, office equipment, entertainment electronics, and sport equipment by auction over the Internet (Beam, Segev et al. 1996, p. 7).

By July 1996 Onsale was averaging $700,000 in gross receipts per week, netting 13-20% margins on sales, and sustaining a company growth rate of 15-20% per month (Mardesich 1996). Onsale uses the "Yankee Auction" format. In a Yankee auction, one or more identical items are offered for sale at the same time. When the auction closes, the highest bidders win the available merchandise at their bid price. Bids are first ranked by price. If bids are for the same price, larger quantity bids take precedence over smaller quantity bids. If bids are for the same price and quantity, then earlier initial bids take precedence over later initial bids (Onsale 1999).

---

[52]   http://www.auction.net
[53]   http://www.internetauctionlist.com
[54]   http://www.bidfind.com
[55]   http://www.auctionhunter.com
[56]   http://www.ebay.com
[57]   http://www.onsale.com

90

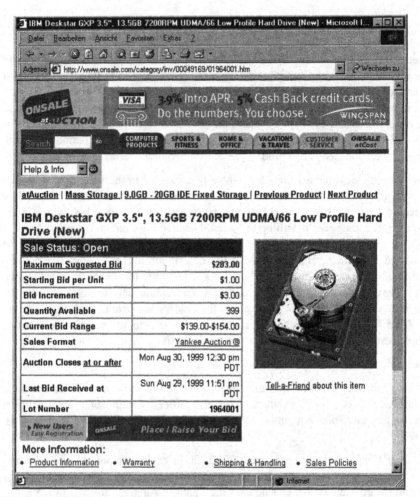

Figure 16:   Product page for an Onsale auction of a computer mass storage device.
Source: http://www.onsale.com

For each item auctioned the user can access a product page which lists information
about the current auction, e.g. the starting bid per unit, the bid increment,
scheduled closing time for bidding, and the current bid range (cf. Figure 16).
Moreover, a list of highest bids is presented which reveals each bidder's
pseudonym, location, date and time of the bid, and the amount of goods the bidder
is interested in purchasing (cf. Figure 17). If the scheduled closing time is reached
but there is still bidding activity, then the auction extends into a "Going, Going,
Gone" period. This period ends, and the auction closes, when five minutes pass
without any further bidding activity (Onsale 1999).

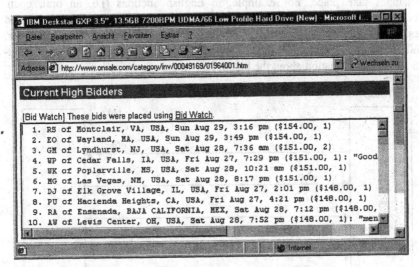

Figure 17: Product page (continued) with the current high bidders.
Source: http://www.onsale.com

A necessary condition of making electronic auctions accessible to further automation is that the auction process is described in a formal way. Furthermore, to enable automatic interaction between a greater number of auction hosting sites, bidders, and bid-takers the formalized description must be sufficiently known and widespread in the software of the participants. While there are different approaches to formalizing the trading-process which takes place in an electronic auction, none of these attempts has gained widespread acceptance. In the following, we give an example of a formal description as it is proposed by Reck (Reck 1997, pp. 19-20).

Reck identifies a number of generic auction messages exchanged during a trading process. Figure 18 illustrates a possible flow of messages between an individual trader, i.e. seller or potential buyer, and an auction center.

The message bid.b denotes the placing of a bid. The parameter b includes information on the trader placing the order and the price the trader is willing to pay for the item offered. Accordingly, offer.f describes the placing of an offer with the same parameters as a bid. Subsequently information about the bid (publish.b) and offer (publish.f) is delivered to the auction participants. With hit.b the seller indicates that he or she is willing to accept the conditions of the bid that has been placed and published immediately before, whereas with take.f the buyer signals the acceptance of an offer. Finally, with publish.d the market is informed that a trade is taking place. Parameter d carries information on the price at which the auctioned good is exchanged as well as a reference to the buyer and seller engaged in the transaction. Depending on the type of auction, some or all of the message exchanges take place. For example, in English auctions (i.e. an oral, open, ascending-bid auction) and first-price sealed-bid auctions[58] there are no dedicated messages indicating the acceptance of a bid or the taking of an offer. Moreover, while in an open-bid auction all bids are published to the participants, in a sealed-bid auction, information about the bids is known only to the seller.

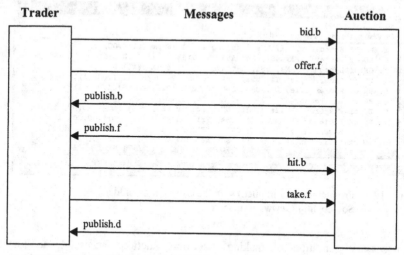

Figure 18:   Types and directions of auction messages, following (Reck 1997, Figure 1).

While trading messages are the basic elements of auction processes, the message sequences allowed for a particular type of auction are defined by trading process rules. In (Reck 1997, pp. 20-22) the author defines trading process rules for the auction start (e.g. start with offer or start with bid), the posting of bids and offers (e.g. publish offer before any bid is placed and ascending bids or descending offers), the publishing of bids and offers (e.g. immediate publication), hitting bids and taking offers, auction timing (e.g. the existence of time intervals for bids), the occurrence and publishing of trades, trade formation (e.g. highest bid constituting a trade and the existence of a fixed period of time for bidding), price determination (e.g. highest bid setting trade price), and the number of messages (e.g. at most one offer allowed in the auction of a single good).

Due to the simplicity of the auction process, researchers in the field of software agents quickly discovered the potential for automation and constructed software agents which make bids on behalf of a human (Beam and Segev 1997, 264-265; Wurman, Walsh et al. 1998). These approaches, however, did have not yet gotten beyond the experimental stage. An interesting example in this field is the

---

[58]   For a description and comparison of the most common auction types see section 2.1.5.1.2.

AuctionBot[59], which is a server for Internet-based auctions at the University of Michigan. It is has been operating since September 1996 with the general purpose of supporting research into negotiation protocols for electronic commerce and multiagent systems. Besides allowing human agents to create auctions and submit bids via Web forms, it provides an application program interface (API) for users to create their own software agents to compete in the AuctionBot marketplace autonomously. To enable automated interaction between software agents and AuctionBot, interaction protocols which are based on generic messages are specified, similar to the formal description by Reck previously discussed. Users can create new auctions to sell products by choosing from a selection of auction types and then specifying its parameters (e.g. clearing times, method for resolving bidding ties, and the number of sellers permitted). Buyers and sellers can then bid according to the negotiation protocols of the auction created. In a typical scenario, a seller would bid a reserve price after creating the auction and let AuctionBot manage and enforce buyer bidding according to the auction protocol (Guttman, Moukas et al. 1998; Wurman, Wellman et al. 1998).

3.2.3.2 Negotiation support systems

As soon as not only the price of a product but also qualitative dimensions are negotiated, goods are exchanged using decentralized market mechanisms and due to the increased complexity of the negotiation cognitive limitations as well as socio-emotional problems become more significant (Anson and Jelassi 1990, p. 185). So far there are no consistent standards for negotiations and therefore, apart from experiments in laboratories, negotiations on decentralized markets have not yet been successfully automated in practice (Foroughi 1995). However, as a first step towards negotiation, automation negotiation support systems (NSS) have been developed. NSS are a special kind of decision support systems with the purpose of helping human negotiators to make better decisions and negotiate more productively (Beam and Segev 1997, p. 264).

In (Foroughi 1995, pp. 122-123) the author identifies a number of cognitive and socio-emotional problems that impede the success of negotiations. These problems are:

- cognitive limitations of negotiators;
- formulation of decision problem influencing the decision frame;
- assumption of participating parties that their interests are in direct conflict with each other (fixed-pie mentality);
- premature finalization of positions;

---

[59]   http://auction.eecs.umich.edu

- biased information reception;

- face-saving behavior;

- distraction due to physical appearance of opposing parties and differences with respect to status and power of the negotiators; and

- overconfidence of negotiators.

A brief discussion of these issues follows, together with suggestions about how NSS are used to alleviate these problems.

Due to cognitive limitations it is difficult to evaluate the utility of alternative settlements. Hence, negotiators may possibly regard issues in isolation, so that potential trade-offs between these issues are not considered. Displaying the entire contract for discussion rather than arguing about the issues one-by-one, for example by help of a NSS, could encourage participants to focus on many issues simultaneously. In experiments this "logrolling among issues" (Pruitt 1983) turned out to lead to better solutions (Jelassi and Jones 1988, p. 80).

In the course of discussion during negotiations the negotiator's "decision frame", i.e. the conception of the acts, outcomes, and contingencies associated with a particular choice, can be influenced by the formulation of the decision problem. Choices involving gains are often risk averse, while choices involving losses are frequently risk taking (Tversky and Kahneman 1981, p. 453). In (Tversky and Kahneman 1981, p. 453) the authors illustrate the effect of variations in framing by presenting an experiment and its results conducted at Stanford University and the University of British Columbia. In this experiment two groups of respondents were confronted with the fictive problem of choosing between two alternative programs to combat a disease, which was expected to kill 600 people. Two different descriptions of the alternatives of the decision problem were presented:

- Description 1: If program A is adopted, 200 people will be saved. If program B is adopted, there is 1/3 probability that 600 people will be saved, and 2/3 probability that no people will be saved.

- Description 2: If program A is adopted, 400 people will die. If program B is adopted, there is 1/3 probability that nobody will die, and 2/3 probability that 600 people will die.

The majority choice when confronted with description 1 was risk averse. The prospect of certainly saving 200 lives was more attractive than a risky prospect of equal expected value, that is, a 1/3 chance of saving 600 lives, whereas when confronted with description 2 the majority choice was risk taking. The certain death of 400 people was less attractive than the 2/3 chance that 600 will die. This shift from risk aversion to risk taking was observed in several groups of respondents, including students, university faculty, and physicians. NSS can help to construct a risk-averse frame by establishing interaction rules and providing pre-negotiation modules requiring parties to identify their interests (Anson and Jelassi 1990, p. 184).

The assumption of the participating parties that their interests are in direct conflict with each other and that one side can only win at the expense of the other side prevents contracts which provide an improved position for both parties being negotiated (Jelassi and Jones 1988, p. 76). NSS can alleviate this problem by displaying conflicting views and providing analytical methods of identifying alternative solutions (Anson and Jelassi 1990, p. 184).

Sometimes negotiators tend to finalize their positions prematurely before considering all possible solution alternatives. Here NSS can help by presenting a single negotiation text of equivalent value for both sides as a starting point and by providing rules requiring consideration of all issues (Jelassi and Jones 1988, pp. 79-80).

The tendency to recall and value most information and/or solutions which are most salient or familiar can cause solutions to be overlooked which might possibly be better. This can be avoided by NSS suggesting possible concessions, solutions, and trade-offs.

Face-saving behavior of negotiators leads to the avoidance of agreements in which they feel they are giving in, even if these agreements are beneficial for both sides (Jelassi and Jones 1988, p. 75). NSS can suggest possible concessions to permit negotiators to compromise.

Communication during negotiations can become ineffective when participants are distracted due to the physical appearance of opposing parties, semantic differences, and status and power differences. By providing equal access to the electronic communication channel NSS can help to counteract power imbalances that emerge between parties if one person dominates the verbal channel. Moreover, each party has the opportunity of expressing its views, free from critical evaluation or interruption by the other party. Thus, NSS facilitate separate idea generation by the participants (Anson and Jelassi 1990, p. 185).

Finally, overconfidence on the part of negotiators can cause them to overrate their own judgment and/or lead to the belief that neutral parties will judge in their favor. NSS can sharpen the sense of rationality by providing analytical processing of subjective preference and/or external objective data and the determination of possible solutions.

The issues described above are experienced as more or less severe depending on the kind of negotiations conducted. In (Foroughi 1995) the author presents a survey of negotiation and bargaining practices in organizations with empirical results[60]. With respect to labor-management negotiations, procurement/purchasing negotiations, and sales negotiations the survey was intended to help identify specific problems encountered by negotiators, determine if computers have been used to support negotiations, and to provide information about the willingness of organizations to try such computer support in the future. In particular, respondents could rate 20 items that described possible attitudes with which one can go into negotiations. The rates described how often a particular attitude is taken and ranged from 1 (never) to 7 (always). In purchasing contract negotiations, the competitive attitude turned out to be an attitude taken significantly more often than all other factors. This result indicates that a fixed-pie mentality, i.e. the assumption of participating parties that their interests are in direct conflict with each other, is potentially a major source of inefficiency.

An example of a NSS is INSPIRE[61]. INSPIRE is software which has been developed at the Center for Computer Assisted Management at Carleton University with collaborators in several countries. INSPIRE supports all the basic steps that are usually followed in negotiations, i.e. it provides support for preparing for negotiations, for conducting negotiations, and for post-settlement activities (see section 2.1.5.1). To help in preparing the negotiations, the software provides a detailed description of the negotiation case and then guides the user through a sequence of pages on which the system asks the user about the importance of each issue and each alternative. This step is also called "preference elicitation" (InterNeg 1998). The information obtained in this way is used by INSPIRE in the next step to give the user a helpful feedback when constructing new offers or evaluating a counterpart's offers. During the conduct of the negotiations, menus are provided by which offers can be constructed, and boxes for messages. The user is further supported by displaying a rating (score) beside each offer based on the preference information from the first step, and by plotting a graph of the history of both sides of the negotiation. Based on the preference information provided by both parties, INSPIRE determines whether the agreement reached is Pareto-optimal, i.e. neither of the parties can improve their position without loss to the other side. If the software finds better solutions than the one agreed so far, then alternative solutions are shown and the option of continuing the negotiation until another agreement is reached is given (InterNeg 1998).

While in NSS essential activities are still being done manually there are efforts to automate these activities by using multi-agent systems. In what follows we

---

60   In this survey, 642 questionnaires were sent to 214 organizations with forty or more employees in the Midwest of the USA. A total of 69 completed survey forms were returned, 24 for purchasing contract negotiations, 22 for sales contract negotiations, and 23 for labor/management negotiations (Foroughi 1995, p. 126).

61   INSPIRE stands for InterNeg Support Program for Intercultural Research. InterNeg is the name of a Web service that contains information about Internet-based negotiations (http://interneg.carleton.ca).

introduce the concept of two multi-agent systems: Kasbah and Tete-a-tete. While Kasbah is an example of an approach to automate bilateral negotiations in a decentralized market[62] considering only the dimension of price, in Tete-a-tete multiple terms of a transaction and/or product are considered.

Kasbah[63] has been developed by the MIT Media Lab and is an online multi-agent classified ad system where users who want to buy or sell goods create software agents, give them a strategic direction, and send them off into a centralized agent marketplace. Kasbah agents proactively seek out potential buyers or sellers and negotiate with them on behalf of their owners. Each agent's goal is to complete an acceptable deal while considering a set of user-specified constraints such as a desired price, a highest (or lowest) acceptable price, and a date by which the transaction must be completed (Guttman, Moukas et al. 1998). Moreover, buyers (sellers) can choose among one of three negotiation strategies that are "anxious", "cool-headed", or "frugal" ("greedy"). While these basic strategies determine the shape of the raise (decay) function, i.e. whether the bids (offers) for a product increase (decrease) over time in a linear, quadratic, or exponential manner (Moukas, Guttman et al. 1998), the user-specific constraints determine the starting and end point of these functions (see Figure 19).

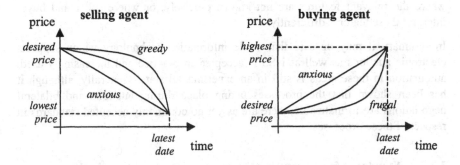

Figure 19:   Agents' strategies in Kasbah, following (Moukas, Guttman et al. 1998, Figure 1).

The software agents automate the tasks of finding potential transaction partners and negotiating with them for buyers and sellers. Negotiations in Kasbah are simple. After buying agents and selling agents are matched, the only valid action in the negotiation protocol is for buying agents to offer a bid to selling agents to

---

62   Kasbah actually provides a central marketplace. Nevertheless, the coordination of the software agents in this marketplace happens in a decentralized way by bilateral negotiations.

63   http://agents.media.mit.edu/Kasbah

which selling agents respond with either "yes" or "no".[64] The simplicity of these negotiation heuristics makes it intuitive for users to understand what their agents are doing in the marketplace. As was observed in experiments conducted on the basis of Kasbah, this is a particularly important issue for user acceptance (Guttman, Moukas et al. 1998).

Our second example, Tete-a-tete[65], is an approach in which an attempt is made to automate the activities of bilateral negotiations of multiple terms of a transaction, e.g. warranties, delivery times, service contracts, return policies, loan options, and other value-added services. As in Kasbah, negotiations take the form of multi-agent, bilateral bargaining (Guttman, Moukas et al. 1998). However, instead of using simple raise or decay functions, Tete-a-Tete's buying agents follow an argumentative style of negotiation (Parsons, Sierra et al. 1998) with sales agents, and use the evaluation constraints captured during the product and seller search as dimensions of a multi-attribute utility. This utility is used by a buyer's agent to rank the sellers' offerings based on how well they satisfy the purchaser's preferences (Guttman, Moukas et al. 1998). It is obvious that the concept of Tete-a-tete is based on the assumption that the ontology problem has been solved, i.e. both trading parties have a common understanding of the relevant product and/or transaction features. Hence, Tete-a-tete seems to be appropriate for commodities (which may still be complex in structure), while it is of limited use for products where the relevant features are not known precisely, or where seller and buyer interpret these features differently.

In summary it may be said that while information technology which supports electronic auctions as well as NSS is accepted in practice and increasingly used, automation in these areas is still in an experimental state. Generally, although it has been shown that the processes taking place during auctions and bilateral negotiations are formalizable, there are as yet no commonly accepted standards in respect of these processes.

3.2.4   Standards for structuring the communication process in the settlement phase

As we have seen in the previous sections, the potential for automating activities which take place in the evaluation phase of a business relationship is rather restricted. Apart from auctions, there are no standard procedures the decision maker can follow and non-trivial decisions have to be made. For example, if the good an organization is looking for is not standardized then the purchaser has to weigh up possible features of the good and make comparisons between offers

---

[64]   For further details about the implementation of the software agents cf. (Chavez and Maes 1996).

[65]   http://ecommerce.media.mit.edu/tete-a-tete

from different potential suppliers. Moreover, while in the settlement phase communication is characterized by the exchange of trade data such as order information and invoices, in the evaluation phase the exchange of information primarily relates to product data and data about the potential transaction partner. Although efforts have been made to standardize this information (e.g. STEP), these endeavors are usually limited to a relatively narrow domain, mainly because the ontology problem with respect to the semantics of the exchanged data has not yet been solved. Consequently, there are no standardization approaches focusing the whole process from searching for a potential transaction partner to the specification of a contract that is ready for signature. Instead, information technology which supports the evaluation phase of a supplier relationship has often a more auxiliary character in supporting subsidiary functions.

On the other hand, the settlement phase is characterized by the exchange of a comparatively well-defined set of business documents. Approaches to standardization in terms of business documents exchanged over the course of the settlement phase can be traced back to the early 1970's[66]. Nevertheless, there are as yet no generally accepted standards for the semantics and context of the use of those documents. For example, the type of response to the receipt of a purchase order can differ from organization to organization. One organization may reply with a purchase order acknowledgement, whereas another organization may reply with a shipping notice (EURIDIS 1999a). Hence, although each party uses standardized documents, the terms and conditions that are their style of doing business must still be negotiated (EURIDIS 1999b). In the worst case this has to be done for each transaction partner and contract.

One way to avoid the coordination of information exchange for each transaction anew is to define standard scenarios that guide the sequence and interpretation of business documents. This path has been followed by a number of approaches which, though differing in scope, have in common the fact that different possibilities of doing business are captured in computational form, calling the results electronic trade procedures, transaction models, or trade scenarios (EURIDIS 1999b). Mostly, the focus of these approaches lies in the settlement phase of a business relationship. This is because the product being exchanged is known and the terms of the exchange often follow a pattern evolving from established forms of contracts. Moreover, these approaches can build on well-established standards for the communication objects exchanged in the settlement phase of a supplier relationship.

The specification of trade procedures is one thing. The ways of sharing trade procedures among transaction partners is a different question. Here, generally

---

[66] EDI standards and other approaches to the standardization of business documents are discussed in detail in section 3.2.5.

three broad modalities can be distinguished: centrally standardized procedures, unilateral coordination, and bi- or multilateral coordination (EURIDIS 1999c).

In the case of centrally standardized procedures it is assumed that there is a generally accepted style of practice to which all parties conform. This is typical of situations where an organized market has been established which means that standard contracts for the exchange of goods are available. In electronic form, this entails standardized trading procedures being made available, e.g. through a publicly accessible library, downloadable and executable by all transaction parties.

The second case of unilateral coordination is characterized by situations where one trading partner dominates the relationship. This is typically true for relationships between large corporations and their suppliers. Here, the dominant trading partner dictates the modalities of the trade and possibly provides trading procedures which are downloadable by the other parties.

The bi- or multilateral way of sharing trade procedures includes situations where several of the transaction parties have established control policies. This is typical of situations where multiple regulatory agencies are involved. Here as well the major players have their trade procedures available in network accessible form. However, there is the potential for conflict between the control policies of the participating parties. In conventional trading circumstances, such conflicts are resolved either by negotiating a compromise, or by seeking other partners.

In the following sub-sections we present and discuss a number of major approaches to standardizing the exchange of business documents during the settlement phase of a transaction. These are:

- Open-EDI initiative, which has the aim of developing a concept and framework for the definition of trade scenarios (section 3.2.4.1);

- Interorganizational Procedures (InterProcs), which denote a pilot system representing an alternative approach of a general framework for the specification of electronic trade scenarios (section 3.2.4.2);

- OAGIS, which aims unlike the frameworks of Open-EDI and InterProcs at the formulation of concrete business scenarios (section 3.2.4.3);

- OTP, which contains building blocks usable in trade scenarios aimed at business-to-consumer relationships, but which may be transferable to business-to-business relationships in certain cases (section 3.2.4.4); and

- OBI, which contains trade scenarios aimed at the purchase of non-strategic, indirect materials by large, distributed requisitioner populations (section 3.2.4.5).

3.2.4.1 Open-EDI

Open-EDI is a reference model presently under development by the Joint Technical Committee 1/Subcommittee 30 (JTC1/SC30)[67] which is subordinated to the International Organization for Standardization/ International Electrotechnical Commission (ISO/IEC). As a reference model, Open-EDI is a guideline for standards development that is used by standard bodies (see Figure 20). In particular, the specification of Open-EDI does not include the definition of standard business scenarios. The Open-EDI reference model instead serves the purpose of supporting the development of standards related to the Business Operational View (BOV) and the Functional Service View (FSV) of a business scenario. While the BOV is used to describe the business aspects of a data exchange in a scenario, the FSV is used to describe the technical implementation (ISO/IEC 1997).

BOV related standards are tools and rules by which users who understand the operating aspects of a business domain can create scenarios. If a scenario developed for a particular exchange is found to be applicable to other situations, it can then be registered with an appropriate body and become part of a scenario repository. In this way, the description is available for use by others (Rawlins 1998). Registration authorities will reference the BOV related standards when considering scenarios for registration. On the other hand, FSV related standards are used by information technology experts, who are those people within an organization who design and/or build information technology used to support the execution of Open-EDI transactions (ISO/IEC 1997).

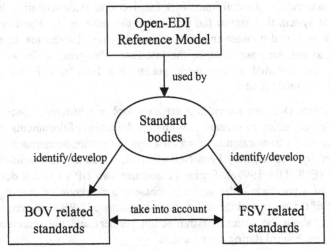

Figure 20:   The creation of BOV and FSV related standards. Source: (ISO/IEC 1997, Figure 2)

---

[67]   http://www.disa.org/international/sc30tag.htm

The interrelationship between BOV and FSV related standards is a critical issue. FSV related standards must take into account the BOV related standards and vice versa. This is because Open-EDI scenarios that are built using BOV related standards contain requirements that lead to demands on information technology and services, which on their part must conform to FSV related standards. These demands include e.g. the identification of the functional capabilities necessary to support Open-EDI transactions and the quality of service required from the functional capabilities for these Open-EDI transactions. The intention is that once an Open-EDI scenario is agreed, if implementations conform to the FSV related standards, there is no need for prior agreement about technical implementation between the organizations (ISO/IEC 1997).

The major purpose of Open-EDI is to facilitate an application-to-application data exchange without prior agreement, other than the agreement to use a particular scenario (Rawlins 1998). Open-EDI is only a framework enhancing the definition of business scenarios and exists only as a committee draft (currently in the second version ISO/IEC JTC1/SC30 Committee Draft (CD) 14662.2). In particular, there are no business scenarios specified yet. It will be interesting to see whether Open-EDI will be successfully completed, introduced, and adopted or whether XML based approaches will be develop faster, thus making Open-EDI obsolete.

3.2.4.2 *Interorganizational Procedures (InterProcs)*

InterProcs is a system designed within the scope of the Open Electronic Commerce project conducted by EURIDIS[68]. The overall objective of this project has been to develop a general framework for electronic trade scenarios. InterProcs is the pilot system that serves the purpose to demonstrate the feasibility of this framework with real transactions based on various model scenarios. InterProcs is divided into two separate systems, the InterProcs Designer, which supports the modeling and knowledge base development, and InterProcs Executor, which utilizes this knowledge base.

The InterProcs Designer provides a graphics tool and different concepts which facilitate the definition of scenarios. While the definition of documents exchanged in the course of a transaction is based on a specific syntax, scenarios are formally represented by Documentary Petri Nets (DPN's), which are an extended form of petri nets (EURIDIS 1999e). Figure 21 contains two DPN's which describe the exchange of a purchase order and a purchase order acknowledgement from the viewpoint of the buyer and the seller. The extensions of DPN's concern additional information about the actions of transaction partners and the representation of documents exchanged during a transaction.

---

[68] Euridis stands for "Erasmus University Research Institute for Decision and Information Systems" which is located at Erasmus University in the Netherlands.

Transitions are interpreted as actions of contracting parties. In the example, this is represented by naming the transitions e.g. "send_po" and "receive_ack". Moreover, the representation of documents takes place syntactically by drawing additional place nodes which are drawn as rectangles. In the example the purchase order sent by the buyer to the seller leads to an additional rectangle labeled with the name of the document ("purchase_order") and the addressee ("seller"). Finally, whereas basic petri nets represent relative time, in DPN's absolute time notations can be used in the form of timer events which indicate deadlines (EURIDIS 1999e).

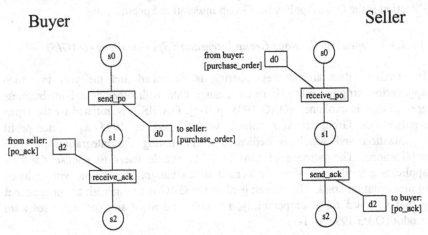

Figure 21: Documentary Petri Nets for the exchange of a purchase order and purchase order acknowledgement between buyer and seller. Source: (Lee 1999, p. 4)

Scenarios in InterProcs can be of a fixed form and parameter driven. Fixed scenarios, which are usually designed manually, lead to the problem that adaptations to meet the additional needs of a given situation are costly. This problem is addressed in InterProcs by breaking down scenarios into reusable components, which can then be flexibly reassembled to meet the needs of a wide variety of situations. The computational formalism employed is called "procedure constraint grammar" (PCG) which enables the descriptions of procedures by their temporal ordering constraints, rather than the absolute sequence of steps (EURIDIS 1999d). The idea is that these reusable scenario components are made accessible for other users, e.g. through a central library.

After using the Designer to define a scenario and documents that will be exchanged over the course of a scenario, the InterProcs Executor is a system component which facilitates multiple concurrent transactions among distant parties. It operates over the Internet using Java applets and Java applications. Currently central and decentralized architectures are supported by Executor. When using the central architecture, parties utilize the Executor as an applet from the

Web site of a VAN provider who fulfills post-master and archiving functions. Alternatively, in the decentralized architecture the Executor is used as a stand-alone application, where documents are transmitted using normal Internet email facilities. Each party is then responsible for maintaining its own local transaction files (EURIDIS 1999d).

As in Open-EDI, in InterProcs the focus is also on the development of a concept that helps to specify the scenarios underlying a transaction between different organizations, rather than on the provision of predefined standard scenarios for selected business activities. An approach which goes a step further in this direction is the Open Application Group Integration Specifications.

3.2.4.3   Open Applications Group Integration Specifications (OAGIS)

In OAGIS[69] data and process sharing is described and the way in which application program methods can exchange data with other compliant business applications is explained (OAG 1998, p. 1-1). OAGIS was initiated by the Open Applications Group (OAG), which was formed in 1995 as a non-profit organization and which is dedicated to promoting the integration of open applications. The purpose of OAGIS is to enable users to choose the best application while achieving the benefit of an integrated solution with reduced implementation costs. The overall goal of the OAG is to establish an independent global standard for interoperability, i.e. independent of any particular software vendor (OAG 1998, p. 1-1).

The idea is that application software used to support business processes can be interpreted as collections of business objects that interact through the exchange of business object documents (BOD). The specification of which BOD's are to be exchanged between the originating and destination business applications and in which sequence this exchange is to take place is done through integration scenarios. Here the technical integration, e.g. between operating systems, databases or middlewares, is assumed to be given (OAG 1998, p. 1-2). In the current release there are definitions of 48 integration scenarios, covering virtually every part of an organization's value chain. Figure 22 shows the example integration scenario "purchasing ordering process" which describes the data exchange between the sub-systems "order management" and "purchasing sales force automation", the latter usually being a procurement application. The communication between the participating sub-systems takes place by the exchange of BOD's, which is in OAGIS terminology also called "service request". In the example, the BOD "process PO" (PO stands for purchase order) is first transferred from the procurement system to the order management. The purpose of this BOD is to transmit a purchase order to a supplier's order management application (OAG

---

[69]   http://www.openapplications.org

1998, p. 3-1). After receiving the "process PO" BOD, the BOD "acknowledge PO" is returned by the order management. The purpose of this BOD is to acknowledge the receipt of the purchase order and to reflect any changes (OAG 1998, 4-1).

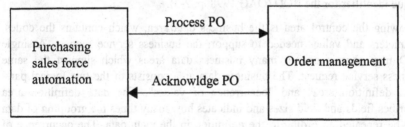

Figure 22:   Integration scenario "purchasing ordering process". Source: (OAG 1998, Section 2, p. 12)

Currently, there are 106 BOD's defined in OAGIS. The general structure of a BOD is described in Figure 23. According to that, a BOD consists of a control area and a business data area and is wrapped with a beginning marker MBBOD and an ending marker MEBOD. Markers are five character strings used as reference points for grouping areas of the BOD (OAG 1998, p. 2-2).

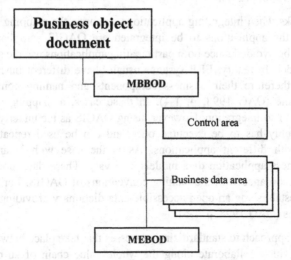

Figure 23:   Structure of a business object document. Source: (OAG 1998, p. 2-2)

The control area segment is located at the beginning of the BOD. It contains the business service request segment, the sender, and the datetime segment. While the business service request segment provides information about the action that the sender application wants the receiver application to perform, the Sender segment contains information about the characteristics of the sender application that created the BOD (e.g. the logical location of the application, the application, and the task that was processed to create the BOD). Finally, the datetime segment gives information about the date and time at which the BOD had been created. The combination of the information given in the control area serves as a globally unique identifier for the BOD (OAG 1998, p. 2-3).

Following the control area is the business data area, which contains the codes, parameters and values needed to support the business service request. A single BOD may contain one or many business data areas which support the same business service request. The business data area consists of the two logical parts "data definition area" and "occurrence of values". The data definition area describes fields and field sizes and indicates how many times the grouping of data may be repeated according to the definition in the meta data. The occurrence of values represents the string(s) of data described by the data definition area (OAG 1998, p. 2-12). While the control area segment is the same for all BOD's, the business data area may contain different compulsory and optional data types depending on the particular BOD.

The meta data architecture for BOD's was developed in 1995 and is similar to the syntax of traditional EDI[70]. Since the advent of XML[71] the OAG has specified a Document Type Declaration that can be used to exchange BOD using XML syntax (OAG 1998, p. 2-1).

Important tasks when integrating applications comprise the mapping of processes and data. If the applications to be integrated are OAGIS compliant, then this mapping can be avoided since both participating applications use the same process and data model. In reality, ERP systems usually have different business process models and therefore their business components and naming conventions are rarely the same (OAG 1998, p. 1-4). In these cases, a mapping must still be conducted prior to integration. However, using OAGIS as the underlying standard this activity only has to be executed once and can be used repeatedly for the integration with different applications. As is the case with business process models, business application data models also vary. These data models must be mapped in accordance with the naming conventions of OAGIS. For this purpose the OAG is establishing an open accessible data dictionary providing field names and definitions (OAG 1998, p. 1-5).

OAGIS is an approach to standardizing processes that take place between different applications which collaborate along the whole value chain of an organization. Although initially the emphasis is on the integration of applications used within a single organization, the concept can be applied to support interorganizational relationships. Basically it makes no difference whether the participating applications are situated in a single, in two, or more different organizations.

---

[70] Cf. section 3.2.5.1.

[71] The concept behind the Extensible Markup Language is introduced and discussed in section 3.2.5.1.3.

While OAGIS follows a broad approach, other standardization activities put the focus on certain selected business processes. Examples here are the Open Trading Protocol and Open Buying on the Internet, which are treated in the following two sections.

3.2.4.4 Open Trading Protocol (OTP)

OTP[72] is an IETF[73] specification for the exchange of documents between trading partners over the course of a market transaction. The development is conducted by a consortium of 26 leading enterprises and associations of the information technology and banking sectors[74].

In OTP nine generic transactions, which are referred to as OTP transactions, are defined. By combining OTP transactions all common variants of trading goods can be represented. The OTP concept tries to encapsulate existing payment methods on the Internet so that it can be freely combined with established payment standards without the need to synchronize the different standardization activities. Major OTP transactions are (OTP-Consortium 1998, p. 1):

- Purchase involves an offer, a payment, and optionally a delivery;

- Refund is the refund of value as the result of an earlier purchase;

- Value exchange involves two payments which result in the exchange of value from one combination of currency and payment method to another;

- Authentication supports the authentication of a party to make sure that the other party is who it appears to be;

- Withdrawal of electronic cash from a financial institution; and

- Deposit of electronic cash at a financial institution;

Each of these OTP transactions involves a number of organizations and/or individuals playing a trading role and a set of trading exchanges, each involving the exchange of trading data between the trading roles. The exchange occurs in the form of a set of trading components (see Figure 25). Trading roles identify the parts that organizations can take in a trade. As shown in Figure 24, trading roles comprise a consumer purchasing the good, a merchant customer care provider

---

[72] OTP is also referred to as Internet OTP (IOTP) to signal that it is primarily aimed on Internet-based Electronic Commerce transactions.

[73] IETF stands for Internet Engineering Task Force, which is an open international community of network designers, operators, vendors, and researchers concerned with the evolution of Internet standards (http://www.ietf.org).

[74] For latest information about OTP cf. http://www.ietf.org/html.charters/trade-charter.html. The actual homepage of the OTP consortium (http://www.otp.org) does not reflect recent developments since it is rarely updated.

resolving consumer disputes, a payment handler accepting value for the merchant, a merchant selling the product, a delivery handler supplying the good on behalf of the merchant, and finally a payment instrument customer care provider resolving problems with a particular payment instrument (OTP-Consortium 1998, pp. 2-3). Roles may be carried out by different organizations or by the same organization, i.e. a single organization can act in multiple roles.

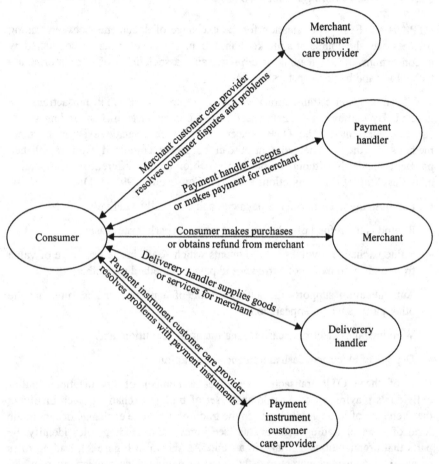

Figure 24:   Trading roles in OTP. Source: (OTP-Consortium 1998, p. 2, Figure 1)

As roles are taken by different organizations, there is a need to exchange data, i.e. in OTP terminology to carry out trading exchanges. In OTP four trading exchanges are identified (OTP-Consortium 1998, p. 3):

- Offer, resulting in the merchant providing information about what is being bought and how much to pay;

- Payment between the consumer and the payment handler. This can occur in either direction;

- Delivery, i.e. the transmission of goods (if they are consisting of bits and bytes) or the delivery of information about physical goods from the delivery handler to the consumer; and

- Authentication, which is usable by any trading role to authenticate whether the other party is who it claims to be.

OTP transactions consist of a combination of a number of trading exchanges. For example, the OTP purchase transaction comprises an offer trading exchange between the customer and the merchant, a payment trading exchange between the customer and the payment handler, and a delivery trading exchange between the customer and the delivery handler (see Figure 25), while an OTP value exchange transaction is composed of an offer and two payment trading exchanges. Trading exchanges are further subdivided into trading components which contain the actual data. The purpose of using trading components is the enhancement of communication efficiency, which is achieved by reducing the number of round-trip delays in an OTP transaction by packing the components from several trading exchanges into combination OTP messages (OTP-Consortium 1998, p. 3).

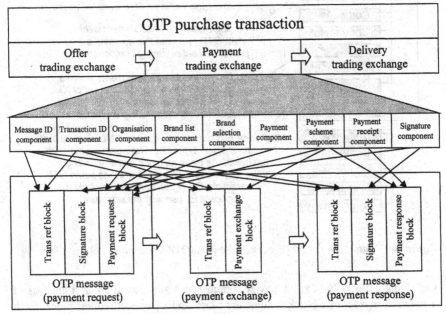

Figure 25:   Structure of an OTP purchase transaction.

Before describing how trading components are combined to form OTP messages, a short note on the structure of OTP messages in general. OTP messages are

110

physically sent in the form of XML documents between the different organizations that take part in a trade and generally consist of a number of blocks (see
Figure 26). Every OTP message starts with a "transaction reference block" which
contains a globally unique identifier for the OTP transaction and for the message
within the OTP transaction. Furthermore, a message contains one or many trading
blocks, each consisting of one or more trading components and optionally one or
more signature components. In the example of Figure 25 a payment trading
exchange takes place over the course of three OTP message exchanges. At first, a
payment request is sent by the customer to the payment handler, e.g. a bank. Then
payments are exchanged between customer and payment handler. Finally, a
payment response is transmitted from the payment handler back to the customer.

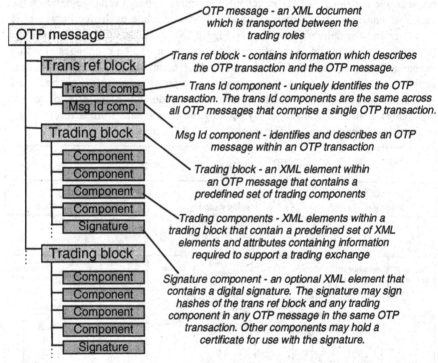

Figure 26:   Structure of an OTP message. Source: (OTP-Consortium 1998, p. 13)

On taking a closer look at the payment request message, we see that it consists of
a transaction reference block, a signature block and a payment request block. Each
of these blocks is composed of either different or the same trading components.
While the trans ref block contains a transaction ID component and a message ID
component, the signature block contains one or more signature components and
associated certificates, which sign the data of the trading block. Finally, the
payment request block contains information which requests the start of a payment,

e.g. a number of compulsory and optional organization components with information about the participants, a brand list component in which it is coded which payment methods are supported by the merchant, and a brand selection component for the brand list in which the payment method chosen by the purchaser is coded (OTP-Consortium 1998, pp. 98-99). The payment exchange and payment response messages are composed analogously, though consisting of an alternative combination of trading blocks.

The focus of the OTP approach is on consumer-to-business relationships for which it is typical that the purchase transactions take place directly between the main protagonists, i.e. the consumer and the merchant. As soon as the consumer is an organization, so that one can speak of a business-to-business relationship, the communication between the purchasing and selling organizations becomes more complex. In particular, the buying organization has employees acting on behalf of their employer who participates in the purchasing process by authorizing and controlling activities. An approach to standardizing the purchasing process in an organization is Open Buying on the Internet, which is examined in the next section.

3.2.4.5 *Open Buying on the Internet (OBI)*

The OBI[75] standard is an open, flexible framework for business-to-business Internet purchasing solutions. The focus of OBI is on the automation of high-volume transactions of low-price goods. The first version of the OBI standard was published in May 1997. Currently OBI is available in version 2.0.[76] OBI has been developed by the OBI consortium, which is a non-profit organization with 64 members managed by CommerceNet. The actual work is done in track groups. The membership in the OBI consortium and participation in its track groups is open to buying and selling organizations, technology companies, financial institutions, and other interested parties on an annual fee basis.

In the OBI concept there are four interacting entities: requisitioner, buying organization, selling organization, and payment authority (see Figure 27).

---

[75] http://www.openbuy.org
[76] OBI has been implemented in commercial procurement software and is supported, e.g., by Intelisys Electronic Commerce (Minahan 1999) and Netscape BuyerXpert, which is part of the Netscape CommerceXpert software (Dolmetsch, Fleisch et al. 1999, p. 80).

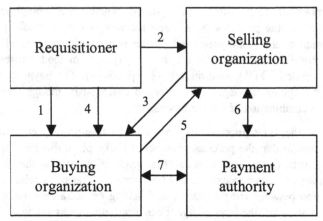

Figure 27:   OBI system entities and (simplified) information flows, following (OBI-Consortium 1999, p. 10, Figure 2-2).

The requisitioner has a need for a product or service. The primary activities of a requisitioner are to query the catalog of the selling organization, generate order requests, specify or confirm accounting and payment information for orders, view and update the requisitioner profile, and query order status from a desktop computer if desired (OBI-Consortium 1999, p. 2).

The buying organization, which employs the requisitioners, has an internal business process and information systems infrastructure for managing the acquisition of goods and services. The primary functions are to maintain the electronic purchasing homepage with links to preferred selling organizations, maintain requisitioner profiles, receive and approve order requests from selling organizations, create OBI orders, and send OBI orders to selling organizations (OBI-Consortium 1999, p. 2).

The selling organization has an electronic product catalog, an electronic ordering capability and an internal process for filling traditional as well as electronic orders. Thus its primary functions are to provide electronic catalogs, create order requests based on requisitioner's selections, forward order requests to buying organization, maintain order status information, request payment authorization from payment authority, and process orders through order fulfillment system (OBI-Consortium 1999, p. 2).

Finally, the payment authority, which can be either a third party or the selling organization, authorizes transactions for particular payment types, records completed transactions, issues payment to selling organization and invoice to buying organization, and receives payment from buying organization (OBI-Consortium 1999, p. 2).

In purchase transactions the four roles interact through the exchange of information, which is described in the OBI architecture by seven steps (see Figure 27). Steps 2, 3, and 5 are subject to the OBI specification, i.e. the focus is on the communication which takes place directly between the selling organization on the one side and the buying organization and requisitioner on the other side (OBI-Consortium 1999, p. 9).

Step 1: In the first step of a purchase transaction the requisitioner accesses supplier catalogs on the purchasing server located at the buying organization. This is done using a Web browser to connect to a local purchasing server located at the buying organization. The requisitioner selects a hyperlink to a selling organization's merchant server containing an online catalog of goods and services. The portfolio of available suppliers and catalogs is preselected by the buying organization.

Step 2: The requisitioner browses the catalog and selects items. Before the requisitioner can browse the catalog, the selling organization's server authenticates the requisitioner's identity and organizational affiliation based on information presented in the requisitioner's digital certificate. Authentication information is used, in conjunction with profile information optionally presented by the requisitioner's browser, to uniquely identify the requisitioner and to construct an individualized catalog view.

Step 3: The selling organization sends an order request to the buying organization. The content of the requisitioner's virtual shopping basket and identity of the requisitioner is mapped into an order request (EDI-compatible). Optionally, a digital signature is calculated. The order request (and digital signature, if used) is encapsulated in an OBI object that is encoded and transmitted securely to the buying organization over the Internet using HTTP and SSL[77]. The buying organization server receives the encoded OBI object, decodes it, extracts the order request, verifies the signature (if appropriate) and translates the order request into an internal format for processing.

Step 4: The buying organization approves the order request. Administrative information (including payment type) is added to the order request at the buying organization (automatically from a profile database and/or manually by the requisitioner), and the order is processed internally either automatically or through a workflow-based process.

Step 5: The buying organization creates an order and sends it to the selling organization. The completed and approved order is formatted as an OBI order

---

[77]   Actually, OBI/2.0 knows two alternative methods for transmitting an encoded OBI object containing an order request over the Internet using HTTP, a the server-to-server and (step 3 in Figure 27) and server-browser-server transmission. In the latter case the communication is routed over the requisitioner's browser, so that the requisitioner has the opportunity to append further data to the order request.

(EDI-compatible) and a digital signature is calculated if desired. The order (and digital signature, if appropriate) is encapsulated in an OBI object that is encoded for transport and transmitted securely from the buying organization server to the selling organization server via the Internet using HTTP and SSL. The selling organization receives the encoded OBI object, decodes it, extracts the order, verifies the signature (if appropriate), and translates the order into its internal format.

Step 6: The selling organization obtains credit authorization, if necessary, and begins order fulfillment.

Step 7: Finally, the payment authority issues an invoice and receives payment.

Basically, two types of documents are exchanged between the selling and buying organization: order requests and OBI orders. The specification of these documents is based on ANSI X12 850 Version 3040 data standard, whereas transport is provided by Internet standard transport protocols. ANSI X12 850 is a complex and flexible standard for formatting orders and provides a syntax that can be used to code purchasing transactions of any kind[78]. Since the OBI order format specification has been designed specifically to support the data requirements of transactions of low-price goods, it allows the use of only a subset of the available ANSI X12 850 data segments, data elements, and codes (OBI-Consortium 1999, p. 23). Although ANSI X12 is used as standard for the exchange of order request and order, trading partners still need to review the use of the data segments, elements, and codes jointly as part of an OBI implementation. This review typically covers topics such as the use of organization codes, how tax calculations will be handled, whether shipping address will be based on codes or street addresses, the type of part numbers to be used to identify items, and how payment will be handled (OBI-Consortium 1999, p. 73).

Comparing Open-EDI, InterProcs, OAGIS, OTP, and OBI it becomes clear that the applicability of these approaches changes from universal to specific. While Open-EDI on the one side of these two poles is actually only a framework giving advice on how standardization processes can take place, OBI, on the other hand, is intended to support only a special kind of transaction, namely high volume transactions of low-price goods. As standards are more generic, they are usable in the context of a greater variety of business processes. However, with decreasing applicability the range of necessary additional arrangement between the transaction partners increases. The way in which this trade-off is represented by costs is discussed, among other issues, in section 3.2.6.

As we have seen, standards for structuring the communication process use a mixture of specific formats and widely accepted and established EDI standards for the business documents exchanged over the course of a transaction. While in the

---

[78] A description and discussion of ANSI X12 is provided in section 3.2.5.1.1.

former case standards are used which are restricted to the provision of syntax rules for the specification of the business documents (e.g. XML is used in OTP to specify OTP messages), in the latter case the semantics of the exchanged documents is also subject to standardization (e.g. ANSI X12 850 in OBI). In the next section we present and discuss established and new approaches to EDI standards, while distinguishing between the levels of the syntax and the semantics in terms of which standardization can take place.

3.2.5   Standards for structuring communication objects

"Electronic Data Interchange is the inter-organizational, computer-to-computer exchange of business documentation in a standard, machine-processable format" (Emmelhainz 1993, p. 4). The main characteristics of EDI are derived from this definition as follows (Emmelhainz 1993, pp. 4-5): Firstly, EDI happens primarily between organizations. Secondly, EDI happens between computers. As Emmelhainz points out, it is generally accepted that 70 percent of a computer's business data output becomes a second computer's business data input. Using EDI the duplicate data entry associated with paper is eliminated. Thirdly, EDI focuses on business information. Hence, any information that is on a business form, e.g. purchase orders, invoices, quotes, status reports, and receiving advices, is appropriate for the use of EDI. Fourthly, EDI requires a standard, machine-processable format. This means that the data must be in a structured format so that it is understandable to a computer without human interpretation.

To send or receive an EDI message, three elements are necessary: an EDI standard, EDI software, and a network. While EDI standards are agreements on how the data must be structured for electronic communications, i.e. formatting rules for creating an EDI message, EDI software fulfills the task of translating the original data into that format, i.e. the data is reformatted from an organization-specific arrangement to the standard arrangement. Finally, the network is used to transport the EDI message from the sender to the receiver. Traditionally this took place either via a direct link through a communications modem or by the use of a value added network (VAN) (Emmelhainz 1993, p. 13). Recently, there have been new approaches of using the Internet as means of transportation for EDI messages[79].

Over the course of the last 20 years a number of different EDI standards have been developed. These standards relate either to certain industrial sectors, to particular kinds of data, or focus on a certain region (Figure 28).

---

[79]   These approaches are discussed under the key words "Internet-EDI" (Segev, Porra et al. 1999) or "WebEDI" (Buxmann, Weitzel et al. 1998; Westarp, Weitzel et al. 1999).

	Trade data		Product data		Text data
	National	**International**	**National**	**International**	
Independent of industrial sector	ANSI X12 TRADACOMS	EDIFACT XML	IGES	STEP OSD XML	ODA/ODIF
Specific for an industrial sector	VDA SEDAS	ODETTE CEFIC EDIFICE RINET SWIFT	SET VDA-FS		DTAM XML

Figure 28: Overview of selected EDI standards, following (Neuburger 1994, p. 22, Figure 5).

The exchange of text data comprises documents like letters, notes, or complex documentation containing not only text, but also graphics and pictures. Examples of EDI standards for text data are the Office Document Architecture/ Office Document Interchange Format (ODA/ODIF) and the Document Transfer, Access and Manipulation-standard (DTAM) (Neuburger 1994, pp. 21-22).

Standards for the exchange of product data contain elements that primarily provide information about the physical properties of products, e.g. graphic data, drawings, and data about the geometry. An internationally established standard which is not restricted to a particular industry is the Standard for the Exchange of Product Model Data (STEP), which emerged from a number of national approaches like the Initial Graphics Exchange Specification (IGES) in the U.S., the Standard d'Exchange et de Transfert (SET) in France, and the Flächenschnittstelle des Verbandes der Automobilindustrie (VDA-FS) in Germany (Neuburger 1994, p. 21).

In the case of standards for the exchange of trade data in history, three major developments occurred (Neuburger 1994, p. 20). Firstly, in different industrial sectors on the national or international level approaches like the standard of the Verband der Automobilindustrie (VDA standard) in the German automotive industry, the international standard for the exchange of banking data of the Society for Worldwide Interbank Financial Telecommunications (SWIFT), the standard Datenkommunikationssystem (DAKOSY) for the transporting sector, and Standardregeln einheitlicher Datenaustauschsysteme (SEDAS) in German industry for consumer goods had been established. In parallel on the national level, industry independent approaches had been followed such as ANSI X12 in the U.S.

and the Trade Data Communications Standard (TRADACOMS) in the U.K. Secondly, as the demand for an international solution to the standardization of trade data increased, under the auspices of the United Nations the universal standard EDIFACT was developed which, however, had the problem of being too bloated due to the fact that every possible eventuality in all industrial sectors had been considered. Subsequently, thirdly, certain industries again took the EDIFACT specification to derive subsets, as happened, for example, in the automotive industry with the standard adopted by the Organization for Data Exchange by Teletransmission in Europe (ODETTE), the Conseil Européen des Fédérations de l'Industrie Chemique (CEFIC) for the chemical industry, the Electronic Data Interchange Forum for Companies with Interests in Computing and Electronics (EDIFICE), and the Reinsurance and Insurance Network (RINET) for the insurance sector. The approaches based on EDIFACT and ANSI X12 are further referred to as "traditional EDI".

In recent years, a new Internet-based approach has emerged which is generic enough to be used for all kinds of documents, be it trade, product, or text data: XML. Therefore, in all of these areas over the course of the last two years new XML-based standards are being worked on. While a reasonable amount of empirical work has been done on the diffusion of traditional EDI standards, there is as yet no comparable research about XML due to its novelty. A recent empirical study conducted in Germany and the U.S., in which the respondents were asked about the use of EDI standards, showed that EDIFACT is by far most popular in Germany (Westarp, Weitzel et al. 1999). It is used by nearly 40% of the responding enterprises. Other common standards follow far behind (see Figure 29). About 11% of the responding German companies use VDA, 6% use SEDAS, 5% use SWIFT, 3% use ODETTE, only 2% use ANSI X12, and about 1% use DAKOSY.

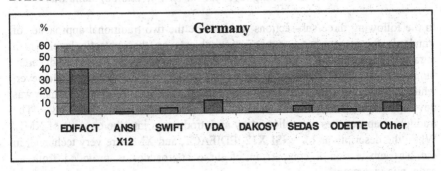

Figure 29:   The use of EDI standards in Germany. Source: (Westarp, Weitzel et al. 1999, Figure 1)

Figure 30 shows that the leading EDI standard in the U.S. is ANSI X12 (more than 48%) followed by EDIFACT (24%). Only two of the responding enterprises use SWIFT or TRADACOMS respectively.

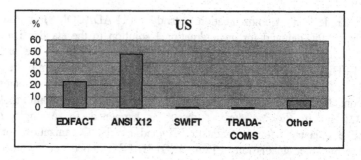

Figure 30: The use of EDI standards in the U.S. Source: (Westarp, Weitzel et al. 1999, Figure 2)

While these numbers offer a snapshot of the use of different EDI standards nowadays, other questions asked by the empirical study revealed the diffusion process over the past 14 years. The respondents were asked when the respective EDI solutions had been implemented and about their future plans. In brief, the answers show that the exponential growth of EDIFACT in Germany will continue in the near future, while in the U.S. the diffusion process of ANSI X12, having reached a high level of diffusion, slows down significantly (Westarp, Weitzel et al. 1999).

In the remainder of this section we discuss and compare major approaches to languages for the specification of standards. Then two examples are given to illustrate how these languages are used to represent standards on the semantic level.

3.2.5.1 The syntactic level: languages for the specification of standards

In the following three sub-sections we describe the two traditional approaches of standards for structuring communication objects on the syntactic level which attracted most attention in the past: ANSI X12 and EDIFACT. These two different families of standard EDI syntax are similar in purpose and approach. However, while in North America ANSI X12 was primarily adopted, EDIFACT, which was developed later, has achieved greater acceptance on the international level. The traditional approaches are followed by an introduction into the concept of XML. While the descriptions of ANSI X12, EDIFACT, and XML are very technical, in the last sub-section a comparison of these approaches is provided from an economic viewpoint.

3.2.5.1.1 American National Standards Institute X12 (ANSI X12)

In EDI terminology a specific document is referred to as a transaction set. Each transaction set is given a numeric code, similar to the way in which most paper forms are assigned a form number. An example is the ANSI X12 purchase order, which is called the 850 transaction set. Each transaction has its own standard designation. In case of the transaction set 850 it is the standard X12.1. Following this schema, different business documents are defined. A purchase order acknowledgement is represented by transaction set 855 and the standard designation X12.9, an invoice has transaction set 810 and standard X12.2, and so on (Emmelhainz 1993, p. 54).

A typical paper document contains numerous lines of information. In a purchase order, the name of the buying organization generally constitutes one line of information, the address of the buying organization constitutes another line of information. In EDI terminology, each line of information is called a data segment. Within each data segment, there are a number of individual pieces of information. The address line, for example, is usually made up of the city, the state, and the ZIP code. Each individual piece of information is called a data element (Emmelhainz 1993, p. 54).

The specification of a document in the X12 format is done by taking the following steps (Emmelhainz 1993, pp. 55-61):

- determine the segments to be used by creating a transaction set table;
- determine the specific structure of each segment by creating a segment diagram key;
- determine the data elements in each segment by specifying element diagrams of the segment diagram key; and
- determine the characteristics of each data element by creating a data element dictionary for each data element.

A transaction set table is used to determine which segments are needed for a particular transaction set. Each transaction set has a number of data segments that are mandatory. In a purchase order, for example, there are some data segments that can be found on all purchase orders, regardless of the industry, the item being purchased, the size of the company, or other variables. In addition to mandatory segments, there are optional data segments that may be used by the trading partners as desired. The standard also allows the repetition of certain segments. For example, most purchase orders include at least two address blocks, one for the buyer and one for the seller.

In a segment diagram what is to be included in each data segment is specified. Moreover, it shows the sequence of the elements and it indicates, whether the use of each element is mandatory, optional, or conditional. The diagram also describes the specific form of each element (e.g. the data type). The segment diagram key consists of five basic components: data segment identifier, data element delimiter, element diagrams, data segment terminator, and notes.

The data segment identifier indicates the data segment. The data element delimiter serves as a separator and is a character selected by the sender. It precedes each element and acts as a position marker. The asterisk is the most commonly used data element delimiter. The element diagrams are boxes that describe each data element. The data segment terminator is a character selected by the sender to indicate the end of a segment. Finally, the notes contain comments and/or syntax rules.

In the element diagrams of the segment diagram key for each data element the following information is given: data element reference designator, data element title, data dictionary reference number, data element requirement designator, data element type, and data element length.

The data reference designator is a two-digit sequence number preceded by the data segment identifier. It indicates the sequence of the data elements. The name of the data element is described by the data element title. With the help of the data dictionary reference number it is possible to access the data dictionary where additional information on the content of the data element can be found. While the data element requirement designator indicates whether the element is mandatory, optional, or conditional (i.e. whether the use of an element is dependent upon the use of another element), the data element type is an indication of the form of the data (e.g. numeric or decimal). Finally, the data element length specifies the minimum and maximum number of characters allowed in the data element.

Finally, the data element dictionary provides the precise content and meaning for each data element. Each data element is described in the dictionary at the reference number shown in the data element box.

The interchange of EDI messages takes place by separating and grouping the documents through the use of interchange envelopes on three levels (Emmelhainz 1993, p. 62): at first, each transaction set is separated from the other transaction sets by a transaction set header (ST) and transaction set trailer segment (SE). Secondly, transaction sets can be bundled to a functional group, which is enveloped by a functional group header (GS) and a functional group trailer segment (GE). A third level of enveloping is the interchange envelope which designates the addresses of both the sender and the receiver and which encloses all of the documents being sent.

3.2.5.1.2   *United Nations Electronic Data Interchange for Administration, Commerce and Transport (EDIFACT)*

The design rules for EDIFACT are similar in many ways to the design rules of ANSI X12. An EDIFACT interchange has the same basic structure as does an X12 interchange (Emmelhainz 1993, p. 70), although the EDIFACT terminology is slightly different. There are five basic levels of hierarchy in the EDIFACT rules, which are used in order to build up a valid transmittable string of characters: interchanges, functional groups, messages, segments, and data elements (Berge 1989, p. 67).

The atomic structure of an EDIFACT message is a data element, e.g. price, weight, or name. Moreover, a number of component data elements can be combined to form a composite data element. The composite data element is a grouping of two or more data elements, which are closely related, e.g. a quantity and quantity qualifier. Furthermore, simple and composite data elements can be combined to form a data segment. An EDIFACT message[80] consists of a number of data segments. Messages can optionally be combined to functional groups. Finally, an interchange contains a number of messages, which are either bundled in functional groups, or stand-alone. The structure of an EDIFACT document exchange is shown in Figure 31.

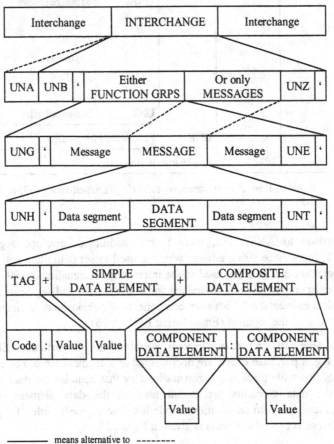

——— means alternative to --------

Figure 31: Hierarchy of an EDIFACT document exchange from interchange level to data element level. Source: (Berge 1989, p. 71, Figure 5.6)

---

[80] In EDIFACT the term "message" is used rather than "transaction set" as it is the case for ANSI X12 terminology (Emmelhainz 1993, p. 70).

Each hierarchical level of a document exchange is enveloped by delimiters. For example, a functional group is introduced by the header "UNG" and closed by the trailer "UNE", while a message is introduced by "UNH and closed by "UNT". The complete enveloping structure as used in EDIFACT is shown in Figure 32.

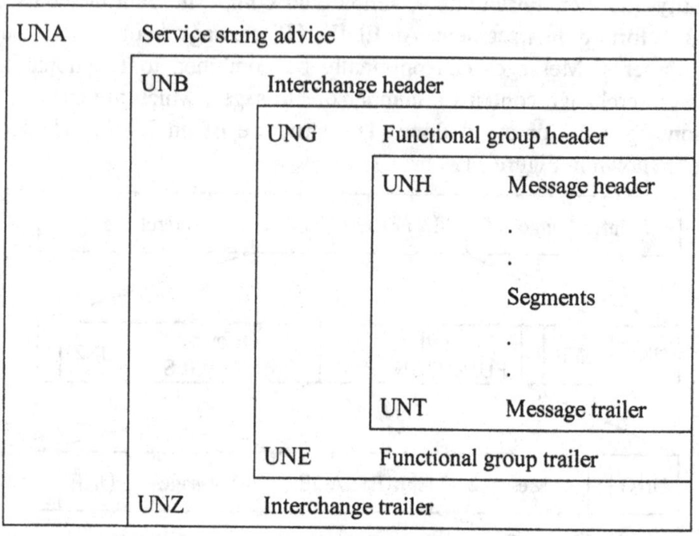

UNA	Service string advice		
	UNB	Interchange header	
		UNG	Functional group header
			UNH Message header
			.
			.
			Segments
			.
			.
			UNT Message trailer
		UNE	Functional group trailer
	UNZ	Interchange trailer	

Figure 32:   EDIFACT enveloping structure, following (Emmelhainz 1993, p. 71, Figure 5-2).

In comparison to ANSI X12, there is one additional envelope segment in EDIFACT, the service string advice, which is used to set delimiters and describe the character set that is being used in the interchange (Emmelhainz 1993, pp. 70-71). The most commonly used delimiters for data elements and segments are a "+" between data elements, a ":" between components of composite data elements, and a "'" at the end of the segment (Emmelhainz 1993, p. 76).

The data segments and data elements permitted for a particular EDIFACT message, e.g. a purchase order, are documented in a segment table. For each data segment of this table there is a segment directory that contains the data elements. Finally, the data elements are documented in the data element directory, sometimes together with an additional code list. The segment table of a purchase order with a selection of segments is given in Figure 33.

The tag describes the segment identifier, which is a string of three characters. Each tag has a description and a status ("S" column). The status can be mandatory ("M") or conditional ("C", i.e. optional). Finally, for each segment the "REPT" column indicates how many times the segment can be repeated. The segments described in a segment table can be organized in groups. The groups in the example are conditional. However, if a segment group is used, then certain elements of this group may be mandatory, as is the case for the NAD data segment in group 1.

Tag	Name	S	REPT
UNH	Message Header	M	1
BGM	Beginning of Message	M	1
RFF	References	C	10
CTA	Contact Segment	C	10
	Segment Group 1	C	20
NAD	Name and Address	M	1
LOC	Location Identification	C	5
	...		
FII	Financial Inst. Information	C	5
	...		
	Segment Group 10	C	9999
LIN	Line Item	M	1
RFF	References	C	10
	...		
CNT	Control Totals	C	5
UNT	Message Trailer	M	1

Figure 33: Purchase order segment table. Source: (Emmelhainz 1993, p. 73, Figure 5-4)

The segment directory for the line item-segment (LIN) of the segment table is shown in a simplified form in Figure 34. In the column "Data Element Tag" the identifier for each segment is given. Identifiers starting with a "C" indicate composite elements. Composite elements can be optional (as defined in the column "Requirement Indicator"). In the last columns the data type and length are described. Data types are either "n" (numeric) or "an" (alphanumeric), followed by the maximum length of an element.

LIN	LINE ITEM		
Function:	To specify the basic and most frequently used line item data for a transaction.		
Data Element Tag	**Data Element Name**	**Requirement Indicator**	**Data Type**
1082	LINE ITEM NUMBER	C	n..6
1229	ACTION REQUEST CODE	C	n..2
C198	PRODUCT IDENTIFICATION	C	
7020	Article Number	M	an..35
7023	Article No. ID	M	an..3
C198	PRODUCT IDENTIFICATION	C	
7020	Article Number	M	an..35
7023	Article No. ID	M	an..3
C186	QUANTITY INFORMATION	C	
6063	Quantity Qualifier	C	an..3
6060	Quantity	M	n..15
6411	Measure Unit Specification ...	C	an..3

Figure 34: Simplified LIN segment directory, following (Emmelhainz 1993, p. 74, Table 5-1).

Each data element is further described in the data element directory, which provides, in addition to the information already given in the segment directory, a plain text description of the data element (Berge 1989, p. 64). In some cases a further specification of the permitted values of a data element may also be necessary. Here, a supplementary code list is given. For example, data element 7023 (Article No. ID) has a code list containing, among other values, the possible code BP with the description "buyer's part number".

In an EDIFACT document exchange each interchange partner knows the sequence of data elements exactly. While mandatory data elements have to appear, conditional data elements are present at the discretion of the sender. However, if data elements are omitted, their absence is denoted by the remaining presence of their separator characters or by the presence of the segment terminator character

(Berge 1989, p. 66). To illustrate the syntax used in EDIFACT following is given a sample interchange of a purchase order (Emmelhainz 1993, p. 77)[81]:

```
#1      UNA:+.?'
#2      UNB+UNOA:1+PETE SENDER+NICK
        RECEIVER+921201:2100+00005'
#3      UNH+NR123+ORDERS:1:10'
#4      BGM+105+PS/98765+921201'
#5      NAD+BU+++STEADYGOING,INC.'
#6      NAD+SE+++NEVERWORRY,INC.'
#7      LIN+1++6666:VP+555:BP+21:100'
#8      UNT+6+NR123'
#9      UNZ+1+00005'
```

This purchase order contains the information, among other things, that Steadygoing Inc. (line #5), represented by Pete Sender (line#2), is purchasing from Neverworry Inc. (line #6), which is represented by Nick Receiver (line #2). The item actually bought is described in line #7, which is explained in detail in Figure 35.

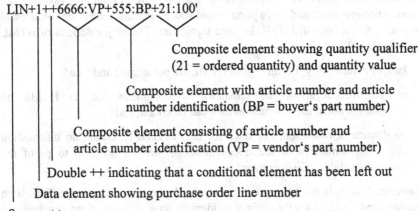

LIN+1++6666:VP+555:BP+21:100'

Composite element showing quantity qualifier (21 = ordered quantity) and quantity value

Composite element with article number and article number identification (BP = buyer's part number)

Composite element consisting of article number and article number identification (VP = vendor's part number)

Double ++ indicating that a conditional element has been left out

Data element showing purchase order line number

Segment tag

Figure 35:   Line item segment with explanation of the data elements, following (Emmelhainz 1993, p. 76).

As we have seen in the description of ANSI X12 and EDIFACT, these concepts are quite complex and the syntax behind these concepts is not intuitively

---

[81]   In an EDIFACT exchange the transmitted string of characters is usually sent as one line, i.e. without line break. To make the interchange readable we have chosen to write each data segment on a single line and assign a number to each line which we can reference in the explanation of data segments.

understandable let alone applicable. Hence, one may expect that a considerable amount of time will be needed to get into the details of these standards. An alternative approach to these traditional EDI standards is XML, which is comparatively simple.

3.2.5.1.3 Extensible Markup Language (XML)

XML is a text based meta markup language which allows the description, the exchange, the display, and the manipulation of structured data (Weitzel, Buxmann et al.) and passed the World Wide Web Consortium (W3C[82]) as a standard in February 1998 (W3C 1998b). XML is extensible, because it does not contain a fixed set of tags, as is the case for HTML. It has instead the character of a meta language that provides a grammar that can be used to define an arbitrary number of markup languages. In this sense, HTML is an application of XML.

XML is a compromise between the markup languages HTML and SGML (Standard Generalized Markup Language). HTML is primarily a language for the description of text presentations in the World Wide Web. Its original purpose was to specify a language that makes it easily possible to present scientific papers on the Web. Hence, HTML contains first of all tags for formatting text. As the Internet became more and more popular and was increasingly used for commercial purposes, the deficits of HTML became significant. The major deficits of HTML are (Bosak 1997):

- lack of extensibility, i.e. all tags in HTML are predefined and fixed;

- no information about the semantics of documents, i.e. in HTML no information about the structure of data can be coded; and

- no document validation, i.e. since the tags in HTML contain no information about the semantics of the document data, there is no help to proof the structural validity of a document.

However, SGML is not appropriate for the use in the Internet, either. SGML is an international standard for the definition, identification, and use of the structure and contents of documents. Like XML, SGML provides a grammar that can be used to specify markup languages. Indeed, HTML like XML is an application of SGML. The problem with SGML is its complexity. The size of documentation necessary to define a language may serve as an indicator for complexity. While the formal definition of XML needs 33 pages to document, SGML is specified on 500 pages

---

[82] The W3C was founded in October 1994 to develop common protocols for the World Wide Web. The W3C is an international industry consortium providing services including a repository of information about the World Wide Web for developers and users, reference code implementations to embody and promote standards, and various prototype and sample applications to demonstrate use of new technology. The web pages of the W3C can be accessed at http://www.w3c.org.

of documentation. Therefore, SGML was inappropriate for the use in the Internet and XML was formed as a subset of SGML, eliminating all features thought to be rarely used and unnecessary for the Internet.

The concept of XML is based on the separation of the content, structure, and layout of documents. Tags can be freely defined and supplied with semantically meaningful names. Moreover, tags can be hierarchically nested. In this way, tags contain information about the contents marked by the tags and through the nesting of tags information about the structure of the data can be provided. Additionally, XML documents can be supplied with a formal description of the grammar they are subject to. The specification of the formal grammar, i.e. of the permitted tags and the nesting of tags, takes place in a document type declaration (DTD).

An XML document is well-formed if it is in conformity with the XML syntax rules. The basic syntax of a well-formed XML document is as follows (Weitzel, Buxmann et al.):

- All tags consist of an opening and a closing tag. Every tag opened must explicitly be closed. In case of a tag without contents, the opening and closing can optionally happen in one tag. For example, a tag
</BR> can alternatively be written as <BR/>.

- Attribute values must be delimited by quotation marks.

- The nesting of tags may only occur hierarchically.

- The letters used for markup (e.g. < and &) may not be used in the contents of a document.

- At the beginning of an XML document a tag must be included to indicate the XML version the current document is subject to, e.g. <? xml version="1.0"?>.

An XML document is valid, if it is well-formed and if it is in conformity with the formal grammar specified by a DTD. An example of a well-formed and valid purchase order formulated with XML is given as follows (Holzner 1998):

```
<?xml version="1.0"?>
<!DOCTYPE order SYSTEM "order.dtd">
<ORDER>

    <HEADER>
        <NAME>
        <LASTNAME>Smith</LASTNAME>
        <FIRSTNAME>John</FIRSTNAME>
        </NAME>
        <DATE>28.07.1999</DATE>
    </HEADER>
```

```
        <ORDERITEMS>

            <ITEM>
                <PRODUCT>harddisk</PRODUCT>
                <NUMBER>6843</NUMBER>
                <PRICE>300</PRICE>
            </ITEM>

            <ITEM>
                <PRODUCT>monitor</PRODUCT>
                <NUMBER>5234</NUMBER>
                <PRICE>500</PRICE>
            </ITEM>

        </ORDERITEMS>

</ORDER>
```

The DTD can be part of the XML document or, alternatively, the DTD can be in an external file, which is then referenced by an XML document. In the example above the latter way was chosen. The second line contains a reference to the external DTD "order.dtd". The DTD of the example purchase order appears as follows (Holzner 1998):

```
<?XML version="1.0"?>
<!DOCTYPE ORDER [
<!ELEMENT ORDER (HEADER, ORDERITEMS)>
<!ELEMENT HEADER (NAME, DATE)>
<!ELEMENT NAME (LASTNAME, FIRSTNAME)>
<!ELEMENT LASTNAME (#PCDATA)>
<!ELEMENT FIRSTNAME (#PCDATA)>
<!ELEMENT DATE (#PCDATA)>
<!ELEMENT ORDERITEMS (ITEM)*>
<!ELEMENT ITEM (PRODUCT, NUMBER, PRICE)>
<!ELEMENT PRODUCT (#PCDATA)>
<!ELEMENT NUMBER (#PCDATA)>
<!ELEMENT PRICE (#PCDATA)>
]>
```

The example DTD specifies a document type "order" and defines the usable tags for this document type, as well as their nesting structure and data types. PCDATA stands for parsed character data, or text, and the "*" means that the item it refers to may be repeated. The element ORDERITEMS, for example, may contain an arbitrary number of ITEM elements, whereas each of the ITEM elements must contain exactly one PRODUCT, NUMBER, and PRICE element in this order, which contain the data. This example provides a simple overview of the basics of XML. The concept of XML is, however, more complex. For example, as an alternative, children elements can be allowed to appear in arbitrary order within the parent element; it is possible to mix data elements and other nested elements; and instead of the arbitrary repetition of a child element as indicated by the "*" symbol, it is possible to declare elements to be optional, alternative, or one can define a minimum number of repetitions (Holzner 1998). However, it becomes clear that by defining the grammar and syntax of a document, one has a powerful instrument at hand, which helps with the validation of XML documents. For example, given the DTD above, it can be proved whether a purchase order is complete and whether it fulfills structural requirements such as that there be a header to which a number of order items belong.

Finally, the visual representation of XML documents is produced with the help of style sheets. Through style sheets the authors as well as the recipients of XML documents can define the appearance of a document, e.g. depending on the output media such as screen or a printer (W3C 1998a; W3C 1998c).

3.2.5.1.4   *Comparing traditional EDI with XML*

Comparing the traditional EDI concepts ANSI X12 and EDIFACT on the one side, and XML on the other side we observe differences in respect of the three necessary EDI elements standard, software, and network.

The network enables the transmission of EDI messages from the sender to the receiver. Although the specification of the traditional EDI standards and XML are in principle independent from the transportation mechanism used to transmit the messages, it is often the case that EDIFACT and ANSI X12 are used together with direct connections between the trading partners or VANs, while XML is founded on Internet transport mechanisms.

With direct connections there is the problem of handling different communication protocols, time zones, and variations in transaction sets (Emmelhainz 1993, p. 102). VANs originally emerged to solve the problems of direct communication between trading partners. A VAN provides EDI communications skills, expertise, and equipment necessary for electronic communication. A basic function of VANs is the provision of electronic mailbox services, i.e. to receive, store, and forward electronic messages (Emmelhainz 1993, pp. 102-103). Through electronic mailboxes the problems of direct communication between the trading partners are solved. One call to the VAN is sufficient to reach all trading partners. Therefore, only compatibility to the VAN needs to be ensured. Compatibility between organizations and their VAN, as well as between different VANs is usually reached by using the communication standard X.400.

As well as the basic functionality of electronic mailbox services, VANs provide a number of additional services, which make up the added value (Emmelhainz 1993, pp. 104-107):

- By the provision of gateways VANs assure the interconnectibility when trading partners participate in different VANs.

- VANs often provide translation and media conversion services, i.e. organizations can use their specific data and/or media formats which will then be translated into a format readable by the receiver of the message[83].

- Encryption and authentication is another important feature offered by some of the VANs. While encryption is the process of changing an EDI message into a coded message, which cannot be read unless the receiver has the key to the code, so that the secrecy of the data is guaranteed, authentication, on the other hand, ensures that the data is not altered.

- Finally, VANs offer installation assistance and training services by providing documentation, implementation guidelines, a hotline for questions and problems, and sales representatives to help with the implementation of EDI.

In the context of EDI the Internet leads to changes, which not only manifest themselves in opportunities for new EDI approaches based on XML, but also the way in which traditional EDI is conducted. The problems of direct communication between trading partners can now be solved by using the Internet as a transport mechanism[84] instead of mailbox services provided by VANs. Whenever there is no need for the additional services of VANs, the Internet may be a valid alternative for current VAN customers as well as for potential EDI users who have not participated in EDI so far because of the high costs of using VANs. An indicator for this development is that many VANs take countermeasures by lowering prices and offering Internet-based services (Tucker 1997; Segev, Porra et al. 1999).

The second necessary element of EDI is EDI software which translates company-formatted data into a standard format, extracts the data from the organization's database, generates the message in a given standard format containing the data previously extracted, and initiates the electronic exchange, e.g. using the Internet or X.400 (Emmelhainz 1993, pp. 80 and 86). Here, XML based solutions may potentially profit from the large installed base of Internet technology (Weitzel, Buxmann et al.). Although the use of the Internet simply as a transport

---

[83] For the optimal number of intermediaries offering translation and conversion services and their optimal service range cf. (Westarp, Weber et al. 1997).

[84] This can be reached, for example, by using Internet-based services such as electronic mail, file transfer, or the World Wide Web. In the current work, we do not go into the technical details. However, the interested reader may be referred to an overview of these concepts in (Buxmann, Weitzel et al. 1998).

mechanism, as we have learnt in the previous paragraph, may not be a lasting advantage, the fact that the philosophy of XML is rooted in the Internet may still be advantageous. The background of traditional EDI was efficient communication in terms of transmitted data volume. Subsequently, the coding is difficult to handle and one needs much time to get into the principles of the standard. However, transmission volume is not a serious problem any more and the usability of a technology in the sense of user-friendliness has become increasingly important. The principles of XML are well known to people in the Internet community, since everybody in this community is quite familiar with the similar syntax of HTML. These learning effects led to the availability of a wide range of cheap tools, e.g. parsers and editors, as soon as XML was specified[85].

Finally, EDI systems need a standard for the messages exchanged. Here, the use of XML possibly has advantages over traditional EDI with respect to portability and flexibility. Due to the broad availability of tools for every platform the contents of XML documents is more accessible for authors as well as for recipients (Weitzel, Buxmann et al.). Moreover, XML can be used in a more flexible way. Because of its generic character it is not restricted to the exchange of trade documents. It can also be used for other kinds of document of almost arbitrary complexity, e.g. product descriptions or text documents.

In summary it may be said that XML, due to its greater portability, flexibility, the availability of software tools, and relatively low communication costs provides new opportunities for small and medium sized enterprises to participate in EDI networks (Tucker 1997). However, traditional EDI will continue to exist, possibly extended by Internet-based transport mechanisms.

3.2.5.2 *Standards on the semantic level*

So far we have discussed different approaches to standards for structuring communication objects on the syntactic level. Clearly, these standards become useful only when applied to the exchange of messages. Examples of standardized trade documents have been introduced in the previous section in the explanations of traditional EDI and XML. In what follows we discuss two commercial applications of XML which go beyond the standardization of trade data, but which can nevertheless be useful in a transaction: OSD for the standardized description of software and WIDL for the standardized description of Internet-based information services.

---

[85] A number of commercial vendors are preparing XML software tools. In addition, aided by XML's relative simplicity, many individuals and academic institutions are undertaking XML efforts. A list of leading examples of XML tools can be accessed under http://www.w3.org/XML/.

3.2.5.2.1 *Open Software Description (OSD)*

OSD was developed by Microsoft in 1997 with the aim of providing an XML-based vocabulary for describing software packages and their dependencies. Software dependencies are represented by a directed graph. Directed means that a software package requires another software package to be able to be run. Graph means that each software package is represented as a node, where any node can have zero or more incident arcs that specify the dependency (Hoff, Partovi et al. 1997).

The OSD syntax allows one to describe one or more dependencies between software components. In addition, OSD provides a syntax for describing different conditional 'dependencies, depending on the operating system, CPU architecture, and language of the machine interpreting the OSD vocabulary. The following example of a software description shows how dependencies are expressed in OSD (Hoff, Partovi et al. 1997):

```
<SOFTPKG NAME="com.foobar.www.Solitaire"
VERSION="1,0,0,0">
   <TITLE>Solitaire</TITLE>
   <ABSTRACT>Solitaire by FooBar Corporation
   </ABSTRACT>
   <LICENSE
   HREF="http://www.foobar.com/solitaire/li-
   cense.html"/>

   <!--FooBar Solitaire is implemented in native
   code for Win32, Java code for other platf. -->
   <IMPLEMENTATION>
     <OS VALUE="WinNT"><OSVERSION
     VALUE="4,0,0,0"/></OS>
     <OS VALUE="Win95"/>
     <PROCESSOR VALUE="x86"/>
     <LANGUAGE VALUE="en"/>
     <CODEBASE HREF="http://www.foobar.org/
     solitaire.cab"/>
   </IMPLEMENTATION>

   <IMPLEMENTATION>
     <IMPLTYPE VALUE="Java" />
     <CODEBASE HREF="http://www.foobar.org/
     solitaire.jar"/>

     <!-- The Java implementation needs the
     DeckOfCards object -->
```

```
        <DEPENDENCY>
            <CODEBASE
            HREF="http://www.foobar.org/cards.osd"/>
        </DEPENDENCY>

    </IMPLEMENTATION>
</SOFTPKG>
```

Each OSD file specifies one level of dependency information. By allowing one OSD file to reference other OSD files, an arbitrarily large dependency graph can be formed. A client must read the OSD file and determine the relevant implementations and dependencies, given the client's local configuration. To fully discover the correct graph of dependencies, the client may have to download additional OSD files. For example, in the above situation, the "cards.osd" refers to an additional OSD file that specifies further second-level dependencies. The client can use the resulting graph to determine which implementations are relevant and need to be downloaded to complete the installation of the package (Hoff, Partovi et al. 1997).

The original purpose of the specification of OSD was to facilitate the automatic distribution of software over the Internet. The idea is that applications can use the OSD vocabulary to automatically trigger downloads of software. Here, the OSD vocabulary provides the necessary information so that only the necessary software components are downloaded and installed. However, other scenarios in the context of business transactions are possible. For example, when purchasing software a standardized description according to OSD may well support the search for products at the sites of different software vendors.

3.2.5.2.2   Web Interface Definition Language (WIDL)

The goal of WIDL is to enable automation of all interactions with HTML/XML documents and forms, providing a general method of representing request/response interactions over standard Web protocols (Wales 1999). WIDL had been developed by webMethods Inc. in 1997 and currently has the status of an acknowledged transmission to the W3C.

The principle of WIDL is simple: service providers in the Internet specify the input and output parameters of their Web pages, e.g. forms, as a WIDL description. Therefore a service defined by WIDL is similar to a function call in standard programming languages. This description can then be accessed and evaluated by visitors to the Web page, e.g. search engines, and used to access the original service automatically. WIDL consists of six XML tags (Merrick and Allen 1997):

- <WIDL> defines an interface, which is a grouping of related services and bindings. In the <WIDL> element an object model to be used for extracting data elements from HTML and XML documents can (optionally) also be specified. Object models are the result of parsing HTML or XML documents. Object references are used in <VARIABLE/>, <CONDITION/>, and <REGION/> elements.

- <SERVICE/> defines a service, which consists of input and output bindings (e.g. a World Wide Web service provided by a CGI script). Services take a set of input parameters, perform some processing, then return a dynamically generated HTML, XML or text document. The attributes of this element map an abstract service name into a URL, specify the HTTP method used to access the service, and designate bindings for input and output parameters.

- <BINDING> defines a binding, which specifies input and output variables, as well as conditions for the successful completion of a service. Input bindings describe the data provided to a Web resource, and are analogous to the input fields in an HTML form. For a static HTML document no input variables are required. Output bindings describe what data elements are to be mapped from the output document returned as a result of accessing the Web resource with the given input variables.

- <VARIABLE/> defines input, output and internal variables used by a service to submit HTTP requests, and to extract data from HTML/XML documents.

- <CONDITION/> defines success and failure conditions for the binding of output variables, specifies error messages returned when a service fails, and enables alternate bindings attempts as well as the chaining of services.

- <REGION/> defines a region within an HTML/XML document. It is useful for extracting regular result sets that vary in size, such as the output of a search engine or news stories.

The following example illustrates the use WIDL-elements[86]:

```
<WIDL NAME="EddieBaeur" VERSION=2.0>

<SERVICE NAME="ProductSearch" METHOD=GET
URL="http://www.ebauer.com/eb/ShopEB/prod_search_resu
lts.asp" INPUT="productSearchInput"
OUTPUT="productSearchOutput"/>

<BINDING NAME="productSearchInput" TYPE="INPUT">
   <VARIABLE NAME="searchstring"
   FORMNAME="searchstring"/>
</BINDING>
<BINDING NAME="productSearchOutput" TYPE="OUTPUT">
```

---

[86]   The example is taken from (Allen 1999).

```
        <CONDITION TYPE="Failure"
        REFERENCE="doc.p['*Sorry*'].text"
        MATCH="*Sorry*"
        REASONREF="doc.p['*Sorry*'].text"/>
        <CONDITION TYPE="Success"
        SERVICE="ExtractPrices"/>
        <VARIABLE NAME="productURL" TYPE="String"
        REFERENCE="doc.table[0].tr[1].td[3].a[0].href"/>
</BINDING>

<SERVICE NAME="ExtractPrices" METHOD=GET
URL="%productUrl%" INPUT="ExtractPricesInput"
OUTPUT="ExtractPricesOutput"/>

<BINDING NAME="ExtractPricesInput" TYPE="INPUT">
    <VARIABLE NAME="productUrl" TYPE="String"
    USAGE="INTERNAL"/>
</BINDING>

<BINDING NAME="ExtractPricesOutput" TYPE="OUTPUT">
    <VARIABLE NAME="Price" TYPE="String"
    REFERENCE="doc.table[1].strong[0].value['*\$$']"/>
</BINDING>

</WIDL>
```

In this example the service "ProductSearch" returns an URL when it successfully finds a product matching the search criteria. Conditions are used to specify a service chain. Service Chains pass the name-value pairs of an output binding into the input binding of the service specified by a <CONDITION/> statement. Any name-value pairs matching the variables of the chained service's input binding are used as input parameters. The success condition in the ProductSearchOutput binding causes the ExtractPrices service to be called. Because the output binding of ProductSearch matches the input binding of ExtractPrices, the variables are passed from one service into the other.

The potential benefit of WIDL in a business transaction lies first of all in the possible automation of search activities. Vendors of goods often provide product catalogues accessible over the World Wide Web. The contents of these catalogues are usually retrieved from a database, and the Web pages presenting the data are dynamically generated. A formal description of the access logic enables the automatic extraction of relevant data matching previously specified search criteria.

As we have seen in the previous sections, information technology can be used to support purchasing activities at all stages of the procurement process, thus contributing to a reduction of costs incurred over the course of a transaction. The next section provides a recapitulation of the technologies discussed, complemented by a closer examination of potential transaction cost reductions.

3.2.6 Information technology and transaction costs

In the following sub-sections we show how the information technologies as presented in sections 3.2.1 to 3.2.5 influence transaction costs. The analysis is oriented according to the schema of transaction costs developed in section 2.2.1. In this schema we distinguish between evaluation and settlement costs.

The impact of information technology on evaluation costs is only sparsely demonstrated in practice by quantitative data. Therefore the analysis is restricted to qualitative issues, whereas in terms of the settlement costs the qualitative results can be substantiated by case studies and surveys, primarily because the use of EDI systems to support the settlement of transactions has been common practice for about 30 years.

3.2.6.1 *Evaluation cost reductions*

The evaluation costs comprise contact costs of finding a potential transaction partner and of establishing initial contact and the costs of gathering further information on potential transaction partners, in what follows we refer to these two components as information costs, and the negotiation costs, incurred through negotiations, contractual arrangements and agreements between partners[87].

3.2.6.1.1 *Information costs*

Contact costs and the costs of gathering further information about potential transaction partners are reduced by Internet-based applications which support the search for potential transaction partners. These applications extend from search engines using differently sophisticated search mechanisms to software agents. The benefit of such applications can potentially be increased by using advanced concepts such as smart catalogs which enhance the bundling of different vendors' catalogs so that the necessity of further inquiries about the vendors' product offers is reduced. In cases where the products purchased are judged primarily on the basis of price the, example of BargainFinder has shown that the activity of further examining supplier offers can be entirely omitted. Furthermore, collaborative filtering methods may contribute to a better judgment of potential transaction partners. Connected with this effect are cost reductions due to the reduced risk of opportunistic behavior on the part of transaction partners. Finally, for information cost reductions the provision of a single gateway which not only supports the

---

[87]   We focus on the major cost components, neglecting the decision costs which are mentioned in section 2.2.1 as part of the evaluation costs.

finding of potential transaction partner but also negotiations in a single and integrated step is particularly appropriate.

An important component of applications which support supplier search and evaluation are standards for structuring the information exchanged during search activities. The exchanged information comprises primarily descriptions of products, suppliers, and contracts. Furthermore, information is exchanged enabling the purchaser to access the relevant information on the supplier's side. As examples of standards in these fields we introduced to the concepts of OSD as a standardized software description and WIDL representing catalog structure and its input and output parameters. These standards reduce the costs of gathering information about potential transaction partners and their products. This is because closer inquiries of suppliers can frequently be avoided, if it becomes clear that a product is not suitable for the purchaser by using a standardized product description. In the example of OSD, searchers may be able to specify the requirements of a software component they are looking for, e.g. in terms of the hardware and/or dependencies on other software used in the organization. On the assumption that software vendors provide a standardized description of their products which is accessible e.g. for Internet search engines, then the searcher can use these requirements as selection criteria for suppliers. In effect, the search leads to more precise results. However, once a number of potential vendors are identified, there may still be the need to evaluate properties of the product that are not covered by the standardized description.

3.2.6.1.2 *Negotiation costs*

Once a potential transaction partner is found and contacted, we have seen various ways of supporting negotiations between purchaser and supplier. Electronic auctions are a way of automating the determination of prices when the traded good and contract conditions are given, thus reducing negotiation costs. In cases where negotiations are more complex, so that auctions are replaced by decentralized market mechanisms, we have seen that negotiation support systems can still contribute to better decisions over the course of negotiations by mitigating cognitive limitations and socio-emotional problems.

In negotiations in particular a common vocabulary is crucial to ensure that the participating parties are referring to exactly the same good and that there is a common understanding of the attributes describing the product and the terms of the transaction, e.g. delivery time, delivery quantity, and financing terms (Beam and Segev 1997, p. 264). Hence, the development and use of standards for the description of products and terms of a transaction facilitates negotiations by reducing costs incurred by misunderstandings between the negotiating parties due to the lack of a common vocabulary.

3.2.6.2   Settlement cost reductions

The settlement costs consist of initialization costs when a relationship to a new supplier is established, costs of exchanging the traded goods and payments, and adjustment costs[88]. All these components are subject to reductions when information technology is used.

3.2.6.2.1   Initialization costs

The expected amount of initialization costs is influenced by information technology use as far as transaction partner change is connected with the introduction of new application software or the adaptations of existing software solutions. These changes lead to implementation costs. In (Emmelhainz 1993, pp. 162-164) and (Niggl 1994, pp. 66-67) implementation costs are broken down into a number of components:

- hardware costs, which include the purchase and maintenance of the computer equipment;

- software costs, which comprise the purchase of a standard system and possible costs of customizing the system, e.g. when the EDI software must be integrated with internal application systems, as well as ongoing maintenance costs. These costs also comprise the costs of negotiating common formats for the exchange of information, the mapping of data to internal formats, and possible costs of interconnecting the participating information systems;

- costs of training the personnel;

- personnel costs;

- outside support costs for services of outside consultants; and

- membership costs, e.g. when becoming member of an EDI associations. For example, to obtain a communication identification code[89] from the Uniform Code Council (UCC[90]) one must become member of the UCC, which is

---

[88]   As is the case for evaluation costs, in the case of settlement costs we also focus on major cost components, i.e. costs of signing a contract, decision costs, and costs of resolving a relationship are neglected.

[89]   The communication identification code is a globally unique number that identifies a UCC member company. This company number allows a company to build ID numbers that uniquely identify products, assets, or shipments in the global supply chain (http://www.uc-council.org/membership/mp_getting_a_upc_bar_code.html).

[90]   The UCC is a non-profit standards organization that began in 1972 as a company originally known as the Uniform Grocery Product Code Council. The primary function of this organization was to administer the Universal Product Code (UPC). In recent years, the traditional role of the UCC as administrator of the UPC has been supplemented by the administration and maintenance of electronic communication

connected with a one-time payment ranging from \$500 to \$15,000 based upon annual sales volume.

These costs can be reduced using standards on the level of the business process as well as of business documents. Software costs, personnel costs, and outside support costs are reduced by the use of information technology standards since the interface with the current transaction partner remains unchanged when changing supplier. Moreover, training costs are reduced because, due to the unchanged process model, employees do not have to do much rethinking. In addition, both transaction parties profit from enhanced flexibility concerning the selection of transaction partners and the information technology used to support the relationship.

The flexibility in decisions about information technology use is enhanced, because solutions from different vendors and/or in different functional areas of the organizations can be more easily integrated. An example is the use of OTP to support purchasing transactions. If one needs to change the software which supports purchase transactions over the Internet, then OTP compliant software from different vendors can be used without changing the underlying process model and interfaces to other intra- or interorganizational information systems.

The flexibility in terms of transaction partner selection is enhanced, because as soon as common standards are used to support a business relationship, the activities of negotiating formats and procedures to exchange data are reduced when changing transaction partner. Therefore, initialization costs decrease in importance and the purchasing organization can be choosier concerning supplier selection. However, the extent to which initialization costs can be reduced depends heavily on the diffusion of standards among potential transaction partners. The more potential transaction partners use the same standards as the purchasing organization, the higher the probability that initialization costs are reduced when changing transaction partner.

Besides diffusion, another determinant of cost reductions is the level of detail of a standard specification. For example, for a given transaction the initialization costs are reduced differently, depending on whether one can rely on existing detailed specifications of a business process fitting to the given transaction (e.g. as OBI fits to purchase transaction of low-price goods in distributed organizations) or whether there is only a framework allowing the (though reasonable) specification of a business process together with the transaction partner (as it is the case, e.g., with Open-EDI). In the latter case there might be still a considerable amount of cost of negotiating common formats for the exchange of information. These costs can be reduced by using appropriate means to negotiate and distribute customized format specification. In particular, standards based on XML provide a reasonable

---

standards and the mapping of standards with business processes (http://www.uc-council.org).

potential for cost reductions. In comparison to traditional EDI the XML approach is easy to handle and new specifications can be negotiated and easily distributed using DTD's. Moreover, it is founded on Internet standards which are ubiquitous in virtually all organizations and application areas, so that, compared to traditional EDI, the introduction and use of XML is connected with minor cost.

3.2.6.2.2 Costs of exchanging goods and payments

The costs of exchanging goods and payments are directly influenced by information technology inasmuch as they are incurred by the transfer of data (EDI) between the trading organizations. The use of information technology to automate or support the exchange of trade data during a transaction improves the cost efficiency of this process. This occurs by reducing communication costs, document processing costs, and inventory costs. Moreover, due to less redundant data entry, there is less resource consumption, because trade data is directly transferred into the recipient's database (e.g. fewer personnel and because of a reduced error rate lower follow-up costs due to inconsistent data) (Emmelhainz 1993; Kilian 1994; Neuburger 1994; Westarp, Weitzel et al. 1999). In (Emmelhainz 1993, pp. 20-29) the author identifies a number of additional indirect effects since the automation of electronic data interchange is often accompanied by an internal reassessment of business processes. This can possibly lead to an improved integration of intra- and interorganizational business processes with the overall result of improved personnel productivity, a better access to information, a better supply chain management, and thus enhanced customer satisfaction and competitiveness.

While there is limited empirical work concerning potential reductions of initialization costs, the impact of (traditional) EDI on the costs of exchanging goods and payments has been substantiated through a wide selection of case studies. Two illustrative examples are 3Com and Procter & Gamble[91]:

- As Westarp et al. state, 3Com uses EDI for order and invoice processing with about 15 percent of its approximately 200 suppliers and distributors. Using EDI 3Com succeeded in reducing the costs of order processing from about $38 per order if it is done manually to $1.35 using EDI. Thus, in total $750,000 is saved in sales order and invoice processing. Taking the reduction of data entry errors, efficiency increases due to better warehouse management, and reduction of processing delays into account, the overall savings add up to $1.3 million (Westarp, Weitzel et al. 1999).

---

[91] Quantitative examples of cost reductions, extending from savings in communication costs through reduced personnel, to time savings and business process related costs are quoted in (Neuburger 1994, p. 36). Case studies following a more qualitative approach can be found in (Gifkins 1990, pp. 165-212).

- According to Emmelhainz, the Procter & Gamble Company uses EDI for the processing of freight bills with over 75 percent of its outbound carriers resulting in a 50 to 75 percent reduction on errors due to the elimination of redundant data entry activities. Additionally Procter & Gamble realized a reduction in telephone expenses, improved cash flow, and enhanced personnel productivity. Overall, in this way cost savings of $3.50 per freight bill could be achieved (Emmelhainz 1993, p. 36).

3.2.6.2.3   Adjustment costs

Adjustment costs are incurred in the supervision of agreements and planned or unplanned changes of the original provisions of the contract. Planned and unplanned changes of the original provisions of the contract are connected with (re-)negotiation activities. The expositions on the use of information technology in negotiations during the evaluation phase (cf. section 3.2.6.1.2) can be applied to contract renegotiations as well. Cost reductions can be achieved by reducing cognitive limitations and socio-emotional problems and providing a common ontology by the use of standards.

Contracts are supervised by monitoring activities, which comprise the collection of data characterizing the fulfillment of the contract and reporting of this data. An example of monitoring costs is the cost of monitoring the quality of the purchased goods as agreed in the contract. Since monitoring activities primarily consist in the collection and distribution of information, information technology can contribute to a more efficient fulfillment of these tasks.

From the discussion of the impact of information technology on transaction costs, we realize that its direct influence finds expression primarily in the enhanced efficiency of information exchange, while the extent to which this benefit can be realized depends on the diffusion of the relevant information technology among current and potential transaction partners[92]. This benefit is compensated for by implementation costs as soon as the information technology to be applied has to be introduced before its use.

An indirect influence of information technology on transaction costs occurs through decreasing opportunism risk. As the costs of changing transaction partner decrease, the power of suppliers in the (re-)negotiation of purchasing contracts diminishes as well.

Finally, lower transaction costs have an impact on the expected acquisition costs when purchasing the goods. As search activities can be accomplished more cheaply and the purchasing organization can be choosier, in effect lower prices (or

---

[92]   Of course this statement is only true for information technology that is subject to network effects (which we focus on).

better quality, respectively) can be achieved so that the overall costs of a supplier relationship decrease.

As we have seen in chapter 2.2 transaction costs determine the way in which supplier relationships are organized. Hence, one could state that information technology through its influence on transaction costs has an indirect impact on supplier contracts. This hypothesis was analyzed theoretically and empirically in a number of works. These works have in common the fact that they generally confirm the existence of a dependency between the use of information technology and the way in which supplier relationships are realized. However, how supplier relationships are actually changed is still subject to scholarly dispute. A brief review of the relevant works in this area is provided in the next section.

3.3 Information technology and changing supplier relationships

In the literature of recent decades a number of different hypotheses have been proposed concerning the influence of information technology on business relationships. In the beginning the focus of research was on the investigation of the vertical integration of organizations and how it was likely to be changed by the use of information technology. In the early years it was forecasted that the use of information technology would lead to increased vertical integration. This conclusion was drawn due to the fact that efficiency gains in the exchange of data had only been possible when using hardware and software from the same manufacturer. Due to a lack of standardization, interorganizational systems did not yet exist (or had been too expensive to realize). Hence, automated information processing between business functions had inevitably been connected with organizational unity (Bauer 1997, p. 198). As the connectivity and computing capacity of information systems increased, this opinion was revised. Since the 1960s, key characteristics of computer hardware technologies such as price, reliability, and density have improved at a rate of 30 to 50 percent per year (Benjamin and Blunt 1992). This means that for the same amount of money computers and networks with increasing performance capacities in processing and transmission speeds as well as accompanying storage media can be purchased. The increasing speed and power of electronic components result directly from miniaturization, the process of creating smaller electronic components with greater capabilities. The miniaturization of electronic components together with advances in communication technology has led to much greater portability of computers and communication devices, i.e. users can carry them around conveniently. Hence, increasing computing capacity goes together with enhanced connectivity. Connectivity is the ability to transmit data between devices at different locations (Alter 1996, p. 23). It has been increasingly possible to transmit computerized data almost instantly anywhere in the world, e.g. by electronic mail or EDI. In particular, it became easier to obtain computerized business information from outside sources such as customers and suppliers and vertical integration was no longer a necessary condition for exploiting benefits from the integration of information systems. Subsequently a move to less vertical integration was forecasted, i.e. supplier relationships moved into the center of analysis. Malone, Yates, and Benjamin proposed the move to the market hypothesis (Malone, Yates et al. 1987) according to which the use of information technology leads to an overall shift toward the use of electronic markets.

3.3.1 The move to the market hypothesis

In (Malone, Yates et al. 1987) the authors argue that information technology reduces the unit cost of coordination, the complexity of product descriptions, and the transaction specificity of investments in inter-organizational interactions. They suggest that the increasing adoption of information technology will lead to a greater degree of outsourcing and hence less vertically integrated organizations.

According to their argumentation, the use of information technology makes the use of hierarchies as well as markets more efficient. The relative costs of market and hierarchy are assumed to be as described in Table 3.

Malone et al. say that the use of information technology gives rise to the electronic communication effect, which means that more information can be communicated in the same amount of time (or the same amount in less time) while the costs of communication decrease dramatically. The electronic communication effect causes an overall reduction in the unit costs of coordination, so that the importance of the transaction cost dimension on which markets are weak is reduced and markets become more desirable in some situations where hierarchies were previously more favored (Malone, Yates et al. 1987, p. 488).

Table 3: Relative costs of markets and hierarchies, following (Malone, Yates et al. 1987, p. 485, Table I).

Organizational form	Production costs	Transaction costs[93]
Markets	Low	High
Hierarchies	High	Low

A second argument is based on the shifts of the transaction determinants asset specificity and complexity of product descriptions (Malone, Yates et al. 1987, p.

---

[93] Malone et al. use the term "coordination costs" rather than transaction costs (Malone, Yates et al. 1987, p. 485). However, according to their notion of coordination as tasks connected with "information processing involved in tasks such as selecting suppliers, establishing contracts, scheduling activities" (Malone, Yates et al. 1987, p. 489) the terms of coordination costs and transaction costs can be used synonymously.

489). As Figure 36 shows, items that are highly asset specific and highly complex in product description are more likely obtained through a hierarchical relationship, whereas items of low asset specificity and having simple product descriptions are more often acquired through a market relationship. Whether in the remaining two quadrants markets or hierarchies are preferred depends on the relative importance of the two factors.

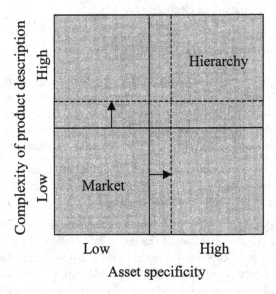

Figure 36: Product attributes affect forms of organization. Source: (Malone, Yates et al. 1987, p. 487, Figure 1)

Information technology reduces the complexity of product descriptions, and the transaction specificity of investments in inter-organizational interactions. By the use of databases, multimedia systems, and high-bandwidth electronic communication complex, multidimensional product descriptions can be handled and communicated much more readily than by traditional modes of communication. Thus the horizontal line between high and low complexity in Figure 36 is shifting upward so that due to the capabilities of information technology some product descriptions previously classified as highly complex may now be considered to be low in complexity (Malone, Yates et al. 1987, p. 489).

A similar argumentation holds for the dimension of asset specificity. Flexible manufacturing technology, for example, allows a rapid change of production lines from one product to another. Thus asset-specific components that are similar to other, rather non-specific components may begin to be produced by more companies because small numbers of these components can be manufactured without significant switching costs. Therefore, the vertical line in Figure 36 moves to the right because some asset-specific components have become less specific (Malone, Yates et al. 1987, pp. 489-490).

As well as the electronic communication effect, Malone et al. identify the electronic brokerage effect of information technology use, which means that in the evaluation phase of a supplier relationship more alternatives can be considered, the quality of selected alternatives is increased, and the cost of the entire product selection process is decreased[94]. Therefore, since search costs are decreased, organizations rely more on search, leading to the emergence of electronic markets (Malone, Yates et al. 1987, p. 488).

However, Malone et al. also identify a phenomenon they term "electronic hierarchies" (Malone, Yates et al. 1987, p. 489), which are inter-firm relationships characterized by less use of search and market competition and more use of tightly coupled operations with few long-term partners. Electronic hierarchies may possibly emerge where the use of information technology gives rise to the electronic integration effect. This effect occurs when information technology is used not just to speed communication but also to change and lead to tighter coupling of the processes that create and use the information. One benefit of this effect is the time saved and the errors avoided because data need only be entered once. Moreover, there are the benefits of close integration of processes in specific situations. In procurement, for example, systems linking the procurer's and supplier's inventory management processes, e.g. with the aim of delivering products just in time, enable the purchasing organization to eliminate inventory holding costs. The benefits of electronic integration are usually captured most easily in electronic hierarchies (Malone, Yates et al. 1987, pp. 488-489).

Malone et al. see electronic hierarchies as a preliminary stage in the development from infirm production to an electronic market. Depending on the relative strength of the electronic brokerage and the electronic integration effect and depending on whether standards for the trade of products in a particular markets are established, the organization of business relationships changes from electronic hierarchies to electronic markets.

Critics of the move to the market hypothesis argue that Malone et al. do not consider the risk connected with market relationships. In particular, investments in information technology may be specific so that an additional opportunism risk turns up (Bauer 1997, p. 206). Indeed, the move to the market hypothesis could not be confirmed by empirical results[95].

---

[94]   The correctness of this statement is shown in section 2.1.5.1.1.

[95]   Efforts to explain the choice of governance structure going beyond the simple question of "make or buy" are rare. The few studies dealing with the question of contract duration indicate more of a move to long-term relationships, but whether this can be attributed to the use of information technology is still an open question (cf.,

Subsequently Clemons et al. developed the move to the middle hypothesis in which it is explained, why the idiosyncratic character of investments in information technology and the risk connected with supplier relationships result in long-term cooperation rather than short-term contracts (Clemons, Reddi et al. 1993, p. 12).

3.3.2 The move to the middle hypothesis

According to Clemons et al. the purchasing organization is confronted with two kinds of risks in a transaction: operations risk and opportunism risk. Operations risk "is the risk that the other parties in a transaction willfully misrepresent or withhold information, or underperform [...] their agreed-upon responsibilities" (Clemons, Reddi et al. 1993, p. 15), whereas "opportunism risk includes the risks associated with a lack of bargaining power or the loss of bargaining power directly resulting from the execution of a relationship, that is, a difference between ex ante and ex post bargaining power" (Clemons, Reddi et al. 1993, p. 16). Information technology is likely to reduce both kinds of risk, thus leading to less vertical integration. However, there are three reasons why this is likely to happen with a reduced set of suppliers and rather in long-term than short-term relationships: the time to recoup investments, learning curve effects, and incentives.

In order to recoup investments in information technology that is used to support a relationship, a purchasing organization may prefer to procure from a particular supplier over an extended period of time (Clemons, Reddi et al. 1993, p. 26).

Furthermore, there are learning costs associated with the use of most information systems. Each supplier may have their own unique method of doing business incorporated into different procedures for different situations. The degree to which information technology reduces the coordination cost and facilitates monitoring depends on the duration for which those systems have been used to coordinate the activities between the purchasing organization and the supplier. Long-term contracts with the same set of suppliers enable both parties to benefit from the learning curve (Clemons, Reddi et al. 1993, p. 26).

The arguments of recouping of investments and learning curve effects still neglect the possible impact of standardization. The same information system can be used for cooperation with different suppliers. Hence the recouping of investments and learning effects are less important as systems become standardized and open.

Finally, Clemons et al. apply the argumentation in (Bakos and Brynjolfsson 1993) to the problem of determining contract duration. According to Bakos et al. it is to the benefit of purchasing organizations that their suppliers should invest in the

---

e.g., (O'Neal 1989) and (Crow and Wildemann 1988); for an overview of empirical studies in this context cf. (Bauer 1997, pp. 65-81)).

quality of the goods exchanged, information sharing, innovation, and responsiveness (Bakos and Brynjolfsson 1993, p. 42). Since these investments may not be verifiable by a third party, such as a court or an arbitrator the contracting parties cannot specify conditions based on the outcome of these investments, i.e. they are non-contractible (Bakos and Brynjolfsson 1993). By reducing the number of suppliers, the purchasing organization signals its transaction partners that it readily grants negotiation power to them, so that the supplier can expect to receive a share of the gains achieved by its investments (see also chapter 2.1.4.2). The same effect can be obtained when the contract duration is extended, because the supplier can expect that its (non-contractible) investments will be recouped over the extended period of time (Clemons, Reddi et al. 1993, pp. 26-27).

In a further publication, Clemons and Reddi refined their initial argumentation and presented a mathematical model representing the product complexity, the variability of product prices over time and among suppliers, relationship-specificity of information technology, and cost-effectiveness of information technology (Clemons and Reddi 1994). As in (Clemons, Reddi et al. 1993) it is assumed in the analysis of the model that the use of external suppliers instead of in-house production is primarily caused by transaction risk, i.e. high transaction risk leads to vertical integration. Furthermore, it is assumed that the decision between long-term and short-term relationships is determined by price risk. As price risk decreases the benefits from searching among suppliers to locate the best price decrease and thus long-term purchasing arrangements begin to replace the use of spot markets. The impact of information technology is represented by the two variables "relationship specificity of information technology" and "cost-effectiveness of information technology" (Clemons and Reddi 1994). They examine how a change of these variables influences the choice of the governance structure. As regards supplier relationships, the choice of contract duration is restricted to the two poles of selecting a new contractor for every period or, alternatively, keeping a single supplier for all periods in which the traded product is needed. The authors came to the conclusion that an increasing cost-effectiveness of information technology as well as a decreasing specificity of investments in information technology leads to a decision on long-term relationships by the purchasing organization under the conditions of low product complexity and a high degree of supplier opportunism (Clemons and Reddi 1994, pp. 861-863).

Criticizing that Clemons et al. only consider the direct effect of information technology through technical integration, in (Bauer and Stickel 1998, p. 439) the authors analyze the indirect effect of information technology, which comes about by increasing organizational, and in effect institutional, integration. A redesign of business processes triggered by the use of information technology, e.g. the realization of just in time delivery concepts, leads to organizational integration (Davenport and Short 1990, pp. 17 and 21; Bauer and Stickel 1998, pp. 440-441). According to Bauer and Stickel this development is inevitable in an economy of increasing competitive pressure. Since the cost savings reached by technical integration alone are only short-term in nature, because due to standardization technical integration can be easily imitated by competitors, organizational integration is necessary to reach long-term advantages (Bauer and Stickel 1998, p. 440). Investments in organizational integration, however, are usually greater than investments in technical integration and there are hardly any standards which support organizational integration. Hence the resulting opportunism risk is often mitigated by choosing certain institutional arrangements, particularly long-term relationships.

3.3.3 Provisional results

When considering the work so far carried out on the issue of information technology and its influence on supplier relationships, we see a number of open questions. The major aim of this work is to contribute to a settlement of these questions.

As stated in the previous section, in (Clemons, Reddi et al. 1993) a major argument for explaining the move to the middle hypothesis is the provision of incentives for suppliers to make non-contractible investments. While the original argumentation of Bakos and Brynjofsson in (Bakos and Brynjolfsson 1993) does not hold when one assumes that due to increasing standardization the switching of suppliers becomes less expensive, the adaptation of this argumentation by Clemons et al. in (Clemons, Reddi et al. 1993) seems to be plausible at first sight. Long-term contracts are incentive compatible for suppliers in cases where the procuring organization provides credible signals that it will not prematurely terminate the contract and change transaction partner, e.g. by granting contract penalties. However, the general question arises, why incentives for suppliers should only be provided by the self-restraint of the procuring organization. Assuming that suppliers are able to act proactively and that they are generally interested in a continuous business relationship, then the threat that the supplier can be quickly changed in case of opportunistic behavior is an incentive not only to behave well but also to make (non-contractible) investments which lead to cost savings for the purchasing organization. In this way, for the procuring organization the costs of changing transaction partner are increasing, primarily because it is more costly to find a supplier who provides a better performance than the current one. Hence the current supplier can be confident that in spite of a restricted contract duration its investments will be recouped through contract prolongation.

In the refined analysis of the move to the middle hypothesis in (Clemons and Reddi 1994) this problem remains. The assumption that the procuring organization has the choice of either exclusively purchasing the good from a single supplier or changing supplier in every period neglects the dynamics inherent in the process of transaction partner selection. In particular, once a supplier is found which provides excellent conditions, there is no reason to change transaction partner later on. Basically, long-term relationships can occur in two ways. One is that ex ante a decision is made to sign a long-term contract over a particular period of time. Secondly, a long-term relationship can arise ex post, e.g. by the prolongation of a short-term contract. Moreover, an ex ante long-term contract can be terminated prematurely resulting ex post in a short-term contract.

In this context the impact of information technology on transaction partner selection works in different ways. The benefit obtained by the use of information technology in the settlement phase comes about repeatedly, directly depending on the number of goods purchased, e.g. because the unit costs of exchanging the products are reduced, whereas information technology in the evaluation phase unfolds its benefit only once, until a transaction partner is found who provides conditions according to minimum requirements which depend on the search strategy and the resulting reservation values for price and/or qualitative properties of the purchased goods.

A further phenomenon connected with the dynamics of transaction partner changes over time is a change in the dispersion of the properties according to which the suppliers and/or their products are distinguished, e.g. the price dispersion. As is commonly known from microeconomic theory, if transaction costs equal zero, all suppliers will provide the same price. The greater the transaction costs, the greater the expected price dispersion. Hence, as transaction costs decrease due to progress in information technology, the observable price dispersion is reduced, either through price adaptations of the suppliers or through a concentration process. Another reaction of suppliers can be to justify differences in price by product differentiation, e.g. by the provision of complementary services.

In the following chapter 4 we introduce a decision model in which the issues mentioned above are taken into account. In this model, we differentiate information technology in terms of the transaction phase in which it is used, the costs of implementing the respective technology, and its dissemination among potential suppliers. Integration, be it technical or organizational, is represented by expenses at the beginning of a relationship and benefits in the form of cost savings during the settlement phase. Whether these investments can be transferred to alternative relationships depends on the degree to which the underlying technology and business process is standardized and if so, whether this standard is widely disseminated. By regarding progress in information technology rather than its mere use, we represent the dynamics underlying the transaction partner decision. Particularly in extensions of the model, the contract duration becomes a decision variable, so that time-dependent changes of contract duration ex ante as well as ex post can be determined.

4 Decisions about Supplier Relationships and Information Technology

In the present chapter we present a microeconomic model which helps to analyze the effect of the information technology used to support transactions on decisions about supplier selection and the design of purchasing contracts. In section 4.1 the notion of progress in information technology is systematized by means of a state preference approach. In section 4.2 a model of supplier selection decisions is introduced and discussed. This basic model helps to explain how information technology influences the selection of transaction partners and the stability of supplier relationships. In a brief excursus the basic model is applied to outsourcing decisions in order to discuss how information technology is likely to influence the vertical integration of organizations. Finally, in section 4.3 the basic model is extended to incorporate decisions on the selection of information technology into the analysis.

4.1 The progress of information technology and the state preference approach

We are interested in the *progress* of information technology, rather than simply the use of information technology. At the center of the analysis is a single organization, a single good, and the decision about from whom the good should be purchased as well as what information technology should be used to support the procurement. To be able to handle progress in information technology conceptually, it is assumed that at the starting point of the analysis the current supplier has been chosen optimally and information technology is used to support the transaction with this supplier optimally, i.e. at a previous point in time an optimal decision on the use of information technology and the design of the supplier relationship had been taken. Progress in information technology may change the conditions of the original decision, so that the alternatives to be considered are reevaluated and the decision is revised. This may result in new or different information technology to be used as well as in a new design of the supplier relationship.

To systematize the notion of progress in information technology we apply the concept of the state preference approach (Schneeweiß 1966; Ferschl 1975; Janko, Taudes et al. 1993; Laux 1995). A simple state preference model is represented by two components: a matrix containing prospective decision results and an objective function. The matrix with the decision results is represented in Figure 37.

| | $p(S_1)$ | ... | $p(S_s)$ | ... | $p(S_S)$ |
	S_1	...	S_s	...	S_S
A_1	r_{11}	...	r_{1s}	...	r_{1S}
...	...		...		...
A_a	r_{a1}	...	r_{as}	...	r_{aS}
...	...		...		...
A_A	r_{A1}	...	r_{As}	...	r_{AS}

Figure 37: Matrix of prospective decision results in a risky situation. Source: (Laux 1995, p. 32)

The header column contains the designation of the possible decisions, i.e. alternatives A_1 to A_A, while the header line comprises the possible states of the environment S_1 to S_S. The fields of the matrix contain the results r_{as} which are realized when alternative a is chosen and the state s occurs. In risky situations the right state cannot be definitely predicted. In this case the matrix is supplemented by probabilities $p(S_s)$ (with $0 \leq p(Ss) \leq 1$) for the occurrence of different states (Laux 1995, p. 32).

The objective function is intended to enable the comparison of the possible results of different alternatives. For example, if the results in the fields of the matrix are costs which depend on the state of the decision environment, then a possible objective function is to minimize the expected costs of an alternative, i.e. the chosen alternative would be the one with the lowest expected costs.

Many phenomena and developments in the area of information technology can be represented on the basis of the state preference model. Technical development finds expression in increasing computing power and growing bandwidth, i.e. an increasing amount of data that can be transmitted in a fixed amount of time.

According to Moore's law[96] the development of computing power has been considerable during the past years and is expected to continue in the near future. Besides the computing power, the bandwidth available to connect computers in a network is increasing as well. During the last 30 years the possible transmission rate of data increased from barely a kilobit per second achieved by the first modems up to about one gigabit per second, as is attainable using ATM[97] (Geihs 1995, p. 4; Knetsch 1996, p. 31). This development has been accompanied by a continuous reduction in the prices of microprocessors as well as the transmission of data. Therefore, increasing performance capacities in computers and networks in processing and transmission speeds as well as accompanying storage media can be purchased for the same money. In the same way the same amount of performance capacity can be purchased for less money. Interpreting transaction costs as the result of decisions about the use of a particular information technology, then these costs are represented by values in the fields of the matrix in Figure 37. If we assume that a major part of transaction costs consists of information processing costs, then technical development in the fields of computing power and computer networks leads to a change in the costs in the fields of the matrix.

Another important determinant of transaction costs is the diffusion of this technology among potential transaction partners, but only in cases where the relevant information technology is subject to network effects. Therefore, changing diffusion is primarily relevant when communication standards are used. As the diffusion of a communication standard among potential transaction partners grows, network effects are more likely to be exploited when using this standard. In terms of the state preference model, this means that the probability of a state in which a newly chosen transaction partner uses the same standard as the decision maker's organization is higher the more potential transaction partners are using this standard.

While the diffusion of information technology has a direct effect on the probability of states, it has an indirect effect on the results of a decision as given in

---

[96]　The performance of a computer CPU varies with the number of transistors per square inch. In 1965 Gordon Moore, co-founder of Intel, observed the increase in computing power and discovered that until 1965 the number of transistors per square inch on integrated circuits had doubled every year since the integrated circuit was invented. Moore extrapolated this trend into the future forming Moore's law. Although in subsequent years the pace slowed down, data density has still doubled approximately every 18 months. Most experts, including Moore himself, expect Moore's Law to apply for at least another two decades (Webopaedia 1999a).

[97]　ATM is the acronym for Asynchronous Transfer Mode which is a network technology based on transferring data in cells or packets of a fixed size. The small, constant cell size allows ATM equipment to transmit video, audio, and computer data over the same network, while assuring that no single type of data hogs the line (Webopaedia 1999b).

the fields of the matrix. The provision of a basic infrastructure for the transmission of information over long distances (WAN[98]), for example, incurs fixed costs which are passed by the provider to its customers over the price. As the number of customers using the infrastructure grows, the price for using the infrastructure decreases due to a degression of fixed costs. Hence the costs of running information technology which uses this infrastructure decrease as well.

As the results in the fields of the matrix change or the probabilities of the states are altered, in both cases decision alternatives are reassessed. If the ratio of decision results for alternative solutions in different states changes, this may in effect lead to the profitability of alternatives which have previously been too expensive, while solutions currently used possibly become too expensive in comparison. An example of this effect is the growing popularity of distributed computing[99]: though an old concept this approach is increasingly being used as the capacity of networks and the computing power grows.

Technical progress and the increasing diffusion of information technology is often the trigger for the development and application of new concepts or methods to solve a given problem. One example is systems based on the implementation and collaboration of software agents like Kasbah (multiagent systems are briefly discussed in section 3.2.3). Kasbah helps to solve the problem of mediating supply and demand on a market. This is done by hosting a number of different software agents on a computer, which demand a considerable amount of computing power when taken together. Moreover, the users communicate with their agents using computer networks. The communication standards which enable the communication between the users and the software agents must be sufficiently widespread so that there are enough potential users to enable the exploitation of network effects. The availability of new solutions to solve a given problem leads to a new alternative in the matrix of decision results and consequently possibly to an altered decision. In the example of Kasbah this means that the problem of finding a transaction partner is solved more efficiently, i.e. a transaction partner is found faster and with lower costs so that one may in effect decide to use Kasbah to change supplier.

To sum up the previous discussion, progress in information technology affects the decision parameters as given in the matrix basically in three ways:

1. Progress leads to a change in the results r_{as} for a given alternative and a given state. This comes about through general technical progress (e.g. in terms of computing power).

---

[98] WAN stands for Wide Area Network.

[99] The term of distributed computing describes a type of computing in which different components and objects comprising an application can be located on different computers connected to a network.

154

2. Progress is also represented by a change in the probabilities $p(S_s)$ for the occurrence of states. This usually happens when the diffusion of information technology changes.

3. Finally, another type of progress takes place when new approaches to a solution of a given problem are developed, implemented, and made available. This leads to a new alternative being added to the matrix of results.

The considerations of the next section are directed to the question of how progress in information technology in the first sense influences the decisions about transaction partner selection and contract duration. Progress in information technology in the second and third sense is addressed in section 4.3.

4.2   The basic model of supplier selection decisions

The basic model outlined and discussed in this section represents the decision between the two alternatives "maintain the existing supplier relationship for the procurement of a certain product" and "dissolve the relationship to the current supplier and change transaction partner". The model is customer driven, i.e. it focuses on the customer selecting a supplier for a given good from the set of potential transaction partners. In this decision suppliers are only evaluated with respect to their prices. It is assumed that a supplier can neither influence the customer's decision, apart from the price offered, nor refuse the conclusion of an agreement once a customer has decided to sign a contract[100]. As regards the technological dimension, we assume in the basic model that the information technology for the support of the supplier relationship is given and perfectly disseminated, i.e. the problem of selecting the proper information technology to support the transaction is taken as read[101].

Furthermore, the model is based on the following assumptions:

1. The decision maker is risk neutral and acts rationally.

2. The goods of different suppliers are distinguished only in price, and not in quality.

3. The suppliers' prices follow a known distribution with the expected value μ_p and the standard deviation σ_p.

---

[100]   In (Born 1998, p. 68) the author states that there is a change in the way market parties see themselves. "Push" approaches focusing on the supplier as a starting point for business transactions are increasingly replaced by "pull" approaches, which focus on the customers' demand as triggers for transactions. The increasing relevance of just in time concepts supports this hypothesis.

[101]   This assumption is dropped in section 4.3.

4. The quantity of goods being purchased is determined in advance, i.e. independent of the price at which the purchase takes place.

5. The marginal search costs are known and constant.

6. The discount rate equals zero.

Assumptions 1 and 3 to 5 were made by Stigler in his pioneering work on the consumer search problem (Stigler 1961). In the following years a large volume of work has been published, extending and building upon the framework erected by Stigler. In particular, the relaxation of his assumptions has been subject to a number of publications[102]. For example, in (Hey 1981, p. 63) the author generalizes the consumer search model, using utility functions to represent the benefit from search activities. Hey shows that the results achieved by the application of the basic search model apply if the utility function is monotonic, which includes linear utility functions (representing risk-neutral consumers) as well as concave utility functions (representing risk averse consumers). For the second assumption, there are a couple of works dedicated to the extension of the basic search model under the label of multiple search strategies, residual uncertainty, or multi-stage search in the case of quality dimensions of a good which are only discoverable by experience (MacQueen 1964; Wilde 1980; Hey 1981, pp. 76-78; Hey and McKenna 1981; McKenna 1987). Similarly the relaxation of the third assumption has been examined in adaptive search approaches, considering that the seeker gets to know about the parameters of the underlying distribution as the search process progresses (see e.g. (Hey 1981, pp. 80-99) or (McKenna 1987, pp. 104-107)). Finally, the fixed-quantity assumption (fourth assumption in the list above) was dropped by Hey in (Hey 1979b). He extended the search model by quantity which was modeled as a function of price. From the analysis of the resulting model he concluded that the original results from Stigler are not qualitatively affected by the extension. We refer to the fourth assumption in sub-section 4.2.5.3 where the amount of goods exchanged between customer and supplier is made endogenous to the decision.

Before we go into the detailed description of the decision model, here is a short note on the price distribution underlying the model: as formulated in assumption 3, the decision-maker is aware of the distribution of supplier prices and has complete information about the parameters of this distribution. In the literature there are only scant hints about what price distributions look like. Stigler assumed that prices would probably be skewed to the right because the seller would have some minimum but no maximum limit for the acceptable price (Stigler 1961, p. 214). The area in which the distribution of prices in a market is well investigated theoretically as well as empirically is finance. The prices of stocks and treasury bonds, for example, are often assumed to be lognormally distributed (ContingencyAnalysis 1998; Eller and Deutsch 1998, pp. 18-24). In simulation

---

[102] See also our expositions on search theory in section 2.1.5.1.1.

156

scenarios market prices are well represented using the lognormal distribution because.it is skewed to the right and bounded to the left by zero, thus neglecting negative prices. In the following we assume that supplier prices are lognormally distributed[103].

From standard textbooks (e.g. (König, Rommelfanger et al. 1999)) we know the probability density function (PDF) of a lognormally distributed variable as

$$(eq.\ 17) \quad \forall_{p>0} : f(p) = \frac{1}{\sqrt{2\pi}\sigma_L p} e^{-\frac{(\ln p - \mu_L)^2}{2\sigma_L^2}}$$

from which the cumulative distribution function (CDF) is obtained as

$$(eq.\ 18) \quad \forall_{p>0} : F(p) = \int_0^p \frac{1}{\sqrt{2\pi}\sigma_L x} e^{-\frac{(\ln x - \mu_L)^2}{2\sigma_L^2}} \, dx$$

where μ_L and σ_L describe the parameters of the function (Figure 38).

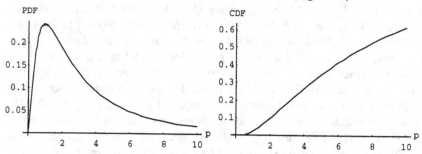

Figure 38:   PDF and CDF of a lognormally distributed random variable.

The mean and the standard deviation of the underlying random variable P are calculated using the distribution parameters by

$$(eq.\ 19) \quad \mu_p = e^{\mu_L + \frac{\sigma_L^2}{2}}$$

and

$$(eq.\ 20) \quad \sigma_p = e^{2\mu_L + \sigma_L^2} \left(e^{\sigma_L^2} - 1 \right).$$

---

[103]   Moreover, for the purpose of simplification we take prices to be continuous.

Depending on the parameters μ_p and σ_p (through μ_L and σ_L) the shape of the PDF and CDF changes, as shown in Figure 39 and Figure 40 for a set of randomly chosen distribution parameters.

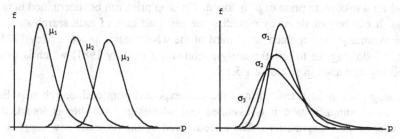

Figure 39: Plots of PDFs in dependence on the parameters μ_p (plot on the left, given σ_p and $\mu_1<\mu_2<\mu_3$) and σ_p (plot on the right, given μ_p and $\sigma_1<\sigma_2<\sigma_3$).

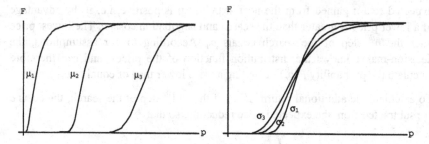

Figure 40: Plots of CDFs in dependence on the parameters μ_p (plot on the left, given σ_p and $\mu_1<\mu_2<\mu_3$) and σ_p (plot on the right, given μ_p and $\sigma_1<\sigma_2<\sigma_3$).

In our basic model the alternative "maintain the existing supplier relationship for the procurement of a certain product" is associated with the total costs C_{change}, which consist of the acquisition costs when purchasing the good from an alternative supplier, the evaluation costs of finding and evaluating potential transaction partners, and the settlement costs when executing the transaction.

4.2.1 Acquisition and evaluation costs

Search costs to find a transaction partner and negotiation costs are a major portion of the evaluation costs. It is assumed that the search takes place sequentially, i.e. suppliers are sought and evaluated one after the other. In this process, the costs of further searching are compared with the expected gain from the search in the form of the expectation of a price reduction. In our model, we represent this process by denoting the costs of evaluating one new supplier as c. The search strategy implies that - if a search is assumed to be promising - a stop price[104] p^* is calculated, which serves as a criterion for stopping the search process. That is, an offer is accepted and the search is stopped as soon as a supplier, who offers the specific good for a maximum price of p^* is found. The stop price can be determined in two ways. It can be calculated by modeling the expected gain of each search step, or by maximizing the expected net reward of the whole search process (Hey 1981). In the following we follow the analysis conducted in (Hey 1981) which is more generally discussed in section 2.1.5.1.1.

The stop price is first derived from the gain expected from each search step. For reasons of simplification it is assumed that whenever a supplier is found, the searcher initiates negotiations. The price offered by the potential new supplier is not known before the negotiations are completed. Hence the evaluation costs incurred by each search step, c, which are further referred to as marginal evaluation costs, comprise not only the costs of finding and contacting a new supplier, but also negotiation costs. A new search will be carried out if the expected return gained from the next search step is positive, i.e. if the advantage of a lower price is greater than the search and negotiation costs c. The lowest price after the nth step of the search equals p_n. According to our assumptions, the decision-maker knows the distribution function of the prices, and can therefore calculate the probability $F(p_n)$ of finding a price lower than or equal to p_n.

To calculate the additional return ΔE_{n+1} of the $n+1^{th}$ step of the search, the costs c are subtracted from the expected price reduction, so that

$$\text{(eq. 21)} \quad \Delta E_{n+1} = vol \int_0^{p_n} (p_n - q) f(q) dq - c.$$

The parameter *vol* denotes the transaction volume, i.e. the number of goods traded on the basis of the intended contract. Transforming the integral leads to

$$\text{(eq. 22)} \quad \Delta E_{n+1} = vol \left[p_n F(p_n) - \int_0^{p_n} q f(q) dq \right] - c.$$

Applying integration by parts to the second term in square brackets on the right-hand side we receive

$$\text{(eq. 23)} \quad \Delta E_{n+1} = vol \int_0^{p_n} F(q) dq - c.$$

---

[104] Synonymously this price is also called "reservation price" or "reservation value".

The search continues until the additional return per unit of the traded good of the next search step is zero. This is the case for the price p^*, which can be evaluated by solving the following indifference condition

(eq. 24) $\quad vol \int_{0}^{p^*} F(p)dp - c = 0$.

The resulting price p^* is the reservation value of supplier search. Interpreting the result graphically, we see in Figure 41 that the stop price is determined by the area under the cumulated price distribution function which equals the marginal evaluation costs divided by the transaction volume.

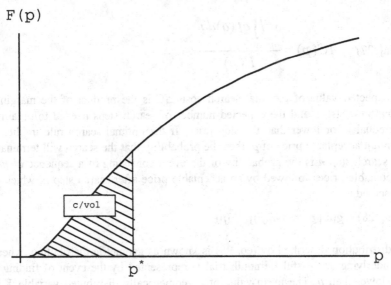

Figure 41: Graphic representation of the indifference condition.

The same result can be obtained by maximizing the expected net reward of the search process. The expected reward of the search process is maximized when the total cost of acquiring the goods, i.e. the sum of the expected price and the expected evaluation costs, is minimized. Assuming that a stop price of p underlies the search and denoting the price resulting from the search process by p_a ($p_a \in [0, p]$), then the expected price $E(p_a)$ is obtained by weighting every price of the interval between zero and p with a probability density relative to the cumulated probability of finding a price lower than or equal to p (Stigler 1961, p. 215; Telser 1973, p. 47):

$$\text{(eq. 25)} \quad E(p_a) = \int_0^p q \frac{f(q)}{F(p)} dq$$

$$\text{(eq. 26)} \quad E(p_a) = \frac{\int_0^p qf(q)dq}{F(p)}$$

The expected acquisition costs AC are then calculated multiplying the expected price resulting from the search by the transaction volume:

$$\text{(eq. 27)} \quad AC(p) = \frac{vol \int_0^p qf(q)dq}{F(p)}$$

The expected value of the total search costs SC is the product of the marginal evaluation costs, c, and the expected number of search steps needed to obtain a price equal to or lower than the stop price. If the optimal search rule implies a maximum acceptable price of p, then the probability that the search will terminate after search step n is the probability of the event consisting of a sequence of n-1 unacceptable prices followed by an acceptable price after search step n, which is represented by

$$\text{(eq. 28)} \quad g(n \mid p) = [1-F(p)]^{n-1}F(p).$$

The distribution described by (eq. 28) is known as geometric distribution, where the underlying successful Bernoulli trial is represented by the event of finding a price lower than p. The mean value of a geometrically distributed variable X is described by the quotient $1/prob$ where $prob$ denotes the probability that the underlying Bernoulli trial ends successfully (Degroot 1970, p. 36). Hence, as the number of expected search steps we obtain (Telser 1973, p. 47; Hey 1981, p. 62)

$$\text{(eq. 29)} \quad E(n \mid p) = \frac{1}{F(p)},$$

leading to expected total evaluation costs of

$$\text{(eq. 30)} \quad EC(p) = \frac{c}{F(p)}.$$

The expected net reward, R, of the search process then follows

$$\text{(eq. 31)} \quad R(p) = AC(p) + EC(p) = \frac{vol\int\limits_{0}^{p} qf(q)dq + c}{F(p)}.$$

The minimum of the function $R(p)$ is determined by solving the first-order condition $dR/dp = 0$, i.e.

$$\text{(eq. 32)} \quad \frac{dR}{dp} = \frac{\left(vol\int\limits_{0}^{p} F(q)dq - c\right)f(p)}{F(p)^2} = 0,$$

which is satisfied if the term in square brackets equals zero. But this is exactly the indifference condition as formulated in (eq. 24). The second-order condition for a cost minimum is given by

(eq. 33)

$$\frac{d^2R}{dp^2} = \frac{\left[F(p)f(p) + \left[vol\int\limits_{0}^{p} F(q)dq - c\right]f'(p)\right]F(p)^2 - 2F(p)f(p)^2\left[vol\int\limits_{0}^{p} F(q)dq - c\right]}{F(p)^4} > 0.$$

The terms in square brackets equals (eq. 24) which evaluates to zero for the stop price so that we receive

$$\text{(eq. 34)} \quad \frac{d^2R}{dp^2}(p^*) = \frac{f(p^*)}{F(p^*)},$$

which is clearly greater than zero.

Using the indifference condition (eq. 24) in (eq. 31) it can be shown that the expected net reward of search equals the reservation value multiplied by the transaction volume (e.g. (Hey 1981); for the derivation of this result cf. appendix A):

$$\text{(eq. 35)} \quad R(p^*) = \frac{vol\int\limits_{0}^{p^*} pf(p)dp + c}{F(p^*)} = vol\, p^*.$$

4.2.2 Settlement costs

The settlement costs of a business relationship consist of a fixed component, a component which depends on the transaction volume, and a time-dependent component. The fixed component is incurred when a new supplier relationship is initialized. They have to be paid at the beginning of a new supplier relationship and comprise expenses for technical or organizational changes, e.g. caused by the integration of information systems on the technical level or on the level of the business process. We denote these costs by *inc*.

The component of the settlement costs which depends on the transaction volume consists of costs incurred by activities when exchanging the traded good, e.g. transportation costs, and costs of controlling the quality of the goods delivered. These costs per unit are further referred to as *exc*.

Finally, during the settlement phase costs are incurred by monitoring the fulfillment of contract conditions and measures which may need to be taken to adapt the agreement. These adaptation costs arise constantly over the course of a business relationship and are greater the longer the relationship lasts. The duration of a business relationship is expressed by the transaction volume which is agreed upon in the supplier contract, divided by the amount of goods being delivered per time unit. Denoting this amount by *frq*, and the adaptation costs by *adc*, yields the following formulation of the settlement costs:

$$(\text{eq. 36}) \quad SC = inc + vol\left(\frac{adc}{frq} + exc\right)$$

The expected total costs of changing transaction partner are formed by the sum of the acquisition, evaluation, and settlement costs by

$$(\text{eq. 37}) \quad C_{change} = AC + EC + SC.$$

4.2.3 Costs of keeping the current transaction partner

For the most part, the costs of the alternative of keeping the current transaction partner, C_{keep}, consist of the same components as C_{change}, i.e. if the current transaction partner is kept there are still adaptation costs, costs of exchanging the product, and acquisition costs to be borne by the purchasing organization, though there are no evaluation costs or costs of initializing the business relationship. Hence we have

$$(\text{eq. 38}) \quad C_{keep} = vol\left(p_0 + exc_0 + \frac{adc_0}{frq}\right).$$

To simplify the analysis of the basic model we define a calculated price p_k by setting

(eq. 39) $\quad p_0 + exc_0 + \dfrac{adc_0}{frq} = p_k$,

so that

(eq. 40) $\quad C_{keep} = vol\, p_k$.

The procuring organization changes supplier if $C_{keep} > C_{change}$. The subsequent frame gives an overview of the basic model of supplier selection decisions which forms the basis of the following analysis.

Synopsis of the basic model of supplier selection decisions

Min (C_{keep}, C_{change}) with

$$C_{keep} = p_k\, vol$$

$$\text{with } p_k = p_0 + exc_0 + \frac{adc_0}{frq}$$

$$C_{change} = AC + EC + SC$$

$$\text{with } \quad AC = \frac{vol \displaystyle\int_0^{p^*} p f(p)\,dp}{F(p^*)}$$

$$EC = \frac{c}{F(p^*)}$$

$$SC = inc + vol\left(\frac{adc}{frq} + exc\right)$$

$$vol \int_0^{p^*} F(p)\,dp - c = 0$$

4.2.4 Properties of the basic model

The costs of the alternatives of keeping the current transaction partner and changing transaction partner depend on a number of parameters. While the costs of keeping the current transaction partner are a function of the transaction volume and the calculated price, the costs of changing transaction partner depend directly on the stop price of supplier search, the cost of initializing a new supplier relationship, the transaction volume, the adaptation costs, the frequency of exchanging goods, and the costs of exchanging the goods. Moreover, an indirect influence on C_{change} comes about through the stop price by the marginal evaluation costs, the transaction volume, and the parameters of the price distribution.

In the following sub-sections we examine the properties of the basic model by analyzing the variability of the decision about transaction partner selection when faced with a change in the underlying model parameters. In the course of this analysis we assume C_{keep} to be constant and make a marginal analysis of the parameters of C_{change}.

4.2.4.1 Marginal evaluation costs

From (eq. 35) we derive

(eq. 41) $$\frac{\partial R}{\partial p^*} = vol$$

and from (eq. 31)

(eq. 42) $$\frac{\partial R}{\partial c} = \frac{1}{F(p)}.$$

The partial derivation of the stop price to the marginal evaluation costs can then be calculated solving

(eq. 43) $$\frac{\frac{\partial R}{\partial c}}{\frac{\partial R}{\partial p^*}} = \frac{\partial p^*}{\partial c} = \frac{1}{vol\, F(p^*)}.$$

As we see, the greater the marginal evaluation costs, the greater the reservation value and hence the higher the expected acquisition and evaluation costs as they are given by (eq. 27) and (eq. 30) (Telser 1973, p. 47). A graphic representation of p^* as a function of c is shown in Figure 42.

Since

(eq. 44) $\dfrac{\partial^2 p^*}{\partial c^2} = \dfrac{-f(p^*)}{F(p^*)^2} < 0$

it is obvious that $p^*(c)$ is always concave.

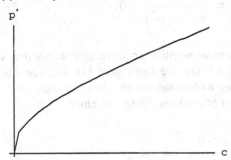

Figure 42: Reservation value as a function of the marginal evaluation costs.

4.2.4.2 *Transaction volume*

To receive the partial derivation of p^* with respect to the transaction volume at first we transform the indifference condition (eq. 24) by dividing by *vol* and setting

(eq. 45) $y = \dfrac{c}{vol}$.

The partial derivation of p^* with respect to y then follows from

(eq. 46) $\dfrac{\dfrac{\partial p^*}{\partial c}}{\dfrac{\partial y}{\partial c}} = \dfrac{\partial p^*}{\partial y} = \dfrac{1}{F(p^*)}$

which can be multiplied by

(eq. 47) $\dfrac{\partial y}{\partial vol} = \dfrac{-c}{vol^2}$

to receive the partial derivation of p^* with respect to *vol*, i.e.

166

(eq. 48) $\dfrac{\partial p^*}{\partial y}\dfrac{\partial y}{\partial vol} = \dfrac{\partial p^*}{\partial vol}$

which evaluates to

(eq. 49) $\dfrac{\partial p^*}{\partial vol} = \dfrac{-c}{vol^2 F(p^*)} < 0$.

Since (eq. 49) is always negative an increasing transaction volume leads to a decreasing reservation value (see also Figure 43). This result reflects the fact that through an increasing transaction volume the evaluation costs can be distributed over a greater number of products. Moreover, since

(eq. 50) $\dfrac{\partial^2 p^*}{\partial vol^2} > 0$

the underlying function is convex, i.e. the influence of a changing transaction volume decreases with an increasing transaction volume.

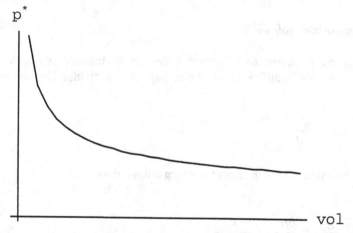

Figure 43: Reservation value as a function of the transaction volume.

4.2.4.3 *Riskiness of the price distribution*

There are different ways of measuring risk. In (Rothschild and Stiglitz 1970) for example, the authors discuss four different approaches. One of these approaches had been applied by Hey to analyze the impact of changing riskiness of a random variable on a searcher's reservation value (Hey 1981, pp. 61-62).

According to Rothschild and Stiglitz a distribution is more risky than another distribution if it has more weight in the tails. Given two CDF's G and F which are defined over the closed interval $[0,1]$, then G has more weight in the tails than F if

(eq. 51) $\quad \int_0^1 [G(x) - F(x)]dx = 0$,

which expresses that both distributions have the same mean, and

(eq. 52) $\quad \forall_{y \in [0,1]} : \int_0^y [G(x) - F(x)]dx \geq 0$,

i.e. the integral between zero and any point in the interval $[0,1]$ of G is always equal or greater than the integral of the function F over the same interval (Hey 1981, pp. 28-29). Hey shows that under these conditions an increased riskiness of the underlying distribution leads to an increasing (decreasing) reservation value when the searcher prefers values as large (small) as possible (Hey 1981, pp. 61-62). However, as is pointed out in (Rothschild and Stiglitz 1970), this result applies to CDF's whose points of increase lie in a bounded interval. This not the case for the lognormal distribution which is open to the right.

In this work we assume that risk is measured by the standard deviation of supplier prices, i.e. for a given mean increasing standard deviation leads to increased risk as measured by Rothschild and Stiglitz. Subsequently we show that (eq. 52) and the conclusions drawn by Hey apply for lognormally distributed prices when risk is measured by the standard deviation of supplier prices and when the interval of prices is open to the right.

Assume there are two lognormal distributions $F(p)$ and $G(p)$, both having the same mean value μ_p but different standard deviations $\sigma_G > \sigma_F$, i.e. G is riskier than F. The two distribution functions intersect in point I which is determined by $p = \mu_p$, where $F(p) < G(p)$ for all $p < \mu_p$ and $F(p) > G(p)$ for all $p > \mu_p$ (see Figure 44).

168

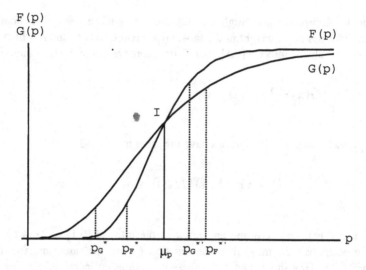

Figure 44: CDFs with different standard deviations of supplier prices and the determination of the reservation value.

As we learnt from (eq. 24) and Figure 41 the stop price is determined by the area which is bordered by the distribution function and the abscissa to the left and whose size exactly equals the marginal evaluation costs divided by the transaction volume $\dfrac{c}{vol}$.

If the marginal evaluation costs are chosen such that the resulting reservation value is lower than μ_p then due to the fact that $\int\limits_0^p F(q)dq < \int\limits_0^p G(q)dq$ for all $p<\mu_p$ (eq. 52) is fulfilled and for the resulting stop prices the relation $p_F^* > p_G^*$ applies. If the marginal evaluation costs lead to a reservation price greater than μ_p, then the difference from (eq. 52) decreases, in other words, the difference between the reservation values of the two CDFs decreases (see $p_F^{*'}$ and $p_G^{*'}$ in Figure 44). However, it can be shown that

$$(eq.\ 53) \quad \lim_{p\to\infty}\left(\int\limits_{\mu_p}^p [F(q)-G(q)]dq\right) = \int\limits_0^{\mu_p} [G(q)-F(q)]dq$$

which means that over the domain of $p=[0,\infty]$ (eq. 52) applies so that a change in the standard deviation of supplier prices leads to a reciprocal change in the reservation value, i.e.

(eq. 54) $\dfrac{\partial p^*}{\partial \sigma_p} < 0$.

Hence, an increasing price riskiness measured by the standard deviation of lognormally distributed supplier prices leads to a decreasing reservation value.

4.2.4.4 Mean value of the price distribution

We distinguish between two kinds of changing the mean value if the prices follow a lognormal distribution:

- The distribution function (including the domain) is moved to the left or to the right (Figure 45); or

- For a given standard deviation and domain the mean of the distribution is changed (cf. the plot on the left in Figure 39 and Figure 40 respectively).

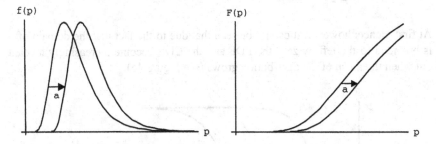

Figure 45:   Moving the PDF and CDF of the lognormally distributed variable p to the right.

While in the first case the shape of the function remains unchanged, the second case leads to a different shape for the function.

To analyze a rightward shift of the distribution we can use a technique described in (Hey 1981, pp. 38-40 and 61). If we initiate a rightward shift of the CDF $F(p)$ in (eq. 24) then we get

(eq. 55) $vol \displaystyle\int_0^{p^*} F(p-a)dp - c = 0$.

Using the standard technique of variable change we receive

170

(eq. 56) $\quad vol \int\limits_{-a}^{p^*-a} F(p)dp - c = 0$

from which it is obvious that

(eq. 57) $\quad \dfrac{\partial p^*}{\partial a} = 1,$

i.e. an increase of a by a certain amount requires an increase of p^* by the same amount.

The analysis is more complex if we change the mean of the distribution, μ_p, leaving the domain of the variable p unchanged. It is obvious that the reservation price increases with μ_p, i.e.

(eq. 58) $\quad \dfrac{\partial p^*}{\partial \mu_p} > 0.$

At first glance, however, it cannot be seen that due to the fact that the domain of p is bounded to the left by zero the PDF and the CDF become increasingly leveled out when the mean of the distribution grows (see Figure 46).

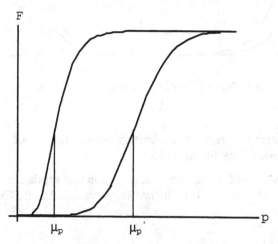

Figure 46:   CDFs when changing the mean price from μ_p to μ_p', holding the standard deviation constant.

In section 4.2.4.3 we stated that an increasing dispersion of a distribution function leads to a decreasing reservation price, i.e. the seeker becomes choosier. This effect is revealed by an increasing distance between the mean price and the reservation value, or, in formal terms, by a partial derivative of p^* with respect to μ_p less than one. As μ_p grows further, however, the distribution becomes less skewed, and the effect of changing mean is approximated to the case of a symmetric distribution, which leads to

$$(\text{eq. 59}) \quad \lim_{\mu_p \to \infty} \left(\frac{\partial p^*}{\partial \mu_p} \right) = 1 .$$

The plot of the stop price as a function of the mean of supplier prices is represented in Figure 47. The dotted line represents the bisector of the first quadrant of the system of coordinates spanned by p^* and μ_p.

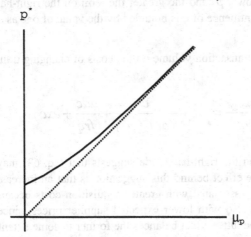

Figure 47:   Reservation value as a function of the mean price.

Therefore, if changing the mean of the distribution function while keeping the domain of the prices unchanged the value of the partial derivation of p^* with respect to μ_p is between zero and one:

$$(\text{eq. 60}) \quad 0 < \frac{\partial p^*}{\partial \mu_p} \leq 1$$

In sections 4.2.4.1 to 4.2.4.4 we have so far discussed the effect of marginal evaluation costs, transaction volume, and distribution parameters on the reservation value. Through the stop price these variables influence the costs connected with the alternative of changing transaction partner, C_{change}. The effect of p^* on C_{change} is given by (eq. 61) $\dfrac{\partial C_{change}}{\partial p^*} = vol\,.$

By means of (eq. 61) the influence of the parameters discussed above on the costs of changing transaction partner can be derived. The partial derivative of these costs with respect to the marginal evaluation costs yields

(eq. 62) $\dfrac{\partial C_{change}}{\partial c} = \dfrac{\partial p^*}{\partial c}\dfrac{\partial C_{change}}{\partial p^*} = \dfrac{1}{F(p^*)}\,.$

The lower c, the lower p^* and the greater the term on the right-hand side of (eq. 62). The minimal influence of c is bounded by the value of one as c becomes very large.

The impact of the transaction volume on the costs of changing transaction partner is given by

(eq. 63) $\dfrac{\partial C_{change}}{\partial vol} = p^* - \dfrac{c}{vol\,F(p^*)} + \dfrac{adc}{frq} + exc\,.$

The second term on the right-hand side suggests that (eq. 63) may evaluate to a negative value. The effect behind this suggestion is that an increasing transaction volume is not only associated with greater acquisition costs because more goods are purchased, but also with lower expected supplier prices, since the seeker is choosier. Hence, the latter effect balances the former to some extent. Nevertheless it can be shown that (eq. 63) is always positive[105], i.e. the gains from more intensified search do not outweigh the increasing expenses caused by more goods being purchased.

Finally, the costs of changing transaction partner through the determination of the reservation value depend on the mean and standard deviation of supplier prices. Changing the price dispersion yields a negative effect on the costs of changing supplier as given by

(eq. 64) $vol\,\dfrac{\partial C_{change}}{\partial \sigma_p} < 0\,.$

Moving the distribution induces a change in C_{change} by a fixed amount according to

---

[105] The proof of this statement is given in appendix B.

$$\text{(eq. 65)} \quad \frac{\partial C_{change}}{\partial a} = vol,$$

whereas changing the mean price results in a degressive growth of C_{change}, which is not greater than the transaction volume:

$$\text{(eq. 66)} \quad 0 < vol \frac{\partial C_{change}}{\partial \mu_p} \leq vol$$

4.2.4.5   Initialization costs

The costs of initializing a supplier relationship simply change the costs of changing transaction partner linearly and with a rate of one, hence the following equation applies:

$$\text{(eq. 67)} \quad \frac{\partial C_{change}}{\partial inc} = 1$$

4.2.4.6   Adaptation costs

A change in the adaptation costs changes the value of the alternative of changing transaction partner by the multiple of the transaction volume divided by the frequency, i.e.

$$\text{(eq. 68)} \quad \frac{\partial C_{change}}{\partial adc} = \frac{vol}{frq}.$$

4.2.4.7   Frequency of a transaction

If the frequency of a transaction, i.e. the amount of goods being exchanged per time unit, increases then the costs of changing transaction partner decrease. However, according to (eq. 69) this influence decreases as the frequency increases:

$$\text{(eq. 69)} \quad \frac{\partial C_{change}}{\partial frq} = \frac{- vol\ adc}{frq^2}$$

4.2.4.8   Costs of exchanging the goods

Finally, a change in the costs of exchanging the goods changes the value of the alternative of changing transaction partner by the multiple of the transaction volume, i.e.

(eq. 70) $\dfrac{\partial C_{change}}{\partial exc} = vol$.

4.2.5   Decisions in the basic model

The basic model of transaction partner selection can be used to examine a number of different decisions with respect to supplier relationships. Firstly, the decision on transaction partner selection can be examined by analyzing how parameter changes lead to a change of suppliers. This happens in section 4.2.5.1. Secondly, by interpreting the costs of keeping the current transaction partner as the costs of in-house production, the model can be used to represent outsourcing decisions. The model then contributes to the analysis of the impact of parameter changes on the vertical integration of organizations, which is discussed in section 4.2.5.2. However, the analysis conducted in sections 4.2.5.1 and 4.2.5.2 is rather static since the transaction volume is assumed to be given and fixed. In section 4.2.5.3 this assumption is dropped while examining how many products should be purchased on the basis of a single contract. Hence, thirdly, we have the compound decision about transaction partner selection and the optimal contract duration.

4.2.5.1   Transaction partner selection

Subsequently, the basic model of transaction partner selection is discussed by

- mapping the model parameters to the transaction determinants as they were introduced in section 2.2.1 in a first step, and then

- examining the sensitivity of the transaction partner decision towards changes of the transaction determinants.

In this way we can verify whether the results obtained by applying the basic model comply with the findings of transaction cost theory.

Figure 48 is an example of the plot of the cost curves C_{change} and C_{keep} in dependency of the marginal evaluation costs. The point of intersection between these curves indicates the marginal evaluation costs c^* at which the decision maker is indifferent towards the alternatives of changing or keeping transaction partner. Generally, the decision-maker will be indifferent if, for the given assumptions, both alternatives have the same expected costs, i.e. when (eq. 71) $C_{keep} = C_{change}$.

Solving (eq. 71) for p_k leads to

(eq. 72) $p_k^* = \dfrac{AC + EC + SC}{vol}$,

which can be interpreted as the indifference curve containing all parameter combinations that lead to indifference towards the alternatives of keeping or changing transaction partner. The formulation of the indifference curve is later used for further analyses.

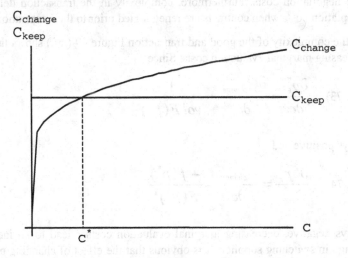

Figure 48:   Cost curves and point of indifference.

4.2.5.1.1   *Complexity of goods and transactions*

Increasing performance capacities of computers and networks create the possibility that in a given period of time an increasing amount of information can be transmitted and processed. This has a direct impact on the capability of handling complexity regarding the transaction and the product traded (for the notion of complexity see section 2.2.1.3). As a result of the increase in the performance capacities of computers, complex product descriptions can be handled with more ease by enabling multimedia descriptions of goods using e.g. (animated) pictures and sound. Moreover, the increasing performance capacity of networks facilitates or even enables the electronic transmission of these descriptions from offering suppliers to inquiring potential buyers of these products. Thus the cost of exchanging the description of a particular product between the potential transaction partners in the evaluation phase of a business relationship is reduced. In terms of the basic model of transaction partner selection this effect can be represented by decreasing marginal evaluation costs c.

The second notion of complexity refers to the contract determining the terms of the transaction. A transaction is more complex the larger the number of possible states that must be considered in the underlying (complete) contract. Information technology can be used in order to support the negotiation process in the evaluation phase of a business relationship (see also section 3.2.5.2). For example, conferencing systems and electronic mail facilities can reduce the costs of exchanging information about proposed contract conditions, thus making negotiations cheaper. In terms of the basic model of transaction partner selection this effect can be represented by decreasing marginal evaluation costs c which also include negotiation costs. Furthermore, complexity in the transaction determines the adaptation costs when contracts are renegotiated prior to their expiration.

Given the complexity of the good and transaction Figure 49 (left) shows the effect of decreasing marginal evaluation costs. Since

$$(eq.\ 73) \quad \frac{\partial p_k^*}{\partial c} = \frac{\partial C_{change}}{\partial c} = \frac{1}{vol\, F(p^*)}$$

is always positive and

$$(eq.\ 74) \quad \frac{\partial^2 p_k^*}{\partial c^2} = \frac{C_{change}}{\partial c} = \frac{-f(p^*)}{F(p^*)^2}$$

is always negative, decreasing marginal evaluation costs c lead to an increasing advantage in switching supplier. It is obvious that the effect of changing marginal evaluation costs is not only dependent on the transaction volume but also, through p^*, on the current value of the marginal evaluation costs and the parameters of the price distribution:

- A high transaction volume and high marginal evaluation costs make the indifference price less sensitive to a change in the marginal evaluation costs.

- A high expected value of supplier prices means that for any price more efforts must be undertaken to undercut this price. Hence p^* becomes greater and the indifference price is less sensitive to a change in the marginal evaluation costs

- A high price dispersion leads to an indifference price which is more sensitive to a change in the marginal evaluation costs.

While a decline of marginal evaluation costs for a given complexity causes a change in the indifference price p_k^* along the indifference curve to the left, a decreasing complexity of the traded good or the transaction leads to a decreasing gradient of the curve (see Figure 49 on the left).

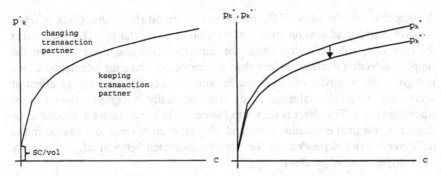

Figure 49: Indifference price as a function of the marginal evaluation costs (left) and in dependence on the complexity of the good/transaction (right).

We have a similar effect with the adaptation costs. Declining adaptation costs lead to a decreasing indifference price and hence to an increasing advantage derived from switching supplier. However, from (eq. 68) we receive

$$(\text{eq. 75}) \quad \frac{\partial p_k^*}{\partial adc} = \frac{1}{frq}$$

from which it is obvious that the ratio of adaptation costs and indifference price is constant and depends on the frequency of the transaction (see the plot on the left in Figure 50). A high (low) transaction frequency makes the indifference price less (more) sensitive to a change in the adaptation costs. This result is plausible, since a high transaction frequency causes the adaptation costs to be distributed over a greater number of goods, so that a change in adaptation costs produces only a small change in the indifference price.

In comparison with the case of decreasing complexity of the traded good, a decreasing transaction complexity causes a downward move of the indifference curve along the axis of ordinates while the gradient of the curve is unchanged (see the plot on the right in Figure 50).

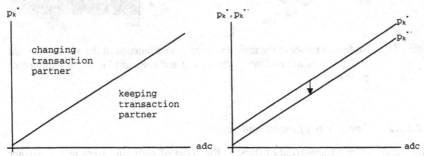

Figure 50: Indifference price as a function of the adaptation costs (left) and in dependence on the complexity of the good/transaction (right).

A comparison of the plots of Figure 49 and Figure 50 shows that while $p_k^*(c)$ is concave, varying adaptation costs lead to a linear change in p_k^*. This means that for high marginal evaluation costs, the impact of changing these costs on the supplier selection decision is less than the impact of changing adaptation costs. But given the concavity of $p_k^*(c)$ and linearity of $p_k^*(adc)$, the leverage effect of decreasing marginal evaluation costs will eventually be greater than that of adaptation costs. The effect is shown in Figure 51. In formal terms, a simultaneous change in marginal evaluation costs and adaptation costs leads to a change in the indifference price dependent on the rate of substitution between adaptation costs and marginal evaluation costs.

$$(\text{eq. 76}) \qquad \frac{\dfrac{\partial p_k^*}{\partial c}}{\dfrac{\partial p_k^*}{\partial adc}} = -\frac{frq}{vol\, F(p^*)}$$

The term on the left hand side of (eq. 76) describes the gradient of the indifference curve displayed in the contour diagram of Figure 51 showing the projection of indifference curves for p_k^* in the coordinate system bounded by c and adc. The steeper the indifference curve, the greater the effect of changing marginal evaluation costs in relation to changing adaptation costs.

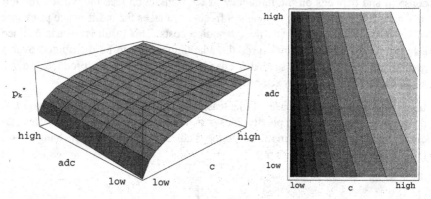

Figure 51:   Surface graphics of the indifference price as a function of the adaptation costs and the marginal evaluation costs (left) and contour plot of the indifference price (right).

4.2.5.1.2   Specificity of assets and goods

The notion of asset specificity refers to the costs of changing transaction partner due to the fact that

- the good traded is highly specific, i.e. alternative transaction partners are difficult to find, so that high marginal evaluation costs are incurred when changing transaction partner, or

- high relationship specific investments have been made to support the transaction, so that high initialization costs are incurred when changing transaction partner.

From the buyer's point of view the specificity of a traded good varies with the number of potential suppliers offering this product. The fewer potential suppliers there are, the more specific the traded good is, and the harder it is to find a transaction partner. Given a good with a particular specificity, then decreasing marginal evaluation costs can make a change of supplier profitable in cases in which it was formerly beneficial to maintain a stable relationship. For example, if there are only a few potential transaction partners who provide a non-standard good it will probably be difficult to trace one of these suppliers. As soon as marginal evaluation costs drop, more search steps can be made and there is a higher probability of finding a potential supplier who was formerly hard to find out. The resulting change in the indifference price p_k^* follows the plot of the curve in Figure 49 (left). Furthermore, in analogy to the impact of a changing complexity a decreasing specificity of the traded good can be represented by a declining gradient of the indifference curve (see Figure 49 on the right).

The specificity of investments in assets supporting a relationship varies with the possibility of using these assets in a relationship with alternative transaction partners. When considering investments in information technology to support a business relationship, human asset specificity and physical asset specificity are of particular interest. Investments in information technology are subject to physical asset specificity when transaction partner change leads to a loss of investments, i.e. if the underlying information technology can only be used with the current supplier. The increasing diffusion of a particular information technology among potential transaction partners makes it more likely that an investment in this technology will not be lost when the transaction partner is changed, so that the expected initialization costs decrease. This effect is treated in section 0 where the decision about information technology selection is discussed.

A similar argumentation applies in the case of investments in human specific assets. For example, when employees acquire specific knowledge about a certain transaction partner, cost reductions due to progress in information technology lead to declining costs of gaining the same level of knowledge about a new transaction partner. Decreasing initialization costs result in an increasing advantage of switching transaction partner. The resulting indifference curve has the same shape as Figure 50, though the gradient of the curve is different, namely

(eq. 77) $$\frac{\partial p_k^*}{\partial inc} = \frac{1}{vol}.$$

180

A decreasing specificity of the assets used to support a relationship leads to a downward move of the indifference curve along the axis of ordinates.

Comparing the indifference curves for c and *inc* respectively we realize that the leverage effect of progress in information technology on transaction partner selection is different for the two interpretations of specificity. The impact of marginal evaluation costs is relatively low for high marginal evaluation costs, but increases as these costs continuously decrease, whereas in the case of specificity of assets supporting the transaction the influence of progress in information technology is constant.

4.2.5.1.3 *Transaction volume and the frequency of a transaction*

As pointed out in section 2.2.1.4 there are different notions of frequency concerning transactions. We distinguish between the number of goods exchanged on basis of a single contract, referring to this notion using the parameter *vol*, and the number of goods purchased per time unit, which is represented by the parameter *frq*.

Figure 52 shows that a decrease in *vol* leads to an increase in p_k^*, thus reducing the likelihood that transaction partner change will be profitable. The dependency can be derived from (eq. 72) resulting in

$$(eq.\ 78) \qquad \frac{\partial p_k^*}{\partial vol} = -\frac{1}{vol^2}\left(\frac{c}{F(p^*)} + inc\right)$$

which is negative for all values of *vol* greater than zero. This result is plausible because the transaction costs per unit of goods exchanged increase progressively when the transaction volume decreases.

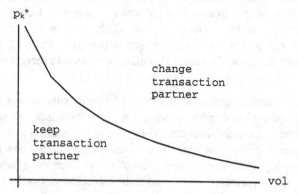

Figure 52:   Indifference price as a function of the transaction volume.

As concerns the frequency of a transaction the dependency between p_k^* and frq is qualitatively the same as between p_k^* and vol, i.e. a decrease in frq leads to an increase in p_k^*. Therefore, the resulting plot is similar to Figure 52. However, the formal representation of this dependency is different:

$$(\text{eq. 79}) \qquad \frac{\partial p_k^*}{\partial frq} = -\frac{adc}{frq^2}$$

While the dependency between p_k^* and vol is determined by the initialization costs of a business relationship and the marginal evaluation costs as well as the parameters of the price distribution, the relation between p_k^* and frq is a function of the adaptation costs. In other words, if there were no costs involved in changing transaction partners, the transaction volume would be an irrelevant parameter. Similarly, if there were no adaptation costs, i.e. if one could succeed in making complete contracts, then the transaction frequency would have no influence on transaction partner selection.

A particular question connected with the transaction volume of a business relationship is how a reduction of the transaction volume affects the decision if it is assumed that the marginal evaluation costs or the initialization costs are decreasing. The practical relevance of this question results from the tendency towards shortening product life-cycles (Christopher 1992, p. 21). According to Christopher, changes in technology and consumer demands make markets more volatile, so that a product can be obsolete almost as soon as it reaches the market. This effect is particularly observable in the markets for computer hardware and automobiles.

If the life-cycle of the final product of a particular manufacturer shortens and if the input goods going into this product are specific to this final product, then the duration of supplier contracts signed to purchase theses input goods decreases as well. As previously shown a decreasing transaction volume makes the decision-maker better off when keeping the current transaction partner, while decreasing marginal evaluation or initialization costs may compensate for this effect. The net effect of decreasing transaction volume, marginal evaluation costs, and initialization costs is the subject of the following analysis.

A simultaneous variation of c and vol yields Figure 53:

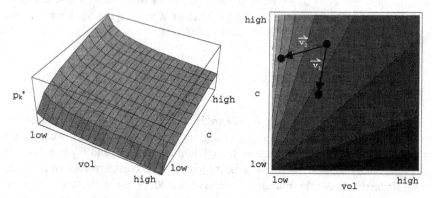

Figure 53:   Surface graphics of the indifference price as a function of the marginal evaluation costs and the transaction volume (left) and contour plot of the indifference price (right).

The trade-off between the marginal evaluation costs and the transaction volume is illustrated by projecting the indifference curves $p_k{}^*$ in the coordinate system bounded by c and vol, which leads to the contour plot in Figure 53. A simultaneous change in c and vol can be represented by a vector in the contour plot in Figure 53, where the length of the vector indicates the ratio of change between the two variables. If both variables are decreasing, then this may lead to a decreasing ($\vec{v}_1$), increasing ($\vec{v}_2$), or even unchanged indifference price. Indeed, the net impact on supplier selection decisions depends on the respective amounts of c and vol actually borne, the initialization costs, and the parameters of the price distribution. The dependence is described by the marginal rate of substitution between vol and c (for the proof of (eq. 80) cf. appendix C)

$$\text{(eq. 80)} \quad \dfrac{-\dfrac{\partial p_k^*}{\partial vol}}{\dfrac{\partial p_k^*}{\partial c}} = \dfrac{F(p^*)}{vol}\left(\dfrac{c}{F(p^*)} + inc\right) = \dfrac{dc}{dvol}$$

which is interpreted as follows: if the ratio of empirically observable changes in c and vol equals the marginal rate of substitution, then there will be no impact on the supplier selection decision. If this ratio is smaller than the rate of substitution, i.e.

$$\text{(eq. 81)} \quad \dfrac{dc}{dvol} < \dfrac{-\dfrac{\partial p_k}{\partial vol}}{\dfrac{\partial p_k}{\partial c}},$$

then the net effect in terms of the indifference price manifests itself in decreasing p_k^* and changing transaction partner becomes more profitable. Consequently,

(eq. 82) $\qquad \dfrac{dc}{dvol} > \dfrac{-\dfrac{\partial p_k}{\partial vol}}{\dfrac{\partial p_k}{\partial c}}$

makes the decision-maker better off when keeping the transaction partner[106].

A simultaneous change in the transaction volume and the costs of initializing a business relationship yields Figure 54. The analysis follows the same line as in the case of c and vol, i.e. the marginal rate of substitution between vol and inc, yielding

(eq. 83) $\qquad \dfrac{-\dfrac{\partial p_k^*}{\partial vol}}{\dfrac{\partial p_k^*}{\partial inc}} = \dfrac{1}{vol}\left(\dfrac{1}{F(p^*)} + inc\right),$

determines the net effect of simultaneously changing these two variables. The interpretation with respect to p_k^* occurs by analogy with (eq. 81) and (eq. 82).

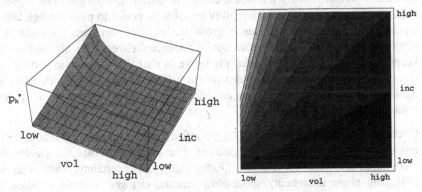

Figure 54: Surface graphics of the indifference price as a function of the initialization costs and the transaction volume (left) and contour plot of the indifference price (right).

---

[106] The proof of (eq. 81) and (eq. 82) follows the same line as for (eq. 80) (see appendix B).

4.2.5.1.4   Uncertainty of behavior and environmental changes

Finally we discuss, how uncertainty is represented within the scope of the basic model and how a change in uncertainty is likely to change the result of decisions on suppliers. As pointed out in section 2.2.1.2 uncertainty can be interpreted for the behavior of transaction partners and the changes of environmental parameters of the supplier selection decision. The former can be represented by marginal evaluation costs, i.e. uncertainty about the reliability of an unknown potential supplier requires exceptional efforts during the evaluation phase. This leads to similar results as received by discussing the complexity of the good and the transaction (cf. 4.2.5.1.1). For (eq. 73) major results are that the greater the uncertainty with respect to the behavior of the transaction partner, the greater the marginal evaluation costs. Progress in information technology leading to decreasing marginal evaluation costs makes the decision-maker better off when changing transaction partner, because the indifference price of transaction partner change decreases. Moreover, the marginal rate of changing indifference price is greater the lower the transaction volume.

While by the use of information technology the risk of opportunistic behavior can be more easily responded to by activities during the evaluation phase, there is another, more indirect effect of information technology. As pointed out in section 2.2.1 opportunistic behavior becomes apparent in the renegotiation of a contract. As soon as it is costly to change supplier, the procuring organization is vulnerable because it cannot reliably threaten a change of transaction partner. The supplier may take advantage of this vulnerability by using its power to push through better contract conditions. The maximum profit the supplier can gain following this strategy depends directly on the cost difference between the alternatives of keeping transaction partner and the alternative of changing transaction partner. As this cost difference diminishes, incentives to behave opportunistically decrease as well, because the procuring organization can credibly threaten to change transaction partner.

Uncertainty about environmental changes influences the number of possible states considered when a contract is negotiated. The evaluation costs are greater the more states are taken into account, i.e. the higher the uncertainty, whereas in the settlement phase uncertainty about environmental changes becomes manifest in the adaptation costs. The greater the uncertainty, the more often renegotiations are necessary and the greater the total adaptation costs over the course of the transaction.

Finally, a short note on the costs of exchanging the good in the settlement phase. In the previous analysis of transaction determinants these costs were negligible. Nevertheless, a change in these costs influences the decision about suppliers. Strictly speaking, a change in *exc* leads to a change in the indifference price to the same extent:

(eq. 84) $\quad \dfrac{\partial p_k^*}{\partial exc} = 1$

This means that progress in information technology which lowers the costs of exchanging the goods ceteris paribus makes the alternative of changing transaction partner increasingly profitable.

The following Table 4 gives an overview of the results of how transaction determinants are represented in the model and how parameter changes are likely to influence decisions on transaction partners.

Table 4: Transaction determinants, respective model parameters, and analysis results.

	Transaction determinant	Influenced parameter	Interpretation	Impact of progress in information technology
Complexity	of the good	c	The more complex the traded good the greater c is.	$c\downarrow \Rightarrow$ The relative importance of complexity as a parameter of C_{change} is increasingly reduced.
Complexity	of the transaction	c, adc	The more complex a transaction the greater c and/or adc are.	$c\downarrow \Rightarrow$ The relative importance of complexity as a parameter of C_{change} is increasingly reduced. $adc\downarrow \Rightarrow$ The relative importance of complexity as a parameter of C_{change} is constantly reduced.
Specificity	of the good	c	The more specific the traded good the greater c is.	$c\downarrow \Rightarrow$ The relative importance of specificity as a parameter of C_{change} is increasingly reduced.
Specificity	of the assets used to support the transaction	inc	The more specific the assets used to support a transaction the greater inc is.	$inc\downarrow \Rightarrow$ The relative importance of specificity as a parameter of C_{change} is constantly reduced.

Table 4: Continued.

	Transaction determinant	Influenced parameter	Interpretation	Impact of progress in information technology
Frequency	number of goods purchased per contract	vol	The more goods are purchased per contract the greater vol is.	undetermined
	number of goods purchased per time unit	frq	The more goods are purchased per time unit the greater frq is.	undetermined
Uncertainty	of the behavior of transaction partners	c	The greater the uncertainty of the behavior of transaction partners, the greater c is.	$c\downarrow =>$ The relative importance of uncertainty as a parameter of C_{change} is increasingly reduced.
	of environmental changes	c, adc	The greater the uncertainty of environmental changes, the greater c and adc are.	$c\downarrow =>$ The relative importance of uncertainty as a parameter of C_{change} is increasingly reduced. $adc\downarrow =>$ The relative importance of complexity as a parameter of C_{change} is constantly reduced.

4.2.5.2   Outsourcing

Using the alternative of keeping the current transaction partner to describe the in-house production of goods, the basic model of supplier selection decisions can be applied to outsourcing decisions. Basically, the results are the same as those derived in section 4.2.5.1 for the general case of transaction partner selection, apart from the different wording, i.e. saying "in-house production" and "outsourcing" instead of "keeping" and "changing transaction partner". In particular, the results of Table 4 keep relevant.

In contrast to the general case of transaction partner selection, in the outsourcing decision the alternative of in-house production is connected with different cost parameters. C_{keep} now consists of internal production and coordination costs, e.g. material costs, costs of production planning and scheduling, but also costs of hiring and monitoring employees. The aggregated parameter p_k is then interpreted as the internal transfer price for the goods being produced. This price multiplied by the amount vol that is put in the production process during the considered period results in the costs of in-house production. Since we focus on the sensitivity analysis of decision results rather than on the detailed interpretation of cost parameters, p_k is simply taken as a black box.

Progress in information technology not only affects the transaction costs of the outsourcing alternative, but also the costs of in-house production insofar as they are attributed to information processing. The aim of this section is to analyze how the outsourcing decision is affected when the costs of in-house production are changed to a lesser, the same, or a greater extent than the costs of the outsourcing alternative. In this way the ceteris paribus assumption of the previous chapter is dropped, according to which the parameters of the keep alternative were supposed to be constant. In the excursus on this topic two scenarios are distinguished:

1. The costs of the outsourcing alternative change in a degressive manner, as is the case when progress in information technology affects the marginal evaluation costs.

2. The costs of the outsourcing alternative are changing linearly, as is the case when the initialization or adaptation costs are subject to progress in information technology.

Scenario 1 is illustrated in Figure 55 which shows the possible plots of C_{keep} (straight lines) and C_{change} (degressive curve, as a function of c). The point of intersection b of the straight line l and the axis of ordinates represents the portion of costs which cannot be further reduced by the use of information technology, even if information-processing costs converge to zero[107]. The slope of l represents the sensitivity of C_{keep} to cost reductions induced by information technology. The case when both, c and p_k, are equally sensitive to progress in information technology is represented by a gradient of one. The simple case in which progress has no effect on p_k is represented by a horizontal line (see dotted line l in Figure 55). As is obvious from Figure 55, as soon as C_{keep} is greater than the settlement costs, there is precisely one point of intersection S between C_{keep} and C_{change}. That means that an internal transfer price p_k exists, at which outsourcing becomes profitable.

As soon as the assumption that internal production costs are not influenced by progress in information technology is dropped, the horizontal line in the simple case has a positive gradient. Depending on the number of intersections between C_{change} and C_{keep} different cases are distinguished.

---

[107] This intersection is determined by calculating $\lim_{c \to 0} C_{change}$ which equals the settlement costs.

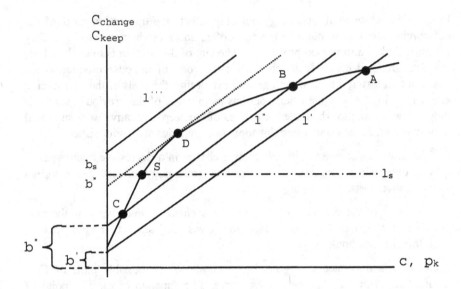

Figure 55:   Paths of development of C_{change} and C_{keep} in scenario 1.

In the first case, which is characterized by

(eq. 85) $b \leq SC$,

there is one point of intersection A between l' and C_{change}. Outsourcing is profitable for all combinations of c and p_k to the right of point A. Technological progress leading to cost reductions on both sides induces a move to the left along the curve formed by the minimum of C_{change} and C_{keep}. Internal production of the good is advantageous for all combinations of c and p_k to the left of A on l'. A rise in b (e.g. from b' to b'') shifts l' upwards to l''. As can be seen in Figure 55 this results in the second case

(eq. 86) $b^* \geq b > SC$.

In contrast to the first case, there is now another point of intersection C between the curve C_{change} and l'', which means that outsourcing is a profitable alternative for combinations of c and p_k to the left of C.

A third case becomes relevant when b is further increased, so that B and C move upwards and closer to each other. Finally, C_{change} and C_{keep} no longer intersect, so that outsourcing is the dominant alternative for every combination of p_k and c (see l''' in Figure 55). This case is characterized by the condition

(eq. 87) $b > b^*$.

In the second scenario it is assumed that the costs of the outsourcing alternative change linearly, as is the case when the initialization or adaptation costs are subject to progress in information technology. An instance of this scenario is represented in Figure 56.

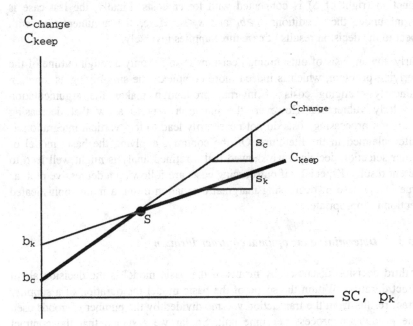

Figure 56:   Paths of development of C_{change} and C_{keep} in scenario 2.

Let s_c be the gradient of C_{change}

(eq. 88) $s_c = \dfrac{\partial C_{change}}{\partial SC} = 1$

and b_c the intersection of C_{change} and the axis of ordinates

(eq. 89) $b_c = AC + EC$.

Moreover, let b_k be the intersection of C_{keep} and the axis of ordinates and s_k the gradient of C_{keep}

(eq. 90) $s_k = constant$.

From these assumptions four cases arise. The first two cases, which fulfill the conditions $s_c \geq s_k$ and $b_c > b_k$ (case 1) and $s_c \leq s_k$ and $b_c < b_k$ (case 2) respectively, represent situations in which one alternative dominates over the other, i.e. in case

1 outsourcing is the predominant alternative while in case 2 in-house production is always preferable; whereas the third case, which is illustrated in Figure 56, is characterized by the conditions of $b_c \leq b_k$ and $s_c > s_k$. This leads to a single point of intersection S which determines whether outsourcing (left of S) or in-house production (right of S) is connected with lower costs. Finally, the last case is relevant under the conditions $b_c \geq b_k$ and $s_c < s_k$. Here, the argumentation with respect to the decision results of case three applies inversely.

Clearly, the analysis of outsourcing decisions is so far only a rough outline of the underlying problem, which is indeed more complex. The simplifying assumption of linearly changing costs of internal production makes the argumentation particularly vulnerable. However, the intention was to show that decreasing information processing costs do not necessarily lead to less vertical integration as is often claimed in the literature. On the contrary, applying the basic model of supplier selection decisions we showed that a refined analysis might well lead to different results. Especially if outsourcing costs are following a degressive plot, as is true in the case of decreasing marginal evaluation costs, a more sophisticated reflection is appropriate.

4.2.5.3 *Determining the optimal contract duration*

The third decision discussed by means of the basic model is the decision about contract duration. Within the scope of the basic model the duration of a supplier contract results from the transaction volume divided by the number of goods used in the production process per time unit. So far we assumed that the contract duration is a given parameter because of the predetermination of *vol* and *frq*. From this an important consequence follows, namely, that by applying the basic model to supplier selection decisions, once a transaction partner had been chosen in an optimal way, the situation arrived at will be optimal until the end of the life cycle of the traded product, i.e. an equilibrium situation is reached. In other words, without a change of model parameters, e.g. decreasing cost parameters caused by technical progress, long-term relationships are predominant. However, if technical progress which lowers cost parameters is assumed, decisions on transaction partner selection may be reevaluated and supplier change may be advantageous. In this way the transaction volume becomes variable.

In the following two sub-sections two decision scenarios are introduced and compared in which decisions about supplier contracts take place: one in which the decision-maker is acting passively, following a simple decision rule, and a second scenario in which the contract duration is optimized actively.

In the first scenario the decision-maker initiates a change of transaction partner as soon as the sum of switching costs and expected acquisition costs is lower than the acquisition costs incurred by the current supplier relationship. The rate at which the marginal evaluation costs decrease over time is assumed to be unknown to the decision-maker. The duration of a supplier contract then results implicitly from the sequence of decision results over time and is determined ex post. In practice this scenario may be implemented by contracts with a duration shorter than the expected life-cycle of the product traded, i.e. as soon as a contract expires the current supplier relationship is reevaluated and the current contract is possibly prolonged. Alternatively, contracts can be designed with unlimited duration but short periods of notice, so that transaction partners can quickly be changed if necessary. However, in practice this strategy may be connected with problems. As Bakos and Brynjolfsson have shown in (Bakos and Brynjolfsson 1993) a lack of commitment on the buyer's side may possibly lead to incentive problems, i.e. the supplier may not be willing to invest in the relationship if it is uncertain whether these investments will be recouped. To encounter these problems, i.e. designing incentive compatible contracts and participating in cost reductions at the same time, in practice it is common to agree on flexible prices, e.g. in the form of constant price reductions over time. Conversely, in the second scenario the decision-maker has expectations concerning the development of marginal evaluation costs over time, so that transaction partner changes and contract duration can be determined ex ante. The latter approach is incentive compatible for suppliers as well as incorporating expected cost reductions into the decision.

Both scenarios are implemented by extending the basic model of supplier selection decisions in the next sub-sections. A comparison of resulting contract durations reveals that both scenarios are associated with different expected costs for supplier relationships.

4.2.5.3.1   Applying the simple decision rule

Before we address the problem of calculating the duration of a contract which results from the application of the simple decision rule, a short note on the extensions of the basic model necessary to incorporate time-dependent phenomena into the decision.

Let T be the final point in time at which the traded product is stopped being purchased. This point may be determined, e.g., by the end of the life-cycle of the traded product. At every point in time t, starting from $t=1$ and ending with $t=T-1$, a decision is made about the prolongation of the current contract. The length of periods between two adjacent points in time can be arbitrarily chosen. The number of goods purchased in each period is given by frq. The transaction volume which forms the basis of the transaction partner decision is a function of time.

(eq. 91) $vol(t) = frq(T - t)$

The transaction volume is less the shorter the period between the decision and T. Furthermore, the marginal evaluation costs are a function of time, modeled by means of an exponential function.

192

(eq. 92) $\quad c(t) = (c_0 - l)t^{-g} + l$ with $t \geq 1$

The resulting function is convex, monotonically decreasing and with an upper bound of $c(1) = c_0$ as starting value for the marginal evaluation costs in $t=1$. The lower bound of $c(t)$ is given by $\lim_{t \to \infty} c(t) = l$ ($l < c_0$). The negative exponent g ($g \geq 0$) indicates the rate of progress in information technology. The greater g, the more convex the resulting curve $c(t)$. If g equals zero, i.e. the marginal evaluation costs are constant, then $c(t)$ equals c_0. The plot of the resulting curve is shown in Figure 57.

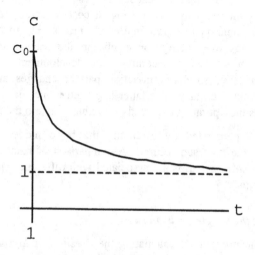

Figure 57:   Marginal evaluation costs as a function of time.

Importantly, the decision-maker has knowledge only of the marginal evaluation costs valid at the relevant point in time at which the decision on transaction partner selection is made.

Furthermore, let us assume that the settlement costs consist only of the costs incurred by initializing the business relationship. The basic decision model is then transformed. At every point in time t between 1 and T the decision-maker evaluates the following model:

Min (C_{keep}, C_{change}) with

$$C_{keep} = p_k \, frq(T-t)$$

$$C_{change} = AC + EC + SC$$

with $\quad AC = \dfrac{frq(T-t)\displaystyle\int_0^{p^*} pf(p)dp}{F(p^*)}$

$$EC = \dfrac{(c_0 - l)t^{-g} + l}{F(p^*)}$$

$$SC = inc$$

$$frq(T-t)\int_0^{p^*} F(p)dp - \left[(c_0 - l)t^{-g} + l\right] = 0$$

Since the transaction volume and the marginal evaluation costs are a function of time and the reservation value p^* depends on c and vol, p^* is now a function of time. From (eq. 43), showing that p^* decreases in c, in combination with (eq. 49) showing that p^* decreases in vol we deduce that there is a minimal reservation price between $t=1$ and $t=T$. To determine the influence of time on the reservation price, the derivations of c and vol with respect to t are first calculated, which are given by

(eq. 93) $\quad \dfrac{dc}{dt} = -g(c_0 - l)t^{(-g-1)}$

and

(eq. 94) $\quad \dfrac{dvol}{dt} = -frq$.

Setting

(eq. 95) $\quad y(t) = \dfrac{c(t)}{vol(t)} = \dfrac{(c_0 - l)t^{-g} + l}{frq(t - T)}$

from (eq. 43) together with (eq. 93), (eq. 94), and (eq. 95) we receive

194

$$\text{(eq. 96)} \quad \frac{\partial p^*}{\partial t} = \frac{\partial p^*}{\partial y}\frac{dy}{dt} = \frac{1}{F(p^*)}\frac{vol(t)\dfrac{dc}{dt} - c(t)\dfrac{dvol}{dt}}{vol(t)^2}$$

which evaluates to

$$\text{(eq. 97)} \quad \frac{\partial p^*}{\partial t} = \frac{-(T-t)g(c_0 - l)t^{(-g-1)} + (c_0 - l)t^{-g} + l}{frq(T-t)^2 F(p^*)}.$$

For reasons of simplification let $l=0$, so that

$$\text{(eq. 98)} \quad \frac{\partial p^*}{\partial t} = \frac{-(T-t)gc_0 t^{(-g-1)} + c_0 t^{-g}}{frq(T-t)^2 F(p^*)}.$$

The first order condition for the minimum of the stop price

$$\text{(eq. 99)} \quad \frac{\partial p^*}{\partial t} = 0$$

satisfies for

$$\text{(eq. 100)} \quad t^* = \frac{Tg}{1+g}.$$

From

$$\text{(eq. 101)} \quad \lim_{g \to \infty}\left(\frac{Tg}{1+g}\right) = T$$

it is obvious that the upper bound of t^* equals T. These results show that there exists a minimum reservation value of supplier prices at t^* which is between zero and T.

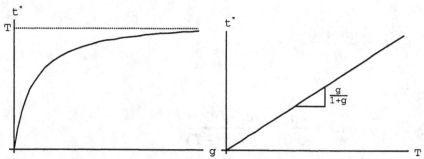

Figure 58: Point in time of minimum reservation value as a function of g (left) and T (right).

As illustrated in Figure 58 the value of t^* is greater the faster the marginal evaluation costs are reduced over time. Moreover, t^* increases linearly in T with the rate $\dfrac{g}{1+g}$.

Due to the fact that supplier change is only advantageous for a purchasing organization if the costs of changing transaction partner decrease over time, it is clear that after t^* it is never optimal to change supplier. However, the question is still open on what conditions it is optimal to change supplier during the period defined by $t=1$ and $t=t^*$. Figure 59 illustrates the dependency between the stop price, the expected acquisition price, the marginal evaluation costs, and the costs of initializing a supplier relationship on the one hand, and the decision to change transaction partner on the other hand.

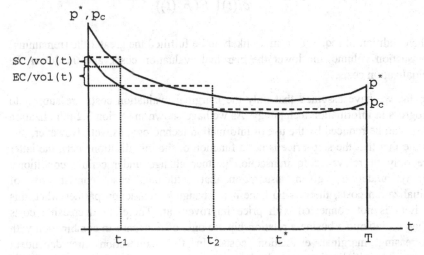

Figure 59:   Contracting sequence when marginal evaluation costs decrease over time.

Figure 59 shows the plot of the reservation value $p^*(t)$ and the expected price $p_c(t)$ per unit of the good when the supplier is changed in t. The price p_c is derived simply by dividing the acquisition costs by the transaction volume. From the definition of the acquisition costs it is clear that p_c is always less than p^*. We assume that the decision-maker starts from an equilibrium situation, i.e. initially it is not beneficial to change transaction partner. The price underlying the initial stage is characterized by the intersection of the topmost dotted horizontal line and the axis of ordinates. As time progresses, the stop price as well as the expected acquisition price go down. As soon as the difference of the price currently paid and the expected unit costs of changing transaction partner is greater than zero, it is beneficial to change transaction partner. This may happen, for example, at t_1. As the expected prices continue to drop, there may be further transaction partner changes. However, since the marginal rate of expected prices as well as the transaction volume from the point of decision to T are decreasing, it may take more time until the costs of switching transaction partner are balanced by prospective price reductions. In our example this happens in t_2.

Generally we may say that there will be at least one transaction partner change between $t=1$ and $t=t^*$ if there is at least one stage t at which the difference between the currently paid price which forms the basis of a contract signed at t' ($t'<t$) and the prospective price expected when signing a contract at t is greater than the sum of the expected evaluation costs and initialization costs per unit of goods traded in the period between t and T, i.e. if the following condition applies:

$$(eq.\ 102)\quad p_c(t') - p_c(t) > \frac{1}{vol(t)}\left(\frac{c(t)}{F(p^*(t))} + inc \right)$$

The condition of (eq. 120) is more likely to be fulfilled the greater the (remaining) transaction volume, the lower the marginal evaluation costs, and the lower the initialization costs.

So far we have assumed that only the marginal evaluation costs are subject to progress in information technology. As we have shown in section 3.2 initialization costs can be reduced by the use of information technology, as well. However, due to the fact that the stop price is not a function of the initialization costs, the latter are only of relevance to transaction partner change under certain conditions. Firstly, under the given assumption that settlement costs consist only of initialization costs, there is no benefit in changing transaction partner when this activity is not connected with price improvement. Therefore decreasing costs when initializing a business relationship are only of relevance in combination with decreasing marginal evaluation costs. In this connection time-dependent decreasing initialization costs lead to reduced contract duration and possibly a greater number of contracts signed between $t=1$ and $t=t^*$. Secondly, the value of initialization costs may be of importance if the decision-maker is not starting from an equilibrium situation. In this case, however, the relevance would be restricted to the first point in time at which the decision on transaction partner is taken.

If the assumption that the settlement costs consist only of costs to initialize the supplier relationship is dropped, and if it is further assumed that a change of supplier is possibly associated with a change of information technology to support the settlement phase, resulting in reduced settlement costs, then this cost reduction may compensate for evaluation costs under certain conditions. This extended question is subject of section 4.3.

If we drop the assumption that the rate at which the marginal evaluation costs decrease over time is unknown to the decision-maker, then the application of the simple decision rule leads to suboptimal results. If the decision-maker cannot foresee the expected minimum of the stop price over time, then for the period between t^* and T a relatively high price for the good will possibly be paid. In consequence more transaction partner changes take place than are necessary in the optimal case. If the minimum stop price can be predicted, the decision-maker is able to calculate the point in time at which supplier change is optimal recursively, going from $t=t^*$ successively back to $t=1$. How the basic model is adapted to enable this calculation is shown in the next section.

4.2.5.3.2 Optimizing contract duration

If the decision-maker has expectations about the development of marginal evaluation costs over time, the optimal number of transaction partner changes can be calculated ex ante by using the concept of dynamic programming. Building on the extension of the basic model of supplier selection decisions introduced in the previous chapter, we can represent the underlying optimization problem with the help of the following recursive formulation[108]:

$$(eq.\ 103)\quad f_t(t') = Min \begin{cases} frq\ p_c(t') + f_{t+1}(t') \\ \dfrac{c(t)}{F(p^*(t))} + inc + frq\ p_c(t) + f_{t+1}(t) \end{cases}$$

The function on the left-hand side of (eq. 103) $f_t(t')$ denotes the minimum costs from t to T if at t a contract is valid which had been signed at t' ($t'<t$), while it is assumed that at t and all following points in time the optimal decision on transaction partner change is made. The formulation of these minimum costs is shown on the right-hand side of (eq. 103). The first line of this term denotes the situation in which at t no transaction partner change takes place, i.e. the current contract is kept. In this case the price $p_c(t')$ is paid in the following period plus the costs connected with the optimal strategy for all following periods $f_{t+1}(t')$, whereas the second line represents the costs of the case when transaction partner is changed at t. This alternative is associated with the costs of searching and evaluating prospective suppliers as well as the initialization costs, the acquisition costs of the following period, plus the costs connected with the optimal strategy for all following periods $f_{t+1}(t)$.

As a first step in the solution process a binary tree is spread out, i.e. at every point in time it is considered that the transaction partner may be changed or kept. The resulting solution space is characterized by t^{*2} possible decision sequences. In the second step the recursive relationship is used, moving backward from t^* stage by stage, each time finding the optimal decision for that stage, until the initial stage

---

[108] For a general description of dynamic programming problems cf. (Hillier and Lieberman 1995, pp. 430-433).

$t=1$ is reached. The resulting decision sequence yields an optimal solution of the entire problem.

As we have already stated, the possible loss associated with the risk of opportunistic behavior decreases with the cost difference between the preferred and second-best alternative. As long as the expected costs of changing transaction partner are decreasing over time, there is no room for opportunism of the supplier, because the buyer can credibly threaten to change transaction partner. As soon as the expected acquisition costs increase due to the reduced transaction volume, i.e. from t^* onwards, the purchasing organization is again increasingly vulnerable to opportunism.

Reviewing the results concerning the decisions on transaction partner change and extending the point of view from the examination of single supplier relationships to all buyers and suppliers of a particular good in a market, then we notice that the application of our model is associated with a concentration of the number of suppliers with whom actually relationships are kept up. According to the model, contracts are signed only with suppliers who provide prices which are equal to or lower than p^*. Therefore, parameter changes resulting in a lower reservation price, e.g. decreasing marginal evaluation costs or increasing transaction volume, but not changes in the settlement costs, result in ever more purchasing organizations buying from a continuously reduced set of suppliers. This statement, however, applies only under the assumption that the suppliers do not react to customer decisions or to their competitors' prices by adapting prices or modifying products.

If we know the reservation price, then we can calculate the share of all potential suppliers of a particular good who remain in the market after all buyers of this good have decided whom they intend to procure from. If in our search model we assume that all potential suppliers have equal opportunity of being found by searching customers, then the relative frequency of suppliers providing a particular price must equal the PDF of this price. After applying the model the share as compared to the total number of potential suppliers then equals the cumulated probability of finding the reservation price in the market $F(p^*)$.

Before we go into the extensions of the basic model of supplier selection decisions let us provide a short summary of the results achieved in section 4.2. From the analysis under the given assumptions and within the scope of our basic model of supplier selection decisions we derive the following conclusions:

- The static analysis of the basic model of supplier selection decisions has shown that it confirms the results of transaction cost theory for transaction partner selection under the conditions of complexity of goods and transactions, the specificity of assets, the uncertainty of transaction partner behavior and the frequency of a transaction. However, it allows an analysis of finer granularity, because progress in information technology is not an aggregated factor as in conventional approaches, but can instead be assigned to different cost components, so that differences concerning the impact on supplier selection decisions can be represented.

- The risk of opportunistic behavior is concerned by the use of information technology in two ways. The use of information technology directly reduces the risk of opportunistic behavior, because for given evaluation costs activities to judge the reliability of potential suppliers in the evaluation phase can be intensified. An indirect effect of information technology derives from the fact that due to reduced costs of changing transaction partner the maximum profit the supplier can gain by opportunistic behavior diminishes, i.e. incentives for suppliers to behave opportunistically are mitigated.

- An application of the basic model to outsourcing decisions showed that progress in information technology does not necessarily lead to a decreasing vertical integration of organizations.

- Time-dependent reductions of marginal evaluation costs might result in transaction partner changes. These changes are restricted to the period of time in which the costs of changing transaction partner decrease. This period ends in t^* and is longer, the higher the rate of cost reductions and the longer the overall period of time in which the good is acquired. The number of transaction partner changes actually taking place depends on the value of potential cost reductions during this period of time. We expect more transaction partner changes to occur, the greater the transaction volume, the lower the marginal evaluation costs, and the lower the initialization costs. As the number of transaction partner changes in the given period of time increases, the expected duration of supplier contracts decreases. Incentives for opportunistic behavior increase after t^*, because from t^* the expected total costs of the supplier relationship when changing transaction partner increase.

- When we consider all buyers and potential suppliers of a particular good in a market, then the (repeated) application of the basic model is associated with a concentration process, i.e. ever more purchasing organizations procure from a continuously reduced set of suppliers.

So far it is assumed that cost reductions are caused exogenously. In practice the decision-maker is likely to influence these costs by the decision about the information technology used to support the supplier relationship. In terms of the state preference model in addition to cost savings this leads to additional alternatives of acting. Moreover, progress in information technology not only influences cost parameters directly but also indirectly by changing probabilities of states due to network effects when using information technology.

The next section is dedicated to the analysis of the compound decisions on supplier selection and technology adoption under the condition of progress in information technology.

4.3 Extending the basic model: the selection of information technology

In this section the assumptions about the technological dimensions of the basic model are dropped. Now the decision-maker can select from a set of potential information technologies to support the transaction. In the decision on the use of information technology a distinction is made between solutions used to support the evaluation phase of a business relationship and the settlement phase. To represent the effects associated with decisions about information technology, the basic model needs to be extended. Firstly, the formulation of the costs connected with the alternatives must be altered. To consider network effects in particular the diffusion of different technologies must be incorporated into the model. Secondly, the number of alternatives the decision-maker chooses from is increased. While so far there have been only two alternatives for action, namely "keep current transaction partner" or "change transaction partner", these two basic alternatives are now subdivided into a number of possibilities of how the change of transaction partner in the evaluation phase and the settlement phase can be supported by different information technology solutions.

4.3.1 Modeling the selection of information technology

In the modified model the decision-maker faces a number of technological alternatives to support the evaluation of potential suppliers. These alternatives can be chosen from the set of available solutions I. Similarly, the settlement phase of a transaction can be supported using a technology chosen from the set of available information technologies J. A particular combination of information technologies (i,j) ($i \in I$ and $j \in J$) determines the expected costs of a supplier relationship. Hence, the acquisition costs, evaluation costs, and settlement costs are a function of the respective technologies used to support the transaction. Furthermore, the information technologies $i=0$ and $j=0$ denote the current configuration of the procuring organization used to support the transaction with the current supplier.

Compared to the basic model, the acquisition costs in the extended model depend on the information technology i used to support the evaluation phase and information technology j used during the settlement phase of a supplier relationship. The acquisition costs are now defined as

$$(\text{eq. 104}) \quad AC_{i,j} = \frac{vol \int_0^{p_{i,j}^*} pf(p)dp}{F(p_{i,j}^*)}.$$

The modified stop price is determined by an altered indifference property and is obtained by solving

$$\text{(eq. 105)} \quad \alpha_i \beta_j vol \int_0^{p_{i,j}^*} F(p)dp - c_i = 0$$

for $p_{i,j}^*$. Compared to the indifference condition of the basic model (eq. 24) the marginal evaluation costs c_i are specific to the applied technology i. Therefore, the diffusion of the technology α_i ($\alpha_i \in (0,1]$) is taken into consideration. A value $\alpha_i=1$ means that the technology considered is perfectly disseminated, i.e. every potential transaction partner uses it. The resulting reservation price then yields the same value as in the basic model. As α_i decreases, it becomes increasingly difficult to reach potential transaction partners so that search activities become more expensive. Behind this modified formulation of supplier search is the assumption that information technology used to support the evaluation phase is of benefit for the seeker only if the same (or a compatible) technology is also present on the side of the potential suppliers. In this way network effects of information technology are represented. For example, using an Internet-based marketplace to discover potential business partners requires both sides of a potential transaction, the purchaser as well as the supplier, to be provided with means of Internet access.

Finally, through (eq. 105) the reservation price is subject to the diffusion of information technology j, which is represented by β_j. Although the formulation of the influence of technology i on the search process is the same as the formulation of the impact of technology j, the interpretation is different. While the influence of α_i can be interpreted as a change in the probability to find a transaction partner possessing technology i, the parameter β_j can be seen as a multiplier affecting the number of search steps necessary to trace a potential transaction partner who has technology j. This influence is illustrated by dividing (eq. 105) by β_j which leads to

$$\text{(eq. 106)} \quad \alpha_i vol \int_0^{p_{i,j}^*} F(p)dp - \frac{c_i}{\beta_j} = 0.$$

The parameter β_j is defined in the domain $(0,1]$. If technology j is perfectly disseminated among the potential transaction partners, i.e. β_j yields a value of one, then every potential transaction partner contacted over the course of the search process is provided with technology j and the resulting costs per search step equal c_i. A value of β_j less than one results in an increase in the expected number of search steps necessary to find potential transaction partners who have technology j. Behind this formulation there are two major assumptions. Firstly, the probability that a potential supplier found during the evaluation phase possesses information technology j is uniformly distributed. Secondly, the probability of finding a transaction partner who uses information technology i and the probability that this potential transaction partner has got technology j for supporting the settlement phase are independent.

Considering the modified reservation value $p_{i,j}{}^*$ the evaluation costs in the extended model are now given by

$$(eq.\ 107) \quad EC_{i,j} = \frac{c_i}{\alpha_i \beta_j F(p_{i,j}^*)} + ime_i.$$

The first term on the right-hand side of (eq. 107) reflects the changes already mentioned in the discussion of (eq. 105). The expected number of search steps necessary to find a potential transaction partner who offers a price lower than or equaling $p_{i,j}{}^*$ and having technology j at the same time is represented by the factor $1/[\beta_j F(p_{i,j}{}^*)]$, while increased marginal evaluation costs due to a lack of standardization with respect to technology i manifests itself in the modified marginal evaluation costs c_i/α_i. Moreover, there is now the additional term of implementation costs ime_i which are incurred as soon as the decision-maker intends to use technology i to support supplier search. Naturally, these costs are only incurred if technology i has not already been acquired and used by the seeking organization.

To make the formulation of the acquisition and evaluation costs more accessible for later analyses the transformation of (eq. 35) can be carried out analogously for the sum of the modified acquisition and evaluation costs which evaluates to[109]

$$(eq.\ 108) \quad AC_{i,j} + EC_{i,j} = vol\ p_{i,j}^* + ime_i.$$

While information technology which supports the evaluation phase of a supplier relationship influences only the evaluation and acquisition costs, the impact of information technology which supports the settlement phase is of benefit due to the expected settlement costs which are now given by

$$(eq.\ 109) \quad SC_j = ims_j + inc_0 - rin_j - vol\left(\frac{rad_j}{frq} + rex_j\right).$$

The settlement costs basically consist of four terms. There are implementation costs that must be borne to enable the use of information technology j, ims_j. Furthermore, the purchasing organization has to bear initialization costs, inc_0, which are already known from the basic model. These initialization costs, however, now can be reduced by rin_j by the use of technology j. Further possible cost reductions are considered in the last term of (eq. 109). When using

---

[109] The derivation of this result is given in appendix D.

technology j the purchasing organization realizes technology-specific reductions of adaptation and exchange costs as they are given in square brackets. Since the components have already been explained in section 4.2.2 we forgo further discussion of these parameters. It is important to say that the reference point for these reductions is given by the fallback alternative, i.e. adc_0 and exc_0 which are paid if the settlement phase is supported by using the current solution[110].

Finally, the alternative of keeping the current transaction partner is now based on a number of different technologies. Therefore, the costs associated with this alternative are a function of technology j which also comprise implementation costs ims_j when new information technology is introduced into the current supplier relationship, so that

(eq. 110) $\quad C_{keep,j} = ims_j + p_{k,j} vol$.

By analogy to (eq. 109) the calculated price p_{kj} reflects potential cost reductions attainable by the use of technology j and is defined by

(eq. 111) $\quad p_{k,j} = p_0 - rex_j - \dfrac{rad_j}{frq}$.

Although theoretically the decision-maker has the choice of implementing any available information technology j to support the settlement phase, due to network effects cost reductions by the use of this technology can only be realized when both the purchasing organization and the supplier jointly decide upon its use. Since the supplier decides independently, there may be room for opportunistic behavior on the part of the supplier. However, this latitude only exists if the best alternative, i.e. the alternative with the lowest cost, is one of the keep alternatives and can be measured by the cost difference between the second-best and best alternatives. The following overview summarizes the extended model.

Synopsis of the extended model of supplier selection decisions

$\underset{i,j}{\text{Min}}(C_{keep,j}, C_{change,i,j})$ with

$C_{keep,j} = ims_j + p_{k,j} vol$

$\quad$ with $\quad p_{k,j} = p_0 - rex_j - \dfrac{rad_j}{frq}$

$C_{change,i,j} = AC_{i,j} + EC_{i,j} + SC_j$

---

[110] Since the reference point defined by adc_0 and exc_0 is the same for all alternatives, it is sufficient to restrict the analysis to cost reductions.

$$\text{with } AC_{i,j} = \frac{vol \int_0^{p_{i,j}^*} pf(p)dp}{F(p_{i,j}^*)}$$

$$EC_{i,j} = \frac{c_i}{\alpha_i \beta_j F(p_{i,j}^*)} + ime_i$$

$$SC_j = ims_j + inc_0 - rin_j - vol\left(\frac{rad_j}{frq} + rex_j\right)$$

$$\alpha_i \beta_j vol \int_0^{p_{i,j}^*} F(p)dp - c_i = 0$$

$$0 < \alpha_i, \beta_j \le 1$$

$$i \in I, j \in J$$

4.3.2 Properties of the extended model

Before discussing the technology selection decisions on the basis of the extended model, a brief analysis of the basic properties of the model in terms of the newly introduced and modified parameters.

The modified indifference condition (eq. 105) implies a different behavior of the stop price in dependence on technology diffusion, the modified marginal evaluation costs, and the transaction volume. The partial derivation of the indifference price for the technology diffusion is defined as

(eq. 112) $\quad \dfrac{\partial p_{i,j}^*}{\partial \alpha_i} = \dfrac{-c_i}{vol\, \alpha_i^2 \beta_j F(p_{i,j}^*)}.$

From this it is clear that the marginal stop price for α_i is negative, i.e. the greater the diffusion of technology i used to support the evaluation of transaction partners, the lower the reservation value and the choosier the seeker is. Analogously, the derivation of the reservation value for β_j is given by

(eq. 113) $\quad \dfrac{\partial p_{i,j}^*}{\partial \beta_j} = \dfrac{-c_i}{vol\, \alpha_i \beta_j^2 F(p_{i,j}^*)}.$

Moreover, the marginal stop price wit respect to the marginal evaluation costs is changed and now yields

(eq. 114)
$$\frac{\partial p^*_{i,j}}{\partial c_i} = \frac{1}{vol\,\alpha_i \beta_j F(p^*_{i,j})}.$$

In comparison with the case without consideration of technology diffusion as given by (eq. 43) there are now the additional arguments of α_i and β_j in the denominator of the fraction on the right-hand side of (eq. 114). Hence, as soon as technologies i and/or j are not perfectly disseminated among potential suppliers, the stop price becomes increasingly sensitive to a change in c_i.

Finally, the modified derivation of the reservation price with respect to the transaction volume is given by

(eq. 115)
$$\frac{\partial p^*_{i,j}}{\partial vol} = \frac{-c_i}{vol^2 \alpha_i \beta_j F(p^*_{i,j})}.$$

Analogously to the interpretation of (eq. 114) the sensitivity of $p_{i,j}{}^*$ with respect to the transaction volume increases as the technology diffusion decreases.

To determine the impact of changes in α_i, c_i, and vol on the costs of changing transaction partner $C_{change,i,j}$ through the reservation value we use (eq. 108) together with (eq. 112) to (eq. 115). The respective partial derivations of $C_{change,i,j}$ for α_i, β_j, c_i, and vol then yield

(eq. 116)
$$\frac{\partial C_{change,i,j}}{\partial \alpha_i} = \frac{-c_i}{\alpha_i^2 \beta_j F(p^*_{i,j})} < 0$$

and

(eq. 117)
$$\frac{\partial C_{change,i,j}}{\partial \beta_j} = \frac{-c_i}{\alpha_i \beta_j^2 F(p^*_{i,j})} < 0,$$

which always evaluate to negative values,

(eq. 118)
$$\frac{\partial C_{change,i,j}}{\partial c_i} = \frac{1}{\alpha_i \beta_j F(p^*_{i,j})} > 0,$$

which is always positive, and

$$\text{(eq. 119)} \quad \frac{\partial C_{change,i,j}}{\partial vol} = p_{i,j}^* - \frac{c_i}{vol\,\alpha_i\beta_j F(p_{i,j}^*)} - \frac{rad_j}{frq} - rex_j\,.$$

As concerns the sign of (eq. 119) the results gained by the analysis of (eq. 63) in section 4.2.4.4 apply as well. By variation of the transaction volume two reversal effects were identified in this analysis: increasing acquisition costs due to more goods being purchased which are balanced by the seeker finding lower prices. In appendix B, however, we have shown that the partial derivation given by (eq. 63) never yields to negative values. The argumentation of this proof applies for (eq. 119).

Finally, a change in the implementation costs effects $C_{change,i,j}$ and $C_{keep,j}$ linearly and without distortion, i.e.

$$\text{(eq. 120)} \quad \frac{\partial C_{change,i,j}}{\partial ime_i} = \frac{\partial C_{change,i,j}}{\partial ims_j} = \frac{\partial C_{keep,j}}{\partial ims_j} = 1\,.$$

4.3.3 Decisions in the extended model

In this section the extended model of decisions on supplier relationships and information technology is first used to determine how progress in information technology understood in the sense of the increasing diffusion of technology among potential transaction partners is likely to influence the duration of supplier contracts. Finally, progress in information technology in the interpretation of newly emerging solutions is analyzed. We show under which conditions new information technology is likely to prevail over well-established solutions.

4.3.3.1 The duration of supplier contracts under the condition of changing technology diffusion

To represent the effect of changing technology diffusion as it effects the stability of supplier relationships the relevant parameters, α_i and β_j, are modeled time-dependently in this section. The diffusion of innovations in markets is examined in innovation diffusion models (Bass 1969; Mahajan and Peterson 1985). The duration of supplier contracts then depends on the shape of the resulting time-dependent diffusion curves of α_i and β_j respectively. Although a wide variety of innovation diffusion processes have been investigated[111], one research finding keeps recurring: if the cumulative adoption time path is plotted, the resulting

---

[111] An overview of diffusion pattern investigations is provided, e.g., in (Mahajan and Peterson 1985).

distribution can generally be described as taking the form of an s-shaped curve (Mahajan and Peterson 1985, p. 8), as illustrated in Figure 60.

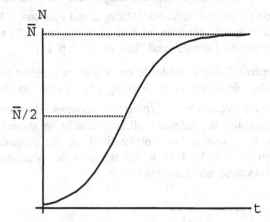

Figure 60:   General case of an s-shaped diffusion curve. Source: (Mahajan and Peterson 1985, Figure 2.2, p.19)

Let the cumulative number of adopters of an innovation in a social system be N and the total number of potential adopters in the social system be $\overline{N}$. Furthermore, let N_0 denote the cumulative number of adopters at time t_0. Then the general case of an s-shaped diffusion curve can be mathematically represented by

(eq. 121) $$N(t) = \frac{\overline{N}}{1 + \frac{(\overline{N} - N_0)}{N_0} e^{-b\overline{N}(t-t_0)}}$$

(Mahajan and Peterson 1985, p. 18). This formulation implies that a symmetric point exists which is also the point of inflection defined by $t = N^{-1}\left(\frac{\overline{N}}{2}\right)$. The curve to the left of this point is progressively shaped while to the right of this point the plot is degressive (hence "s-shaped").

Mahajan and Peterson showed in (Mahajan and Peterson 1985, p. 17) that the interpretation of the parameter b is revealed forming the derivation of (eq. 121), which is

(eq. 122) $$\frac{dN(t)}{dt} = bN(t)[\overline{N} - N(t)].$$

As is obvious from (eq. 122), b reflects the interaction of prior adopters $N(t)$ with potential adopters $\left[\overline{N} - N(t)\right]$. Hence, Mahajan and Peterson describe b as an index of imitation or internal influence (Mahajan and Peterson 1985, p. 18) and diffusion models with the properties of (eq. 121) and (eq. 122) are also called internal-influence models (Mahajan and Peterson 1985, p. 17).

To apply the general diffusion model to our model of supplier and information technology selection decisions we modify (eq. 121). Firstly, we do not consider absolute but only relative numbers of (potential) adopters. Therefore $\overline{N}$ is set to one and the domain of N_0 is restricted to $(0,1]$. Secondly, we assume that t_0 always equals zero, i.e. the curve is horizontally fixed on the abscissa. Taking the example of information technology which supports the evaluation phase of a supplier relationship these modifications lead to

(eq. 123) $\quad \alpha_i(t) = \dfrac{1}{1 + \dfrac{1 - \alpha_{i,0}}{\alpha_{i,0}} e^{-b_i t}}.$

As the plot of (eq. 123) in Figure 61 shows, the mathematical properties of the general diffusion model are preserved. The range of α_i is between zero and one, a point of inflection exists at $t = \alpha_i^{-1}(0.5)$, and the parameter b_i determines the maximum marginal rate of the diffusion curve or, in other words, the rate with which technology dissemination grows: the greater b_i is, the greater the maximum marginal rate of the diffusion curve is.

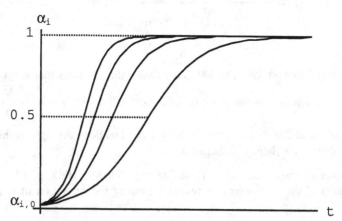

Figure 61:   System of diffusion curves of information technology i for varying b_i.

The analysis of the influence of changing diffusion of technology on the duration of supplier contracts follows the line of the analysis of time-dependent cost changes in section 4.2.5.3. In the analysis we distinguish between the two types of information technology i and j, which support the evaluation phase and the settlement phase of a business relationship respectively.

4.3.3.1.1   Time-dependent dissemination of information technology which supports the evaluation phase of a supplier relationship

The impact of the changing diffusion of information technology i on the duration of a contract is examined under the assumptions that the settlement costs are constant, the information technology j used to support the settlement phase is given, and no implementation costs are incurred. The value of the sum of all contract durations over time is given by the length of the life-cycle of the underlying product, T. Moreover, it is assumed that the decision-maker applies the simple heuristic to determine the point in time at which to change supplier as used in section 4.2.5.3.1 under the condition of restricted information. Assuming that the decision-maker has no ex ante information about the plot of technology diffusion over time the rule says that supplier change is initiated as soon as the costs of changing supplier are lower than the costs of keeping the current supplier.

The dynamics of the model are represented by defining the transaction volume as well as the technology diffusion as functions of time (as they are given by (eq. 91) and (eq. 123) respectively). As time progresses, the decision-maker can potentially realize lower prices from supplier search. A supplier change is initiated as soon as the expected supplier price is sufficiently low, so that the costs of changing supplier are balanced by the expected price reductions realized over the remaining lifetime of the traded product. However, since the transaction volume decreases over time, the costs of changing transaction partner are less and less compensated for. This effect manifests itself in an increasing reservation value, which is a function not only of the diffusion of technology i, but also of the transaction volume. This trade-off is represented in Figure 62 by a convex plot of the reservation value $p_{i,j}^{*}$ with a minimum value at t^{*}. The second curve running below $p_{i,j}^{*}$ represents the expected supplier price when changing transaction partner at t, $p_c(t)$, which is

$$(eq.\ 124)\quad p_c(t) = \frac{AC_{i,j}}{vol(t)}.$$

From the plot of these curves it is clear that a transaction partner change due to an increasing diffusion of technology i can only occur in the period between $t{=}0$ and $t{=}t^{*}$. Whether during this period transaction partner changes actually take place and if so, how often this is going to happen, depends on the marginal rate of $p_{i,j}^{*}$ (and p_c respectively). Given a contract had been signed at t', then at any given point in time t ($t{>}t'$) transaction partner change takes place if the expected price

210

reduction is at least as great as the expected unit cost of changing transaction partner:

(eq. 125) $\quad p_c(t') - p_c(t) > \dfrac{1}{vol(t)}\left(\dfrac{c_i}{\alpha_i(t)\beta_j F(p_{i,j}^*(t))} + inc_0 - rin_j\right)$

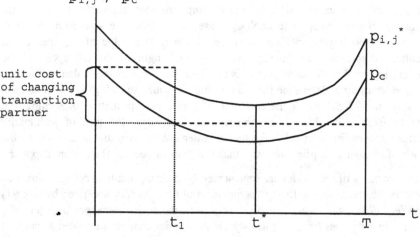

Figure 62: Reservation value and expected supplier prices as functions of time.

To examine which variables the length of the period between t_0 and t^* depends on, as a first step the point in time t^* must be determined. Let y be the marginal evaluation costs per unit of the good and per diffusion of technology i, i.e.

(eq. 126) $\quad y = \dfrac{c_i}{\alpha_i(t)\beta_j vol(t)},$

then the partial derivation of the reservation price with respect to the time is given by

(eq. 127) $\quad \dfrac{\partial p_{i,j}^*}{\partial t} = \dfrac{\partial p_{i,j}^*}{\partial y}\dfrac{\partial y}{\partial t} = \dfrac{-c_i\left(\dfrac{d\,vol}{dt}\alpha_i(t) + \dfrac{d\alpha_i}{dt}vol(t)\right)}{\left[\alpha_i(t)vol(t)\right]^2 \beta_j F(p_{i,j}^*)}.$

An evaluation and simplification of (eq. 127) results in

$$\text{(eq. 128)} \quad \frac{\partial p_{i,j}^*}{\partial t} = \frac{c_i \left(1 + \frac{1-\alpha_{i,0}}{\alpha_{i,0}} e^{-b_i t} \left[1 - b_i(T-t)\right]\right)}{frq(T-t)^2 \beta_j F(p_{i,j}^*)}.$$

Equating (eq. 128) with zero yields the first-order condition which satisfies

$$\text{(eq. 129)} \quad t^* = T - \frac{1}{b_i}\left[1 + W\left(\frac{\alpha_{i,0}}{1-\alpha_{i,0}} e^{b_i T - 1}\right)\right],$$

where W represents the product log function[112]. We can show that the functions of $p_{i,j}^*(t)$ and $p_c(t)$ have a common minimum at t^*, i.e.

$$\text{(eq. 130)} \quad \frac{\partial p_{i,j}^*}{\partial t}(t^*) = \frac{\partial p_c}{\partial t}(t^*) = 0.\,[113]$$

A necessary condition for transaction partner changes to occur is that (eq. 129) evaluates to a positive value. As shown in the following discussion of t^* this is not always the case.

It is obvious from (eq. 129) that t^* is a function of T, $\alpha_{i,0}$, and b_i. With respect to T, t^* is a concave and monotonically increasing function. This means, that as T increases t^* increases as well (with a decreasing marginal rate). The plot of t^* as a function of T is shown in Figure 63.

The parameter t^* evaluates to a value greater than zero only if T is greater than T_0, where T_0 is determined by

$$\text{(eq. 131)} \quad T_0 = \frac{-1}{(-1+\alpha_{i,0})b_i}.$$

---

[112] The product log function gives the solution for w in $z=we^w$. The function can be viewed as a generalization of a logarithm. It can be used to represent solutions to a variety of transcendental equations (Wolfram 1999, p. 772).

[113] The proof of this equation is provided in appendix E.

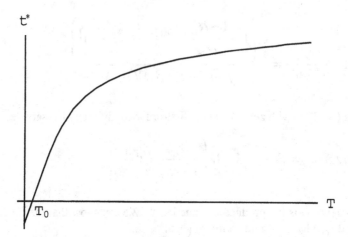

Figure 63: Point in time of minimum reservation value as a function of T.

In comparison to T, a change in $\alpha_{i,0}$ leads to a decreasing t^* (Figure 64).

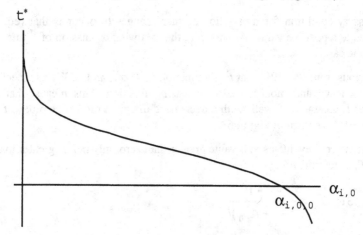

Figure 64: Point in time of minimum reservation value as a function of $\alpha_{i,0}$.

A positive t^* exists only if the condition $\alpha_{i,0} \leq \alpha_{i,0,0}$ applies, where $\alpha_{i,0,0}$ is given by

$$\text{(eq. 132)} \quad \alpha_{i,0,0} = 1 - \frac{1}{b_i T} .$$

Finally, an increasing dissemination growth rate b_i leads to an increasing t^* as long as b_i is less than b_{max}, and to a decreasing t^* as soon as b is greater than b_{max} (see Figure 65).

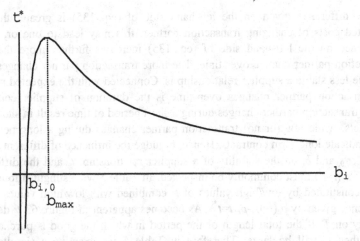

Figure 65: Point in time of minimum reservation value as a function of b_i.

The value of b_{max} is determined by solving

$$\text{(eq. 133)} \quad \frac{\partial t^*}{\partial b_i} = \frac{1}{b_i}\left(\frac{1+W\left(\frac{\alpha_{i,0}e^{b_iT-1}}{1-\alpha_{i,0}}\right)}{b_i} - \frac{TW\left(\frac{\alpha_{i,0}e^{b_iT-1}}{1-\alpha_{i,0}}\right)}{1+W\left(\frac{\alpha_{i,0}e^{b_iT-1}}{1-\alpha_{i,0}}\right)}\right) = 0.$$

However, due to its transcendental nature, (eq. 133) is not easily solved in an algebraic way. A numerical solution may suffice. A positive value for t^* is found only in cases where b_i is greater than $b_{i,0}$, while $b_{i,0}$ is given by

$$\text{(eq. 134)} \quad b_{i,0} = \frac{-1}{(\alpha_{i,0}-1)T}.$$

To understand the influence of changes in the characteristics of information technology diffusion (as expressed by the parameters T, $\alpha_{i,0}$, and b_i) on the stability of a supplier relationship, it is not sufficient to restrict the analysis to t^* alone. Knowing t^* and using the general condition that transaction partner change should be profitable as given in (eq. 125) we can specify the condition under which transaction partner change turns out to be profitable, which is

(eq. 135)

$$p_c(t=0) - p_c(t=t^*) > \frac{1}{vol(t^*)}\left(\frac{c_i}{\alpha_i(t^*)\beta_j F(p_{i,j}^*(t^*))} + inc_0 - rin_j\right).$$

As the difference given on the left-hand side of (eq. 135) is greater than the expected costs of changing transaction partner, this may lead to one or, as the difference on the left-hand side of (eq. 135) increases further, more than one transaction partner change over time. The more transaction partner changes there are, the less stable a supplier relationship is. Connected with the expected number of transaction partner changes over time is the duration of supplier contracts. Many transaction partner changes during a short period of time result in short-term contracts, while few (or no) transaction partner changes during a long period of time indicate long-term contracts. Hence, to judge the influence of different values for T, $\alpha_{i,0}$, and b_i on the stability of a supplier relationship, t^* and the difference $p_c(t{=}0){-}p_c(t{=}t^*)$ must commonly be inspected. In Table 5 we distinguish four basic cases constituted by low/high values of t^* combined with low/high values of the difference given by $p_c(t{=}0){-}p_c(t{=}t^*)$. As becomes apparent in Figure 63 t^* depends directly on T. If the total length of the period in which the good is purchased is long, then t^* will be large. Therefore in Table 5 we examine a simultaneous change in T and t^*.

Table 5: Determining the stability of a supplier relationship and contract duration by values of T, t^*, and $p_{i,j}^*(t{=}0){-}p_{i,j}^*(t{=}t^*)$.

	Low T (low t^* respectively)	High T (high t^* respectively)
High value of $p_{i,j}^*(t{=}0){-}p_{i,j}^*(t{=}t^*)$	Case B: low stability of supplier relationship, short-term contracts between $t{=}0$ and $t{=}t^*$;	Case C: moderate stability of supplier relationship, medium-term contracts between $t{=}0$ and $t{=}t^*$;
Low value of $p_{i,j}^*(t{=}0){-}p_{i,j}^*(t{=}t^*)$	Case A: high stability of supplier relationship, short-term contracts are predominant because of low T;	Case D: high stability of supplier relationship, long-term contracts are predominant;

The relative size of the quadrants A, B, C, and D is determined by the arguments on the left-hand side of (eq. 135), particularly the transaction volume, the marginal evaluation costs, and the initialization costs (see Figure 66).

A decline in marginal evaluation costs or initialization costs causes a downward move of the horizontal line dividing cases B and C on the one side and cases A and D on the other side. Therefore, supplier relationships which were previously highly stable may become unstable or moderately stable. This development is connected with a reduction of the expected contract duration.

$p_{i,j}^{*}(t=0) - p_{i,j}^{*}(t=t^{*})$

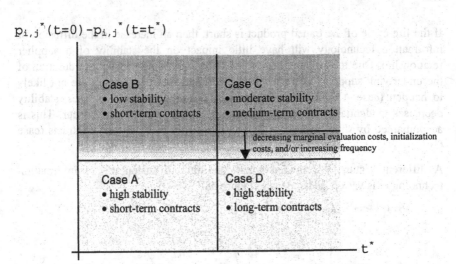

Figure 66: The impact of decreasing marginal evaluation costs, initialization costs, and increasing frequency on the stability of supplier relationships and expected contract duration.

Furthermore, as the parameter values characterizing the diffusion of a particular information technology change, this is associated with a different expected stability of the supplier relationships in which this technology is used. In this case, however, the relative size of the quadrants characterizing cases A to D is unchanged. Figure 67 shows the expected stability and contract duration of a supplier relationship as the life-cycle of the traded product, T, increases.

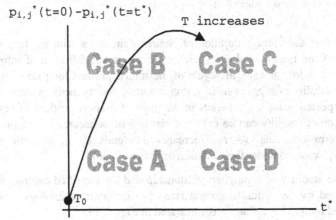

Figure 67: Stability of supplier relationship and expected contract duration as a function of T.

216

If the life-cycle of the traded product is short, then an increase in the diffusion of information technology will have little impact on the stability of a supplier relationship. Due to the short life-cycle of the underlying product the duration of the underlying supplier contract will be short and supplier changes are not likely to happen (case A). As the life-cycle of the traded product increases, stability decreases tendentially, i.e. many transaction partner changes may occur. This is accompanied by short-term (case B) and eventually medium-term contracts (case C).

A different picture is provided when the initial diffusion $\alpha_{i,0}$ of information technology i is varied, as happens in Figure 68.

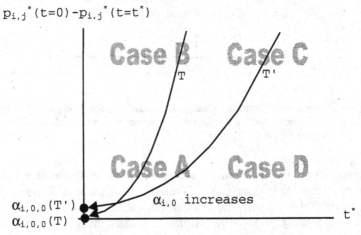

Figure 68: Stability of supplier relationship and expected contract duration as a function of $\alpha_{i,0}$ and T where $T<T'$.

It is clear that the average duration of contracts increases with the length of the life-cycle of the traded product. Therefore, if the initial diffusion of information technology i is low and the life-cycle of the traded product long (say T'), then a moderate stability of supplier relationship accompanied by medium-term contracts can be expected (case C); whereas in the case of a short product life-cycle the same degree of stability can be expected but will be connected with a prevalence of short-term contracts. As $\alpha_{i,0}$ increases this ends up in a stable supplier relationship (case A) under the condition of T as well as T'.

Finally, the stability of a supplier relationship and the expected contract duration is influenced by the diffusion growth rate of information technology i, which is represented by b_i. This influence is illustrated in Figure 69.

If b_i is small, i.e. technology i disseminates slowly and over a long period of time, this is likely to appear in combination with few or no changes of transaction partner (case A). If b_i increases while the product life-cycle is short this is likely to result in less stable business relationships based on short-term contracts (case B). This unstable period, however, only lasts for a short period of time, since t^* decreases. In the case of a long product life-cycle (T) we end up with large values of b_i in case B as well.

$$p_{i,j}{}^*(t=0)-p_{i,j}{}^*(t=t^*)$$

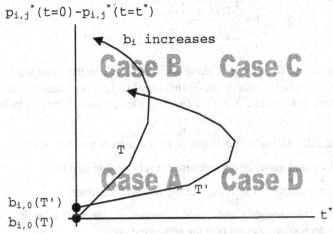

Figure 69: Stability of supplier relationship and expected contract duration as a function of b_i where $T < T'$.

4.3.3.1.2 Time-dependent dissemination of information technology which supports the settlement phase of a supplier relationship

Changing characteristics of the diffusion of technology for the support of the evaluation phase of a supplier relationship lead to more or less unstable business relations primarily because the benefit derived from using this technology evolves repeatedly from transaction partner changes in the form of price reductions, whereas a change in the diffusion of information technology for the support of the settlement phase provides benefits through reduced settlement costs. Settlement cost reductions, however, are obtained not only through transaction partner change, but also by changing the information technology used to support the relationship with the current supplier. Therefore one may assume that the stability of a supplier relationship is less influenced by the diffusion of the information technology used in the settlement phase.

The analysis of the influence of the changing dissemination of technology j on the stability of supplier relationships and the expected duration of supplier contracts is based on the assumptions that the information technology used to support the evaluation phase in the case of supplier change is given and that the starting point $t=0$ is an equilibrium situation in which supplier change is not profitable. Moreover, we ignore implementation costs, and the decision rule of the previous section applies.

218

In analogy to the modification of α_i in (eq. 123) the diffusion curve of technology j is given by

$$\text{(eq. 136)} \quad \beta_j(t) = \frac{1}{1 + \dfrac{1 - \beta_{j,0}}{\beta_{j,0}} e^{-b_j t}}.$$

The parameters of the diffusion curve are interpreted in the same way as in the case of the diffusion curve of technology i, i.e. $\beta_{j,0}$ denotes the initial dissemination in $t=0$ while b_j stands for the diffusion growth rate of information technology j.

Basically, the decision-maker now has three alternatives to select from:

1. Do nothing and leave the current supplier relationship as it is.

2. Introduce technology j with the current transaction partner.

3. Implement technology j and change transaction partner, i.e. seek a supplier who has technology j to support the settlement phase.

While the benefits of the second alternative compared to the first alternative are reduced settlement costs, the third alternative as compared to the second involves additional evaluation costs. Representing the volume dependent costs per unit connected with the three alternatives yields Figure 70.

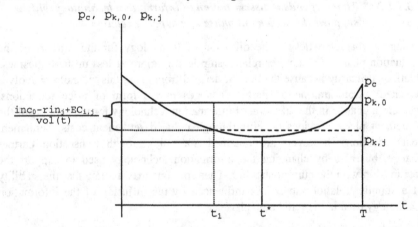

Figure 70: Reservation value and expected supplier prices as functions of time.

The cost of alternative three is represented by the curve p_c, which comprises the expected price paid for the good if the transaction partner is changed at t minus the settlement cost reductions attainable through the common use of technology j:

$$\text{(eq. 137)} \quad p_c = \frac{AC_{i,j}}{vol(t)} - \frac{rad_j}{frq} - rex_j$$

Since β_j influences the determination of the reservation value as well as the expected evaluation costs, p_c changes over time. The reversal effects already known from the discussion of the diffusion of information technology i (see section 4.3.3.1.1) cause a minimum of p_c at the point t^*. While an increasing diffusion of technology j leads to a decrease in the expected price of the good, the diminishing remaining duration of the newly signed contract means that the volume independent costs of changing transaction partner are distributed among a decreasing number of products.

The unit cost of the second alternative is represented by p_{kj}, which denotes the price currently paid minus the reduced settlement costs per unit of the good when introducing information technology j. Finally, the unit cost of the first alternative is denoted by $p_{k,0}$. We assume that supplier selection took place in $t=0$ and the current relationship is based on technology $j=0$ which is perfectly disseminated, so that $p_{k,0}$ is given by

$$\text{(eq. 138)} \quad p_{k,0} = \frac{AC_{i,0}(\beta_0 = 1)}{vol(t)}.$$

As the difference between p_{kj} and $p_{k,0}$ consists in settlement cost reductions, p_{kj} is given by

$$\text{(eq. 139)} \quad p_{k,j} = \frac{AC_{i,0}(\beta_0 = 1)}{vol(t)} - \frac{rad_j}{frq} - rex_j.$$

Since p_{kj} as well as $p_{k,0}$ is independent of the diffusion of information technology j, both values are constant over time. Moreover, from (eq. 137), (eq. 138), and (eq. 139) it is obvious that $p_{k,0} > p_{kj}$ and $p_c > p_{kj}$. The latter applies, because it is assumed that information technology i is not the subject of the decision, i.e. the first term on the right-hand side of (eq. 137) is always greater than the first term on the right-hand side of (eq. 139).

From the analysis it becomes clear that the third alternative dominates the first and the second alternative. However, this dominance applies only when the current supplier willingly accepts the introduction of information technology j in its organization. If this is not the case then the purchasing organization will have to provide incentives to the supplier. The maximum willingness to pay for these incentives is represented by the difference between the outcome of the third and the minimum value of the first and second alternative. But one may expect that the necessity to provide incentives to the supplier diminishes. As the diffusion of j

increases, which leads to increasing network effects for the purchaser, this might also be true for the supplier. So a change of transaction partner is still less likely.

If the third alternative is still excluded, e.g. because the payments necessary to get the current supplier to introduce information technology j make alternative three too expensive, then the transaction partner will be changed under the condition that

(eq. 140)

$$p_{k,0} - p_c(t = t^*) > \frac{1}{vol(t)}\left(\frac{c_i}{\alpha_i \beta_j(t)F(p_{i,j}^*(t))} + inc_0 - rin_j\right)$$

where t^* is given by[114]

$$\text{(eq. 141)} \quad t^* = T - \frac{1}{b_j}\left[1 + W\left(\frac{\beta_{j,0}}{1 - \beta_{j,0}}e^{b_j T - 1}\right)\right].$$

In words (eq. 140) means that the difference of volume dependent costs between the first and the third alternative must be at least as great as the volume independent costs per unit. The volume independent costs are represented by the term in brackets on the right-hand side of (eq. 140) and consist of the evaluation costs and the initialization costs net of initialization cost reductions which are attainable by the use of information technology j. Essentially, the results of the analysis of (eq. 135) in the previous section apply, so that further discussion of (eq. 140) is omitted.

The subject of this section was to show how transaction partner selection is affected by progress in information technology in the form of changing diffusion. Since new information technology does not usually occur in a market without competing alternatives, for example well established solutions with an extended installed base, the question of what conditions a newly emerging solution is likely to gain significant market share under is of particular interest. Therefore the next section is dedicated to the third kind of progress in information technology: the appearance of new information technology.

---

[114] The determination of t^* follows the line of the calculation of t^* when considering information technology i (see section 4.3.3.1.1).

4.3.3.2 The selection of information technology under the condition of newly emerging solutions

Given the current use of an information technology, a new solution is used if the benefit exceeds the costs of changing the solution. In the analysis of this question we assume that the new solution is used to replace the current technology within the scope of the current supplier relationship.

4.3.3.2.1 The acceptance of new information technology for the support of the evaluation phase

Coming from an equilibrium situation for information technology which supports the evaluation phase, the decision-maker can select from two alternatives "keeping the current solution" (i.e. $i=0$) and "introducing the new information technology" (i.e. $i=1$). The latter alternative goes hand in hand with transaction partner change, since it produces benefits only through price reductions realized by supplier change.

The indifference condition of standardization from the point of view of the decision-maker is given by

$$(\text{eq. } 142) \quad ime_1 = AC_{0,j} - vol\, p_{1,j}^* - inc_0 + rin_j .$$

The new information technology is introduced and used to change transaction partner if the implementation costs are balanced by the expected price reduction plus the expected evaluation costs and the initialization costs when the technology which supports the settlement phase is given. As soon as the implementation costs on the left-hand side of (eq. 142) are lower than the net benefit on the right-hand side, the decision-maker initiates the introduction of technology $i=1$ and supplier change.

A necessary condition for supplier change to be beneficial is that either the marginal evaluation costs of technology 1 are lower than those of technology 0 (given $\alpha_1=\alpha_0$), or that the diffusion of technology 1 is greater than the diffusion of technology 0 (given $c_1=c_0$). This leads to prospective price improvements through the use of technology 1. A second condition is that the implementation costs of technology 1 should not completely compensate for the expected gains from price reduction. It is important to notice that low implementation costs alone do not suffice, because a net profit is only achieved by changing transaction partner. Subsequently we analyze critical values of the parameters in (eq. 142) with respect to the profitableness of using technology 0 or 1. After that we briefly discuss the implications in terms of the expected stability of supplier relationships, the market share of technology 1 as compared to technology 0, and the reduction of the number of suppliers being actively in business.

222

If the diffusion α_0 and the marginal evaluation costs of the established technology 0 are given, then the question of what critical values of $\alpha_1{}^*$, $c_1{}^*$ and $ime_1{}^*$ make the introduction of technology 1 worthwhile for the purchasing organization arises. Given

(eq. 143) $\quad y_1 = \dfrac{c_1}{\alpha_1}$

then the graphic determination of the critical values $ime_1{}^*$ (given y_1) and $y_1{}^*$ (given ime_1) respectively is illustrated in Figure 71.

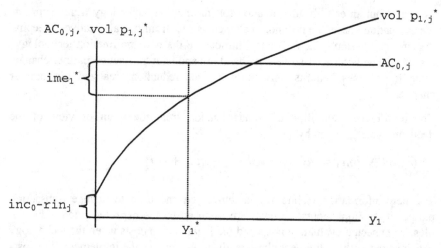

Figure 71: Graphic determination of the critical values $y_1{}^*$ and $ime_1{}^*$.

As y_1 decreases, e.g. by decreasing marginal evaluation costs or increasing diffusion of technology, the critical value of the implementation costs increases as well. Hence increasing diffusion of information technology 1 or decreasing marginal evaluation costs can compensate for implementation costs, or, in formal terms, using (eq. 142) together with (eq. 118) and (eq. 116) we receive

(eq. 144) $\quad \dfrac{\partial ime_1{}^*}{\partial \alpha_1} = \dfrac{c_1}{\alpha_1^2 \beta_j F(p_{1,j}^*)} > 0$

and

(eq. 145) $\quad \dfrac{\partial ime_1{}^*}{\partial c_1} = \dfrac{-1}{\alpha_1 \beta_j F(p_{1,j}^*)} < 0.$

Our primary interest concerns the question of how likely it is that technology 1 will prevail over an established solution. Therefore we are interested in the dependency of the critical values on the parameters which characterize technology 0, which are α_0 and c_0.[115]

The critical costs of implementing technology 1 in dependency on the diffusion and the marginal evaluation costs of technology 0 are illustrated in Figure 72. The critical implementation costs ime_1^* decrease with a decreasing rate as α_0 increases, whereas ime_1^* increases with a decreasing rate as c_0 increases[116].

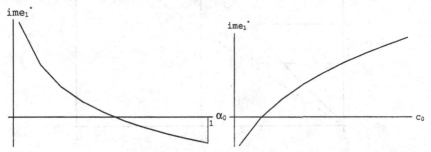

Figure 72:   Critical implementation costs of information technology 1 as a function of the diffusion (left) and the marginal evaluation costs of information technology 0 (right).

There may be a diffusion of information technology 0 and a value of the marginal evaluation costs associated with the use of information technology 0 which leads to negative critical implementation costs, thus excluding technology 1 from the market. The size of the interval $[\alpha_0, 1]$ and $[0, c_0]$ respectively leading to negative values of the critical implementation costs depends on the parameters of the function given by (eq. 142). A decreasing transaction volume or diffusion α_1, as well as increasing marginal evaluation costs c_1 or initialization costs lead to an increase of these intervals.

A further question concerns the determination of the critical values of α_1, given the implementation costs and assuming that $c_1=c_0$ or, alternatively, the critical value of c_1, given the implementation costs and assuming that $\alpha_1=\alpha_0$. Numerical analysis leads to the plot of critical values for the diffusion of information technology 1 in dependence on the diffusion of technology 0 as illustrated in Figure 73. The broken line indicates the bisector of the system of coordinates. The difference between the broken line and the critical diffusion of technology 1

---

[115]   Since it is assumed that solution 1 is already established we omit the costs of implementing this technology.

[116]   In this section we refrain from a formal representation of the partial derivations. Due to the frequently transcendental property of the underlying equations we restrict the examination to numerical analysis.

represents the necessary lead of technology 1 over technology 0 in terms of diffusion. The critical diffusion α_1^*, and therefore the difference $\alpha_1^*-\alpha_0$, increases with a growing rate as α_0 increases.

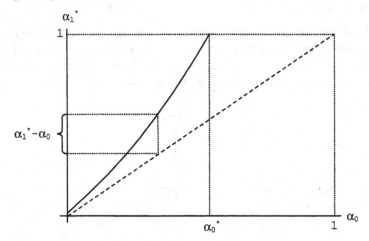

Figure 73:   Critical diffusion of information technology 1 as a function of the diffusion of information technology 0.

From the critical value α_1^* it becomes clear that there is a value α_0^* for the diffusion of information technology 0 which leads to a safe position for this technology. In other words, within the scope of our model, as soon as technology 0 reaches a dissemination greater than α_0^* a new technology has no chance of succeeding in the market, because a diffusion greater than 1 is impossible. The interval bounded by α_0^* and 1 depends on the implementation costs of technology 1 and the initialization costs when changing transaction partner.

The plot of the critical marginal evaluation costs of information technology 1 in dependence on the marginal evaluation costs of technology 0 is illustrated in Figure 74. The difference between the broken line and the critical marginal evaluation costs when using technology 1 represents the necessary lead of technology 1 over technology 0 in terms of reduced marginal evaluation costs. The critical marginal evaluation costs c_1^* increase with a decreasing rate as c_1 increases, so that the difference $c_0-c_1^*$ increases with a growing rate.

The analysis of critical values concerning the adoption of information technology 1 as compared to the characteristics of technology 0 shows under what conditions the new technology is likely to prevail over technology 0. Since the adoption of technology 1 is always accompanied by transaction partner change, these results can be used to assess the impact of a newly emerging technology on the stability of supplier relationships. Having a closer look at the decisions about technology adoption and supplier selection, we realize that there is an interrelation between these decisions. After the initial introduction of the new technology into the market, during the first stage all buyers reevaluate their current technology portfolio at the beginning of a period of time and decide whether to adopt the new solution. The necessary conditions for technology adoption in terms of the critical values concerning the properties of the new technology in dependence on the characteristics of the established solution can be seen in Figure 72, Figure 73, and Figure 74. As a number of procuring organizations adopt the new technology, which is accompanied by supplier change, the initial diffusion of this solution is increased.

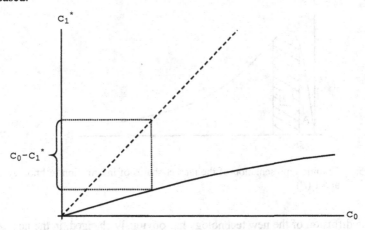

Figure 74: Critical marginal evaluation costs of information technology 1 as a function of the marginal evaluation costs of information technology 0.

We can show the resulting market shares of technology 0 and 1 after the first stage by means of our model. Denoting the initial dissemination of the new technology by $\alpha_{1,0}$, the reevaluation of the technology portfolio turns out in favor of technology 1 only for those organization which currently buy the good for a price greater than $p_{1,j}{}^*$. If we further assume that all buyers not belonging to the group of initial adopters of technology 1 are provided with technology 0, so that $\alpha_0=1-\alpha_{1,0}$, then on the market relationships only exist with a price equal to or lower than $p_{0,j}{}^*$. Moreover, supplier change only takes place in the case of those relationships which are based on a price greater than $p_{1,j}{}^*$. In formal terms, after all purchasing organizations for whom it turned out to be profitable to use the new solution implemented technology 1, the market share of this technology yields

$$(\text{eq. 146}) \quad \frac{\displaystyle\int_{p_{1,j}^*}^{p_{0,j}^*} f(p)\,dp}{F(p_{0,j}^*)} = \frac{F(p_{0,j}^*) - F(p_{1,j}^*)}{F(p_{0,j}^*)}.$$

In Figure 75 the relevant market shares according to (eq. 146) are visualized. The sum of the areas A and B represents the market share of technology 0 before the introduction of technology 1. After an initial diffusion of the new technology has been reached and all buyers of the good have decided upon its use, in the new situation technology 1 has gained a share equivalent to area B (as compared to the sum $A+B$), so that for technology 0 a share of A remains.

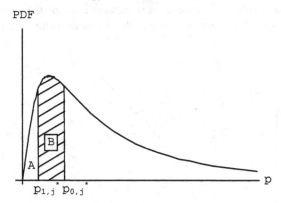

Figure 75:   Graphic representation of the market shares of information technology 0 (A) and 1 (B).

Since the diffusion of the new technology has obviously changed, in the next stage buyers who still use the old technology reevaluate their technology portfolio on the basis of the new data. Consequently, the new technology wins additional adopters who also change transaction partners. Moreover, the organizations which already belong to the installed base of the new technology reevaluate their transaction partner decision on basis of the new dissemination. Eventually the process of interacting decisions about technology adoption and supplier selection ends up in a stable state in which neither further technology adoption, nor transaction partner change is beneficial. This process leads in effect to a diffusion curve for the new technology which is, as regards its qualitative properties, similar to the diffusion functions already discussed in section 4.3.3.1. However the growth of dissemination of the technology is not now given exogenously, but endogenously, as determined by the decision parameters and their interaction during the decision process. In particular, the market share of the new technology does not necessarily end up in a perfect diffusion, but can also be less than 1. Therefore, as the dissemination of technology 1 increases over time, the statements derived in section 4.3.3.1.1 in the analysis of the stability of supplier relationships over time apply in principle, though, if the market share of the new technology ends up in a diffusion less than one, supplier relationships tend to be comparatively more stable.

Finally, the emergence of new information technology is associated with an increasing concentration in the market, as the buyers purchase the good from a reduced set of suppliers. This consequence is compelling because the adoption of technology 1 is always accompanied by transaction partner change. If prior to the introduction of technology 1 a share of $F(p_{0,j}{}^*)$ suppliers had been in business, after the introduction a share of only $F(p_{1,j}{}^*)$ (with $p_{1,j}{}^* < p_{0,j}{}^*$ and therefore $F(p_{1,j}{}^*) < F(p_{0,j}{}^*)$) suppliers is remaining.

4.3.3.2.2   The acceptance of new information technology for the support of the settlement phase

As we have discovered in section 4.3.3.1.2 information technology for the support of the settlement phase of a supplier relationship primarily provides benefits through cost reductions which are independent of transaction partner change. Therefore, in that section we analyzed the impact of changing diffusion of technology taking into account the decision on technology adoption. We came to the conclusion that the alternative of introducing the new information technology to support the relationship with the current transaction partner is dominant compared with the alternative of adopting the technology and changing transaction partner. However, in that section we abstained from analyzing implementation costs and our aim was to determine the influence of changing technology diffusion on the stability of supplier relations. In what follows we extend the analysis of section 4.3.3.1.2 in terms of the decision about the adoption of technology insofar as we now take implementation costs and the expected market share of the new technology into consideration.

We assume that currently information technology 0 is used to support the settlement of supplier relationships by all purchasing organizations in the market. If a new information technology ($j=1$) emerges in the market, then all procuring organizations decide upon the introduction of this new technology to support the relationship with the current supplier. As the reference point in the decision is technology 0, it is sufficient to consider cost reductions which can be achieved through the use of the new technology, thus implicitly considering the settlement costs incurred when using technology 0. In this setting the indifference condition of standardization from the point-of view of the decision-maker is shaped linearly and given by

$$(eq. 147) \quad ims_1 = vol\left(\frac{rad_1}{frq} + rex_1\right).$$

According to (eq. 147) parameters of the decision comprise cost reductions, the transaction volume, and implementation costs. The new technology is introduced if the expected cost reductions exceed the implementation costs. When we consider (eq. 147) we notice that neither β_1 nor β_0 influence the decision[117]. This means that under the given assumptions network effects have no effect on the adoption of the new technology and an initial diffusion is not necessary to achieve acceptance among the market participants.

The prospective settlement cost reductions are specific to the technology and not depending on the organization which uses this technology. Hence, if all procuring organizations had the same transaction volume, then the new technology would either be adopted by all buyers or by none. A difference in the profitableness of the use of technology 1 in different purchasing organizations therefore occurs only as the transaction volume varies. Given the implementation costs and prospective cost reductions, then the critical transaction volume is given by

$$\text{(eq. 148)} \quad vol^* = \frac{ims_1}{\dfrac{rad_1}{frq} + rex_1}.$$

A change in technology occurs for all relationships where the transaction volume exceeds the critical transaction volume. Assume that the transaction volume is equally distributed between zero and an upper bound, say vol_u, then after all buyers decided upon the use of the new technology the market share of technology 1 yields

$$\text{(eq. 149)} \quad \beta_1 = \begin{cases} 1 - \dfrac{ims_1}{vol_u \left(\dfrac{rad_1}{frq} + rex_1 \right)}, & vol^* \leq vol_u \\ 0 \end{cases},$$

from which the market share of technology 0 evaluates as

$$\text{(eq. 150)} \quad \beta_0 = 1 - \beta_1.$$

Therefore, increasing cost reductions or decreasing implementation costs lead to an increasing market share of technology 1, as far as there exists a critical transaction volume smaller than vol_u. However, while the influence of the implementation cost is linear, increasing cost reductions lead to a degressive growth of the market share. Finally, since the adoption of the new technology

---

[117] As one extends the analysis from supplier relationships for the procurement of a single good to the procurement of different goods so that a multitude of supplier relationships is considered, the diffusion of the technology used to support the settlement of a transaction is increasingly important.

takes place independently of transaction partner change, the number of suppliers staying in business is independent of the market share of the technology.

As we explained in section 4.3.3.1.2 the dominance of the alternative of using the new technology with the current transaction partner only holds if the current supplier willingly implements technology 1. If this is not the case, then a new transaction partner must be sought. Assuming that the technology used in the evaluation phase is given, the resulting indifference condition of standardization is given by

(eq. 151)

$$ims_1 = AC_{i,0} - AC_{i,1} - \frac{c_i}{\alpha_i \beta_1 F(p_{i,1}^*)} - inc_0 + rin_1 + vol\left(\frac{rad_1}{frq} + rex_1\right).$$

As compared to (eq. 147) in (eq. 151) additional evaluation costs must be borne. Moreover, a higher price may have to be accepted, because searching for potential suppliers who are provided with the new technology will be relatively expensive if technology 1 is not widely disseminated. The latter is represented by the difference of the expected acquisition costs $AC_{i,0}-AC_{i,1}$. As soon as β_1 is smaller than β_0 the procuring organization may expect greater acquisition costs. Therefore, in contrast to the previous case, the dissemination of the new technology now influences the profitability derived from its adoption. In particular, the decisions about transaction partner change and technology adoption may interact as described in the case of technology which supports the evaluation phase of the transaction.

From the analysis of the stability of supplier relationships under the condition of progress in information technology in terms of increasing technology diffusion and newly emerging information technology the following results can be summarized:

- A changing dissemination of information technology for the support of the evaluation phase of a supplier relationship may have a major impact on the stability of this relationship. Depending on the shape of the (exogenously given) technology diffusion curve, a growing dissemination of this information technology leads to an unstable period of time in which transaction partner changes are likely to occur. The length of this period depends on the initial diffusion of this information technology, the growth rate of its dissemination, and the life-cycle of the traded product.

- While the shape of the diffusion curve determines the maximum length of the unstable period of time, the actual number of transaction partner changes depends on the potential cost savings through supplier change during this period. Potential cost reductions are primarily determined by the marginal evaluation costs, the initialization costs, and the frequency with which the traded goods are exchanged.

- As the dissemination of information technology reaches a certain level, the unstable period ends and the relationship between the purchasing and supplying organization reaches a stabilized state in which no further transaction partner changes occur.

- A changing diffusion of information technology used in the settlement phase has only limited influence on the stability of supplier relations. Excluding implementation cost, when deciding on the use of a particular technology to support the settlement phase the alternative of using this technology with the current supplier is dominant, because no additional evaluation costs must be borne. Therefore, the diffusion of this technology has no impact on transaction partner selection. However, this result holds only if the current supplier willingly adopts the technology. If this is not the case, side payments are necessary, so that transaction partner change may be a profitable alternative. In this case the diffusion of technology influences the supplier decision. A changing diffusion then influences the stability of a supplier relationship in a way which is similar to the case of information technology used in the evaluation phase.

- When a new information technology for supporting the evaluation phase of a supplier relationship emerges in the market, then its adoption depends on the properties of this technology as well as on the properties of the competing solution already established in the market. Properties characterizing a particular information technology within the scope of our model are the implementation costs, marginal evaluation costs, and the dissemination of the technology among potential transaction partners. The new technology is adopted by a purchasing organization if the implementation costs and marginal evaluation costs associated with the use of this technology remain under, or the dissemination of this technology exceeds, a critical value.

- Extending the analysis from the relationship of a single organization to purchase a particular good to all relationships serving the purpose of procuring this good in a market, the determination of the critical values of technology adoption allows us to draw conclusions concerning the expected market share of the new solution. In this way, the diffusion curve of the new information technology becomes endogenous and depends on technology adoption decisions in the market. In terms of the stability of supplier relationships the results derived for the case of the exogenously given diffusion curve apply.

- As regards newly emerging information technology for supporting the settlement phase of a supplier relationship, the adoption of this technology depends on the expected settlement cost reductions which must exceed the implementation costs. Due to the dominance of the alternative of keeping the current supplier over the alternative of adopting the new technology and changing transaction partner, the diffusion of the new technology does not play a role in the adoption decision. Assuming that expected settlement cost reductions and implementation costs are specific to the applied information technology but not to the relationship, the expected market share of the new technology depends on the transaction volume underlying each relationship. The new technology is adopted by all purchasing organizations whose transaction volume exceeds a critical value, which is determined by the implementation costs and prospective settlement cost reductions.

- If dominance does not apply, however, then the adoption of technology may be associated with a change of transaction partner. Therefore, unstable supplier relationships may occur and in principle the results concerning the emergence of new information technology for the support of the evaluation phase apply.

- Progress in information technology in terms of increasing dissemination as well as newly emerging technology is connected with a concentration process on the supply side. Transaction partner changes only take place when a cheaper supplier is found. Hence, the unstable period of a business relationship in which transaction partner changes take place leads to ever more organizations buying from a continuously reduced set of suppliers.

5 Conclusion

In the following sections we review the major results of this thesis (5.1), derive implications for the management of supplier relationships (5.2), and propose how the basic model and its extensions can be used in further research (5.3).

5.1 Summary

In the introductory chapter 1 we stated the following research questions:

- How does information technology influence transaction costs?

- How does a change in transaction costs influence the design of supplier contracts?

- How does progress in information technology, interpreted as a change in the costs and benefits of using information technology as well as the increasing diffusion of a particular information technology, affect the design of supplier relationships?

- How does the availability of new information technology influence decisions on the adoption of information technology and the design of supplier relationships?

The analysis of these questions started in chapter 2 by providing a systematization of supplier relationships and discussing the facets and general set-up of the management of supplier relationships in organizations. Chapter 3 provided a systematization of information technology and it was shown how it can be used to support the procurement function in organizations. Finally, in chapter 4 a model representing decisions about supplier relationships and the selection of information technology was developed and used to answer the initial research questions.

The management of supplier relationships comprises the tasks of selecting vendors, negotiating contracts with them, and issuing purchase orders (Lee and Dobler 1971, p. 13). In chapter 2 we showed that decisions taking place within the scope of these tasks could be systematized according to the phases in the life-cycle of a supplier relationship. We distinguished between the evaluation phase and the settlement phase. In the evaluation phase prospective suppliers are sought, negotiations take place, and activities are carried out to judge the trustworthiness of a potential supplier. In particular we discussed how the concepts of search theory could be used to describe the activities of transaction partner search in a formal way. In addition to the basic search model, which is applied in chapter 4, we introduced a number of extensions to this model in terms of multidimensional and adaptive search strategies. Furthermore, we showed how negotiation activities in the evaluation phase differ depending whether there is a centralized or a decentralized market for a purchased product.

In the settlement phase major activities comprise the signing of a contract, the initialization of the relationship, and the exchange of goods and payments. Moreover, the contracting partner's fulfillment of the conditions of the contract is monitored. These activities are necessary to counteract possible operations risk, i.e. the risk that a supplier does not fulfill the agreed conditions of the contract. Finally, contract adaptations and renegotiations take place during the settlement phase. Here, the purchasing organization faces the risk that a supplier may act opportunistically, particularly when it has made investments specific to the current relationship or if there are only few alternative suppliers for the purchased goods.

Since this work focuses on the efficiency and cost structures of a single supplier relationship we used the concepts of transaction cost economy to assess alternative ways of organizing supplier relationships with different information technology solutions. Depending on the phases of a supplier relationship and the major tasks associated with each of these phases, we distinguished between transaction costs incurred during the evaluation and the settlement phase. The former comprise primarily the contact cost of finding potential transaction partners, the cost of gathering further information about potential transaction partners, and negotiation cost, whereas transaction costs incurred during the settlement phase consist primarily of the cost of initializing a relationship, the cost of exchanging goods and payments, and adjustment cost when adapting contract conditions. Furthermore we showed that beside transaction costs acquisition costs form a major determinant of the total costs associated with a supplier relationship. The value of acquisition costs depends directly on the price paid for the purchased good.

Concerning the determinants of transaction costs we distinguished between asset specificity, uncertainty in respect of the transaction and behavior of transaction parties, complexity in terms of the transaction or traded good, and transaction frequency. We showed, how in transaction cost theory the optimal governance structure of a supplier relationship is determined in dependence on the transaction determinants. We realized that, according to Williamson, when uncertainty is present the governance structure of a supplier relationship is mainly determined by the specificity of investments in a relationship and the frequency of a transaction (Williamson 1985). While the former primarily influences the opportunism risk of a transaction, the latter determines the unit transaction costs. Major expenses for the design of a contract only pay off if the underlying transaction is recurrent. Moreover, relationship specific investments make a long-lasting relationship worthwhile, because more complex and expensive governance structures are necessary as precaution against opportunistic behavior. Therefore, expensive contractual arrangements such as strategic partnerships are preferred in cases of high transaction frequency in combination with idiosyncratic investments, whereas standard contracts are predominant in case of no or low relationship specific investments.

In chapter 3 we introduced the basic aspects of information technology. Focusing the analysis on the externalities connected with the use of information technology, we worked out that information technology for supporting the management of supplier relationships, i.e. procurement applications and services brought to the customer by means of information technology, is based on communication standards. Distinguishing between communication standards for structuring the communication process and communication standards aimed at the information transferred between the transaction parties we introduced a number of traditional, well established solutions as well as new approaches. We evaluated these solutions in terms of transaction costs and showed that all transaction cost components are likely to be reduced by the use of information technology.

We discussed different hypotheses concerning the impact of information technology on supplier relationships. While it is commonly accepted that the use of information technology in relationships between business partners leads to less vertical integration, the influence of information technology on the design of supplier relationships is a controversial issue. We introduced the move to the market hypothesis, according to which the use of information technology is likely to result in the emergence of more electronic markets; and gave an overview of the objections to this hypothesis resulting in the move to the middle hypothesis. Clemons and Reddi, who have made the most thorough analysis of this subject so far, examined the impact of information technology on outsourcing, the number of suppliers, and the duration of contracts representing. They represented the influence of information technology by the two variables "relationship specificity of information technology" and "cost-effectiveness of information technology" (Clemons and Reddi 1994). Restricting the choice of contract duration to the two poles of selecting a new contractor for every period or, alternatively, keeping a single supplier for all periods in which the traded product is needed, the authors came to the conclusion that an increasing cost-effectiveness of information technology as well as a decreasing specificity of investments in information technology leads to a decision on long-term relationships by the purchasing organization under the conditions of low product complexity and a high degree of supplier opportunism (Clemons and Reddi 1994, pp. 861-863). Although the insights gained through these works contribute to the answer to our initial research questions, we identified a number of issues which are still open and could motivate further research. The main subject of criticism was the assumption that the procuring organization has the choice of either purchasing the good from a single supplier all the time or changing supplier in every period thus neglecting the dynamics inherent in the process of transaction partner selection. In particular, once a supplier who provides excellent conditions is found, there is no reason to change transaction partner later on. We argued that long-term relationships are therefore not necessarily the result of an ex ante calculation, i.e. evolving from an explicit decision about the duration of a contract. Long-term relationships can also arise ex post, e.g. by the prolongation of a short-term contract. Moreover, an ex ante long-term contract can be terminated prematurely resulting ex post in a short-term relationship. As we learnt, in this context the impact of information technology on transaction partner selection works in different ways. The benefit obtained by the use of information technology in the settlement phase happens repeatedly, depending directly on the number of purchased goods, e.g. because the unit costs of exchanging the products are reduced, whereas information technology in the evaluation phase unfolds its benefit only once, until a transaction partner is found providing conditions according to minimum requirements depending on the search strategy and the resulting reservation values for price and/or qualitative properties of the purchased goods.

In chapter 4 we identified three types of progress in information technology on the basis of a state preference approach. Firstly, progress leads to a change in parameter values for a given alternative and a given state of the environment. This comes about through general technical progress (e.g. in terms of computing power). Secondly, progress is also represented by a change in the probabilities for the occurrence of states. This usually happens when the diffusion of information technology changes. Thirdly, another type of progress takes place when new approaches to the solution of a given problem are developed, implemented, and made available. This leads to a new alternative from which the decision-maker can select.

Subsequently we gradually introduced a model and extensions to this model representing decisions concerning supplier relationships and the selection of information technology. In this model we distinguished between the fundamental alternatives of "keeping the current supplier" and "changing transaction partner" while considering the use of information technology in the evaluation and the settlement phase of a supplier relationship. We used parameters representing transaction costs in terms of evaluation costs, initialization costs, adaptation costs, and the cost of exchanging goods. Furthermore, we presented different options concerning the use of information technology in terms of implementation costs, prospective cost reductions, and the dissemination among potential transaction partners. In the model formulation, taking into account technology specific costs and benefits, we explicitly considered that transaction partners must be sought and negotiations must be conducted before one can decide upon the acceptance of a certain supplier. Analyzing the properties of the model and discussing decisions taken within the scope of this model we worked out answers to the initial research questions.

5.1.1 Information technology and transaction costs

In chapter 3 we showed that information technology has an impact on every component of the transaction costs. The mathematical description by means of the model showed that this influence works differently in different phases of a transaction. In the evaluation phase, the cost of evaluating potential transaction partners that is incurred during the search process must be compared with prospective price reductions achievable when changing transaction partners, whereas in the settlement phase information technology leads to reductions in terms of the exchange of goods and the supervision of the fulfillment of contract conditions. These cost reductions, however, might be compensated for by initialization costs incurred when transaction partner is changed. We discovered that under the assumptions of the model the total costs of changing transaction partner decrease progressively as information technology is used to support the evaluation phase of a supplier relationship, while the use of information technology in the settlement phase has a linear effect on these costs.

5.1.2 Reduced transaction costs and the design of supplier contracts

We examined how the costs associated with the alternatives "keeping supplier" and "changing transaction partner" change when transaction costs are reduced and analyzed the impact of these cost changes on decisions about transaction partners. In confirmation of the general results of transaction cost theory, we discovered that within the scope of our model an increasing complexity of the traded good and transaction, a growing specificity of the traded good, as well as in terms of the assets supporting the transaction, and an increasing uncertainty in respect of the behavior of the transaction partner and environmental changes, make the alternative of changing supplier comparatively more attractive. However, since in the model transaction costs are not represented in an aggregated form but rather a distinction is made between different cost components, a refined analysis of the effect of cost reductions was possible. In particular, we discovered that the risk of opportunistic behavior is affected by the use of information technology in two ways. The use of information technology directly reduces the risk of opportunistic behavior, because for given evaluation costs activities to judge the reliability of potential suppliers in the evaluation phase can be intensified. An indirect effect of information technology derives from the fact that, due to the reduction in costs incurred by changing transaction partner, the maximum profit the supplier can gain by opportunistic behavior is diminishes, i.e. incentives for suppliers to behave opportunistically are mitigated.

In the analysis of the influence of transaction cost reductions on the selection of suppliers initially, we assumed the number of goods traded on the basis of a contract to be predetermined. Hence the contract duration was not an element of the decision. In the next step of the analysis we dropped this assumption and showed how decisions about the duration of a contract turn out if it is assumed that transaction costs are following an exponential function, thus diminishing over time. In two decision scenarios we examined how the duration of contracts is expected to change. In the first scenario we assumed that the decision-maker had restricted information about the time-dependent development of transaction costs, deciding on basis of the simple decision rule "change transaction partner as soon as the total costs of changing are smaller than the cumulated gains during the term of the newly signed contract". In the second scenario we assumed that the decision-maker had perfect information about the expected development of transaction costs over time. The simple decision rule was then replaced by a calculation in order to determine points in time at which to change transaction partner resulting in optimized contract duration.

Time-dependent reductions of marginal evaluation costs might result in transaction partner changes. We discovered that these changes are restricted to the period of time in which the costs of changing transaction partner decrease. This period ends in t^* and is longer the higher the rate of cost reductions and the longer the overall period of time in which the traded good is acquired. The number of transaction partner changes which actually occur then depends on the value of potential cost reductions during this period of time. We expect more transaction partner changes to occur, the greater the transaction volume, the smaller the marginal evaluation costs, and the smaller the initialization costs. As the number of transaction partner changes in a given period of time increases, the expected duration of supplier contracts decreases. Replacing the simple decision rule by an optimization of contract duration, we showed that the decision-maker is able to anticipate expected price reductions so that overall fewer transaction partner changes occur and the contract duration is comparatively longer. Furthermore, we stated that incentives for opportunistic behavior decrease during the period until t^* but increase afterwards, because from t^* the expected total costs of the supplier relationship when changing transaction partner increase.

5.1.3 Growing dissemination of information technology and the duration of supplier contracts

In a way analogous to the analysis of the impact of time-dependent cost reductions on the expected contract duration we assumed that the decision-maker applies a simple decision rule to determine when to change transaction partner. Moreover, we assumed that the dissemination of information technology follows an (exogenously given) s-shaped diffusion curve. From the analysis of the stability of supplier relationships we discovered that an increasing dissemination of information technology for the support of the evaluation phase of a supplier relationship has a major impact on the profitability of supplier change. This is because the benefit of using this technology evolves directly from transaction partner change. On the other hand, information technology which supports the settlement phase may be also profitable if used within the current relationship. Indeed, we demonstrated that the alternative of retaining the transaction partner dominates in this setting, so that a change in the diffusion of the information technology that supports the settlement phase has no effect on the stability of a supplier relationship.

On taking a closer look at the information technology which supports the evaluation phase of a supplier relationship, we discovered that, depending on the shape of the diffusion curve, a growing dissemination of this information technology leads to an unstable period of time in which transaction partner changes are likely to occur. The length of this period depends on the initial diffusion of this information technology, the growth rate of its dissemination, and the length of the life-cycle of the traded product. As the shape of the diffusion curve determines how long the unstable period is going to last, the potential cost savings from transaction partner change during this period are also considerably influenced by the marginal evaluation costs, the initialization costs, and the frequency with which the traded goods are exchanged. The smaller the marginal evaluation costs, the smaller the initialization costs, and the greater the frequency, the less stable the supplier relationship is. In any case, since the period of time in which transaction partner changes are likely to happen is smaller than the total period of time in which the traded product is acquired, supplier relationships always end up in a stable period in which no further transaction partner changes occur.

5.1.4 The adoption of new information technology

We have shown that when new information technology for the support of the evaluation phase of a supplier relationship appears on the market, then its adoption depends on the properties of this technology as well as on the properties of the competing solution already established on the market. Properties characteristic of information technology within the scope of our model are implementation costs, marginal evaluation costs, and the dissemination of the technology among potential transaction partners. The new technology is adopted by a purchasing organization if the implementation costs and marginal evaluation costs associated with the use of this technology remain under, or the dissemination of this technology exceeds, a critical value.

Extending the analysis from the relationship of a single organization which wishes to purchase a particular good to all relationships in the market of this good, we used the determination of the critical values of the adoption of technology to draw conclusions concerning the expected market share of the new solution. In this way the diffusion curve of the new information technology becomes endogenous and depends on technology adoption decisions in the market. In terms of the stability of supplier relationships the results derived for the case of an exogenously given diffusion curve remain true.

When considering newly emerging information technology for the support of the settlement phase of a supplier relationship, the adoption of this technology depends on the expected settlement cost reductions which must exceed the implementation costs. Due to the dominance of the alternative of keeping the current supplier over the alternative of adopting the new technology and changing transaction partner, the diffusion of the new technology plays no role in the adoption decision. Assuming that expected settlement cost reductions and implementation costs are specific to the applied information technology but not to the relationship, the expected market share of the new technology depends on the transaction volume underlying each relationship. The new technology is adopted by all purchasing organizations whose transaction volume exceeds a critical value, which is determined by the implementation costs and prospective settlement cost reductions. If dominance does not prevail, however, then the adoption of technology may be associated with transaction partner change. Therefore unstable supplier relationships may occur, and in principle the results connected with the emergence of new information technology for the support of the evaluation phase apply.

Finally, we realized that the progress of information technology in terms of increasing dissemination as well as newly emerging technology is connected with a process of concentration on the supplier side. Transaction partner changes only take place when a supplier who provides lower prices is found. Hence the unstable period of a business relationship in which transaction partner changes take place leads to ever more organizations buying from a continuously reduced set of suppliers. Within the scope of our model, this concentration process can be primarily attributed to the influence of the information technology used in the evaluation phase.

5.2 Implications for the management of supplier relationships

Reviewing the results gained by the analysis of our model, we are able to identify implications for the design of supplier relationships in terms of contract types, contract duration, and investments in supplier integration.

The initial hypothesis of this work is that information technology changes the optimal design of supplier contracts. We analyzed the design of supplier contracts by determining points in time at which it is beneficial for the procuring organization to change supplier. The results have implications for the buyer's contracting strategy. In conditions of progress in information technology, one can expect short contract duration to be beneficial at the beginning of a supplier relationship, until a particular point in time, t^*, is reached. This implies either a series of short-term contracts, a long-term contract with dynamic price adaptation, or a contractual arrangement which can easily be terminated by the purchasing organization at any time. The purpose of this contracting strategy is to secure gains by realizing price reductions due to increasing market transparency. The period of short contract duration is also associated with comparatively low opportunism risk, because due to decreasing costs of the alternative of changing transaction partner the purchasing organization can credibly threaten a change of supplier. Since opportunism risk increases after t^*, it is optimal to keep the current supplier from then on. Furthermore, to rule out opportunism risk in contract renegotiations, a single contract is to be preferred for the total remaining time in which the good is purchased.

When procuring goods, a further dimension of interest concerns the integration of suppliers. Supplier integration means that at the beginning of a supplier relationship investments that are more or less idiosyncratic and which lead in effect to cost reductions during the execution of the relationship are made. These investments can be made with the aim of technical or organizational integration. The issue of supplier integration comprises the two questions about the amount of money that should optimally be spent to integrate the current supplier of a particular good and the point in time at which this should take place. Although this work does not focus on the analysis of these questions, our model is already provided with the relevant parameters which would allow an analysis of these issues, so that implications for the purchasing organizations can be deduced. Indeed, decisions about the use of information technology to support the settlement phase of a supplier relationship can also be interpreted as decisions about the integration of suppliers. Although the analysis of investments in information technology indicates an emphasis on the issue of technical integration, investments in organizational integration are in principle subject to the same determinants. The introduction of information technology in the settlement phase, for example, is often associated with the adaptation of business processes. These costs can be interpreted as a part of the implementation costs. High implementation costs, i.e. high integration in terms of technology and organization, may result in high costs when switching transaction partner. The latter is represented in our model by initialization costs. The use of standardized solutions for supplier integration directly affects not only the initialization costs through prospective cost reductions, but also the evaluation costs when changing transaction partner. Technical integration and organizational integration differ primarily in respect of the degree of standardization. While technical integration is often based on communication standards which are disseminated to some extent, organizational integration can hardly be standardized, although, as we have shown in chapter 3[118], efforts at standardization are also undertaken in respect of the organizational dimension. In terms of our model this distinction becomes manifest in different values for the parameter β, which indicates the dissemination of information technology used in the settlement phase.

The optimal amount of money that should be spent for supplier integration within the scope of our model is determined by the trade-off between prospective settlement cost reductions and losses due to opportunistic behavior of the supplier. Using the indifference condition of standardization derived in section 4.3.3.2.2 we can determine the critical values in accordance with which integration is beneficial for the procuring organization. This is done by comparing implementation costs with settlement cost reductions. The smaller the implementation costs and the greater the settlement cost reductions are, the better it is for the purchasing organization. However there are prospective losses associated with these gains due to increased opportunism risk as the costs of changing transaction partner increase. Losses expected due to opportunistic behavior are greater, the smaller β and the greater the initialization costs. This trade-off indicates the existence of an optimal amount of integration in a supplier relationship. Our model of decisions about supplier relationships and information technology can be used to calculate this amount by measuring prospective losses which are caused by opportunism risk in a particular setting, because at any point in time the cost difference between keeping a transaction partner and changing a supplier can be determined.

Beyond the question about the optimal amount of money spent for integration, the second question concerns the optimal point in time at which supplier integration should take place. A delay of investments in integration opens up prospective gains from supplier change due to the price reductions achieved by supplier change. These gains are balanced by losses, because settlement cost reductions deriving from supplier integration cannot be realized. This trade-off indicates a particular point in time at which supplier integration should optimally be carried out. This point in time is situated between zero and t^* and is earlier, the greater β and the lower the initialization costs when changing transaction partner. Therefore, a delay in supplier integration may be profitable and, tendentially, technical integration is optimally carried out earlier than organizational integration.

Accepting the implications in terms of contract duration and supplier integration, we see that supplier relationships under conditions of progress in information technology and on the assumptions of our model can be characterized by short contract duration and low integration at the beginning. One might describe a

---

[118] Particularly OAGIS, by defining standard integration scenarios for business processes, is an approach going beyond the technical dimension.

relationship with these features as market-like. However, due to advances in information technology a transition towards long-term contracts which is associated with increasing supplier integration can be expected. This type of relationship can also be described as a partnership. The transition only occurs when technology progress is sufficiently great to allow gains by transaction partner change and when the transaction volume is great enough to recoup idiosyncratic investments in supplier integration. Otherwise long-term contracts are the predominant strategy from the very beginning of a procurement relationship.

5.3 Outlook

The model of decisions about supplier relationships and the use of information technology can be used for further analyses which may also require additional extensions to the model. These analyses can be carried out to improve decisions by the procuring organization, but also to support the decisions of information technology providers or suppliers, who may use the knowledge about the purchasing organizations' decisions to adapt their own strategies.

Examples of extensions to the model from the procuring organization's point of view concern the joint examination of decisions about the use of information technology in supplier relationships for the procurement of different goods, the search strategy of the procuring organization, and the consideration of dependencies between information technologies at different levels of a supplier relationship.

A strong assumption in the formulation of our model is that decisions about the supplier relationship for the procurement of a particular good and the information technology used in this relationship are taken to be independent from existing relationships for the procurement of other goods or the information technology used to support the procurement of these goods. Using this assumption we have seen that the network effects of information technology used in the settlement phase are restricted to the activities of supplier search. However, as the procurement of different kinds of goods is simultaneously examined, network effects increase in importance, because implementation costs can then be distributed among a greater number of relationships.

Another assumption concerns price as being the single decision criterion of the procuring organization in supplier search. However, as we have shown, the search model that we used can be easily extended or replaced by more complex search strategies (see section 2.1.5.1.1). In this way the analysis can be extended to cases in which particular combinations of quality and price are sought, or to situations in which the searcher has restricted information in respect of the probability distribution of prices or qualities of the products sought.

The model can be further extended by refining the concept of information technology. In chapter 3 we have shown that information technology and communication standards can be differentiated in terms of the different levels at which it is used. We distinguished, for example, between procurement applications which use communication standards for structuring the communication process that takes place in a supplier relationship. These communication standards can focus on the business process or the technical level, which fall back on standards for structuring the information exchanged over the course of a business process. In a top down view the decision in favor of a particular procurement application may restrict the number of alternatives on the other levels. For example, if one decides to use an OBI compliant application in order to support the procurement of indirect materials, this implies the decision in favor of the use of ANSI X12 for the exchange of purchase orders. On the other hand, seen bottom up, the status quo at a lower level may restrict the decision at higher levels. In other words, solutions based on information technology which has already been implemented in the organization have a cost advantage over solutions which imply major investments in information technology at the other levels. In (Weber 2000) we have shown how these dependencies can be incorporated into decisions about the use of communication standards in principle. A transfer of the results to the circumstances of the model used in this work allows a refined analysis of how information technology is likely to influence supplier relationships.

Finally, from the point of view of information technology providers, those results which allow one to draw conclusions concerning the expected market share of a certain technology are of particular interest. Given the characteristic features of competing products in terms of implementation costs, prospective transaction cost reductions, and installed base, one can determine how much a solution may cost, what prospective savings the adopter should expect from its use, and what initial dissemination is necessary in order to prevail over competing solutions. However, the aim of a technology provider is not necessarily the maximization of market share but rather the maximization of profit. Thus, the model must be extended by the specification of a function which represents the profit of the technology provider which depends on the price paid by the adopter, the expected market share of the solution, and the expected expenditure for marketing activities aimed at reaching a particular initial dissemination of the product.

6 References

AberdeenGroup (1999). Strategic Procurement:The Next Wave of Procurement Automation, Aberdeen Group. **1999**. http://oracle.com/html/stratproc/aberdeenwp.html.

Akerlof, G. A. (1970). "The market for 'lemons': quality uncertainty and the market mechanism." *Quarterly Journal of Economics* **84**: 488-500.

Alchian, A. A. and H. Demsetz (1972). "Production, Information Costs, and Economic Organization." *The American Economic Review*: 777-795.

Allen, C. (1999). WIDL: Application Integration with XML, webMethods. **1999**. http://www.webmethods.com/xml/widl_wp1.html.

Alter, S. (1996). Information Systems: A Management Perspective. Menlo Park, CA, The Benjamin/ Cummings Publishing Company.

Anson, R. G. and M. T. Jelassi (1990). "A development framework for computer-supported conflict resolution." *European Journal of Operational Research* **46**: 181-199.

Arnheim, L. A. (1996). Collaborative Filtering Workshop, School of Information Management & Systems (SIMS), Berkeley. **1999**. http://sims.berkeley.edu/resources/collab/collab-report.html.

Arrow, K. J. (1969). The Organization of Economic Activity: Issues Pertinent to the Choice of Markets versus Nonmarket Allocation. The Analysis and Evaluation of Public Expenditures: The PBB-System, Joint Economic Committee, 91st Congress, 1st Session, Washington D.C.

Bakos, J. Y. and E. Brynjolfsson (1993). "Information Technology, Incentives, and the Optimal Number of Suppliers." *Journal of Management Information Systems* **10**: 37-53.

Baligh (1986). "Decision Rules and Transactions, Organizations and Markets." *Management Science* **32**: 1480-1491.

Baligh, H. H. and L. E. Richartz (1967). "An Analysis of Vertical Market Structures." *Management Science* **10**: 667-689.

Bass, F. M. (1969). "A New Product Growth for Model Consumer Durables." *Management Science* **15**: 215-227.

Bauer, S. (1997). Auswirkungen der Informationstechnologie auf die vertikale Integration von Unternehmen. Frankfurt am Main.

Bauer, S. and E. Stickel (1998). "Auswirkungen der Informationstechnologie auf die Entstehung kooperativer Netzwerkorganisationen." *Wirtschaftsinformatik* **40**: 434-442.

Beam, C. and A. Segev (1997). "Automated Negotiations: A Survey of the State of the Art." *Wirtschaftsinformatik* **39**: 263-268.

Beam, C., A. Segev, et al. (1996). Electronic Negotiation through Internet-based Auctions, CITM. http://www.haas.berkeley.edu/~citm/WP-1019.PDF.

Benjamin, R. I. and J. Blunt (1992). "Critical IT Issues: The Next Ten Years." *Sloan Management Review*: 7-19.

Berge, J. (1989). EDIFACT - a technical introduction. EDI technology. M. Gifkins. London, U. K., Blenheim Online: 63-78.

Blouin, M. R. and R. Serrano (1998). A Decentralized Market with Common Values Uncertainty: Non-Steady States. Providence, Richmond, Brown University. http://econ.pstc.brown.edu/wp98/pdfs/98-5.pdf.

Born, A. (1998). "Kettenspiele - Supply Chain Management: optimierte Lieferketten." *iX* **1998**: 68-71.

Bosak, J. (1997). XML, Java and the future of the Web. http://sunsite.unc.edu/pub/suninfo/standards/xml/why/xmlapps.html.

Bössmann, E. (1982). "Volkswirtschaftliche Probleme der Transaktionskosten." *Zeitschrift für die gesamte Staatswissenschaft*: 664-679.

Bretzke, W.-R. (1994). "Make or Buy" von Logistikdienstleistungen: Erfolgskriterien für eine Fremdvergabe logistischer Dienstleistungen. Logistik - Beschaffung, Produktion, Distribution. H. Isermann. Landsberg/Lech: 321-330.

Brynjolfsson, E., T. W. Malone, et al. (1994). "Does Information Technology Lead to Smaller Firms?" *Management Science* **40**: 1628-1644.

Buxmann, P. (1996). Standardisierung betrieblicher Informationssysteme. Wiesbaden.

Buxmann, P. and J. Gebauer (1999). Evaluating the Use of Information Technology in Inter-Organizational Relationships. 32nd Hawaii International Conference on System Sciences (HICCS), Maui, Hawaii.

Buxmann, P., T. Weitzel, et al. (1998). Erfolgsfaktor Standard: Internet-basierte Kooperationen mit WebEDI und XML/EDI. Kooperationsnetze und Elektronische Koordination, Frankfurt am Main.

Buxmann, P., F. Westarp, et al. (1998). Centralized vs. Decentralized Decisions on Software Standards in Enterprises - Results of an Empirical Study. Frankfurt am Main, Sonderforschungsbereich 403.

Chavez, A. and P. Maes (1996). Kasbah: An Agent Marketplace for Buying and Selling Goods. First International Conference on the Practical Application of Intelligent Agents and Multi-Agent Technology, London.

Chou, C. and O. Shy (1990). "Network Effects without Network Externalities." *International Journal of Industrial Organization* **8**: 259-270.

Christopher, M. (1992). Logistics: the strategic issue. London.

Church, J. and N. Gandal (1992). "Network Effects, Software Provision, and Standardization." *Journal of Industrial Economics* **40**: 85-103.

Church, J. and N. Gandal (1993). "Complementary Network Externalities and Technological Adoption." *International Journal of Industrial Organization* **11**: 239-260.

Clemons, E. K. and S. P. Reddi (1994). The Impact of IT on the Degree of Outsourcing, the Number of Suppliers, and the Duration of Contracts. 27th Hawaii International Conference on System Sciences (HICSS).

Clemons, E. K., S. P. Reddi, et al. (1993). "The Impact of Information Technology on the Organization of Economic Activity: The "Move to the Middle" Hypothesis." *Journal of Management Information Systems* **10**: 9-35.

Coase, R. H. (1937). "The Nature of the Firm." *Economica* **4**: 386-405.

ContingencyAnalysis (1998). Lognormal Distribution, Contingency Analysis. **2000**.
http://www.contingencyanalysis.com/glossarylognormaldistribution.htm.

Crow, D. A. and H. Wildemann (1988). Die deutsche Automobilindustrie - Ein Blick in die Zukunft. Frankfurt am Main, Arthur Andersen.

Davenport, T. E. and J. E. Short (1990). "The New Industrial Engineering - Information Technology and Business Process Redesign." *Sloan Management Review* **31**: 11-27.

Degroot, M. H. (1970). Optimal Statistical Decisions. New York, McGraw-Hill.

Dolmetsch, R., E. Fleisch, et al. (1999). "Desktop-Purchasing: I-Net-Technologien in der Beschaffung." *HMD* **1999**: 77-89.

Eller, R. and H.-P. Deutsch (1998). Derivate und Interne Modelle: Modernes Risikomanagement. Stuttgart, Schäffer-Poeschel.

Emmelhainz, M. A. (1993). EDI: A Total Management Guide. New York.

EURIDIS (1999a). Background: Open-EDI, Erasmus University Research Institute for Decision and Information Systems (EURIDIS). **1999**.
http://abduction.euridis.fbk.eur.nl/projects/weboutline/Web.OpenEDI.html.

EURIDIS (1999b). Electronic Trade Procedures, Erasmus University Research Institute for Decision and Information Systems (EURIDIS). **1999**.
http://abduction.euridis.fbk.eur.nl/projects/weboutline/Web.EProcs.html.

EURIDIS (1999c). Sharing of Trade Procedures among Contracting Parties, Erasmus University Research Institute for Decision and Information Systems (EURIDIS). **1999**. http://abduction.euridis.fbk.eur.nl/projects/weboutline/Web.EProc.Coordination.html.

EURIDIS (1999d). InterProcs: A Prototyping Environment for Electronic Trade Procedures, Erasmus University Research Institute for Decision and Information Systems (EURIDIS). **1999**. http://abduction.euridis.fbk.eur.nl/projects/weboutline/Web.InterProcs.Intro.html.

EURIDIS (1999e). Documentary Petri Nets (DPN): A Formal Representation for Electronic Trade Procedures, Erasmus University Research Institute for Decision and Information Systems (EURIDIS). **1999**. http://abduction.euridis.fbk.eur.nl/projects/weboutline/Web.DPN.html.

Farrell, J. and N. T. Gallini (1988). "Second-Sourcing as a Commitment: Monopoly Incentives to Attract Competition." *Quarterly Journal of Economics* **103**: 673-694.

Farrell, J. and G. Saloner (1986a). "Installed Base and Compatibility: Innovation, Product Preannouncements and Predation." *American Economic Review* **76**: 940-955.

Farrell, J. and G. Saloner (1986b). "Standardization and Variety." *Economics Letters* **20**: 71-74.

Farrell, J. and G. Saloner (1987). Competition, compatibility and standards: the economics of horses, penguins and lemmings. Product standardization and competitive strategy. H. L. Gabel. Amsterdam: 1-21.

Farrell, J. and G. Saloner (1992). "Converters, Compatibility, and the Control of Interfaces." *Journal of Industrial Economics* **40**: 9-35.

Fearon, H. E. and B. Bales (1997). Measures of Purchasing Effectiveness, Center for Advanced Purchasing Studies (CAPS). http://www.capsresearch.org/.

Ferschl, F. (1975). Nutzen- und Entscheidungstheorie. Opladen, Westdeutscher Verlag.

Fischer, M. (1993). Make-or-Buy-Entscheidungen im Marketing - Neue Institutionenlehre und Distributionspolitik. Wiesbaden, Gabler.

Foroughi, A. (1995). "A Survey of the Use of Computer Support for Negotiation." *The Journal of Applied Business Research* **11**: 121-134.

Fulk, J. and B. Boyd (1991). "Emerging Theories of Communication in Organizations." *Journal of Management* **17**: 407-446.

Gastwirth, J. L. (1976). "On Probabilistic Models of Consumer Search for Information." *Quarterly Journal of Economics* **90**: 38-50.

Gebauer, J., C. Beam, et al. (1998). Use of Emerging Technologies in Procurement - State of the Art and a Look into the Future. 9th International Conference of the Information Resource Management Association (IRMA 1998).

Geihs, K. (1995). Client/Server-Systeme: Grundlagen und Architekturen. Bonn.

Gifkins, M., Ed. (1990). EDI technology. London, Blenheim Online.

Good, N., J. B. Schafer, et al. (1999). Collaborative Filtering with Personal Agents for Better Recommendations. Conference of the American Association of Artificial Intelligence (AAAI-99), Orlando, Florida.

Grant, R. (1987). The Effects of Product Standardization on Competition: Octane Grading of Petrol in the UK. Product standardization and competitive strategy. H. L. Gabel. Amsterdam: 283-302.

Grossman, S. J. and O. D. Hart (1986). "The Costs and Benefits of Ownership: A Theory of Vertical and Lateral Integration." *Journal of Political Economy* **94**: 691-717.

Gurbaxani, V. and S. Whang (1991). "The Impact of Information Technology on Organizations and Markets." *Communications of the ACM* **34**: 59-73.

Guttman, R., A. Moukas, et al. (1998). "Agent-mediated Electronic Commerce: A Survey." *Knowledge Engineering Review* **13**.

Hansen, R. (1988). "Auctions with Endogenous Quantity." *Rand Journal of Economics* **19**.

Hart, O. and J. Moore (1990). "Property Rights and the Nature of the Firm." *Journal of Political Economy* **98**: 1119-1158.

Hart, O. D. (1988). "Incomplete contracts and the theory of the firm." *Journal of Law, Economics and Organization*: 119-139.

Heinritz, S. F., P. V. Farrell, et al. (1986). Purchasing: Principles and Applications. Englewood Cliffs, NJ, Prentice-Hall.

Hey, J. D. (1979a). Uncertainty in Microeconomics. Oxford, Martin Robertson & Company Ltd.

Hey, J. D. (1979b). "A Note on Consumer Search and Consumer Surplus." *Bulletin of Economic Research* **31**: 61-66.

Hey, J. D. (1981). Economics in Disequilibrium. Oxford.

Hey, J. D. and P. J. Lambert, Eds. (1987). Surveys in the Economics of Uncertainty. New York, Basil Blackwell Inc.

Hey, J. D. and C. J. McKenna (1981). "Consumer Search with Uncertain Product Quality." *Journal of Political Economy* **89**: 54-66.

Hillier, F. S. and G. J. Lieberman (1995). Introduction to operations research. New York, NY, McGraw-Hill.

Hodges, H. G. (1961). Procurement: The Modern Science of Purchasing. New York, Harper & Brothers Publishers.

Hoff, A. v., H. Partovi, et al. (1997). Specification for the Open Software Description (OSD), Microsoft. **1999**. http://www.w3.org/TR/NOTE-OSD.html.

Holzner, S. (1998). XML Complete. New York, NY, McGraw-Hill.

Hough, H. E. and J. M. Ashley (1992). Handbook of Buying and Purchasing. Paramus, N. J., Prentice Hall.

InterNeg (1998). INSPIRE: InterNeg Support Program for Intercultural Research, InterNeg. **1999**. http://interneg.carleton.ca/inspire.

Isermann, H. and M. Kaupp (1996). Logistikkompetenz als Erfolgsfaktor für Speditionen. Jahrbuch der Güterverkehrswirtschaft. F. S. u. L. d. V. i. Hessen. Frankfurt am Main.

ISO/IEC (1997). ISO/IEC 14662:1997(E) Information Technologies - Open-edi reference model, ISO/IEC. http://www.disa.org/international/sc30tag.htm.

Janko, W. H., A. Taudes, et al. (1993). Simultane Datenpräzisierung und Alternativensuche. Wien, Wirtschaftsuniversität Wien. http://wwwai.wu-wien.ac.at/Publikationen/Janko/paper/alternativensuche/paper.html.

Jelassi, M. T. and B. H. Jones (1988). Getting to Yes with NSS: How Computers Can Support Negotiations. Organizational Decision Support Systems. R. M. Lee, A. M. McCosh and P. Migliarese. Amsterdam, North-Holland: 75-85.

Johnston, R. and P. R. Lawrence (1988). "Beyond Vertical Integration - the Rise of the Value-Adding Partnership." *Harvard Business Review*: 94-101.

Kaas, K. and M. Fischer (1993). "Der Transaktionskostenansatz." *Wirtschaftsstudium* 22: 686-693.

Karni, E. and A. Schwartz (1977). "Search theory: The case of search with uncertain recall." *Journal of Economic Theory* 16: 38-52.

Katz, M. L. and C. Shapiro (1985). "Nework Externalities, Competition, and Compatibility." *The American Economic Review* 75: 424-440.

Keller, A. M. (1997). Smart Catalogs and Virtual Catalogs. Readings in Electronic Commerce. R. Kalakota and A. Whinston, Addison-Wesley.

Kerridge, S., A. Slade, et al. (1998). "SUPPLYPOINT: Electronic Procurement using Virtual Supply Chains." *Electronic Markets* 8: 28-31.

Kilian, W. (1994). Electronic Data Interchange (EDI). Baden-Baden.

Killen, K. H. and J. W. Kamauff (1995). Managing Purchasing - Making the Supply Team Work. New York, McGraw-Hill.

Killen&Associates (1997). Operating Resources Management: How Enterprises can make money by reducing MRO costs. Palo Alto, CA, Killen & Associates.

Kindleberger, C. P. (1983). "Standards as Public, Collective and Private Goods." *Kyklos* 36: 377-396.

Klein, S. (1997). "Introduction to Electronic Auctions." *International Journal of Electronic Markets* 7: 3-6.

Kleinemeyer, J. (1998). Standardisierung zwischen Kooperation und Wettbewerb. Frankfurt am Main, Peter Lang, Europäischer Verlag der Wissenschaften.

Klemperer, P. (1987a). "The competitiveness of markets with switching costs." *Rand Journal of Economics* 18: 138-150.

Klemperer, P. (1987b). "Markets with consumer switching costs." *Quarterly Journal of Economics* 102: 375-394.

Klemperer, P. (1989). "Price Wars Caused by Switching Costs." *Review of Economic Studies* 56: 405-420.

Klemperer, P. (1992). "Equilibrium Product Lines: Competing Head-to-Head May Be Less Competitive." *American Economic Review* 82: 740-755.

Knetsch, W. (1996). Die treibenden Kräfte: Der Weg zum vernetzten Unternehmen. Management im vernetzten Unternehmen. A. D. Little. Wiesbaden, Gabler: 15-72.

Knolmayer, G. F. (1993). Modelle zur Unterstützung von Outsourcing-Entscheidungen. Wirtschaftsinformatik '93. K. Kurbel. Heidelberg: 70-83.

König, W., H. Rommelfanger, et al., Eds. (1999). Taschenbuch der Wirtschaftsinformatik und Wirtschaftsmathematik. Frankfurt am Main, Verlag Harri Deutsch.

Kreis, R. (1993). Handbuch der Betriebswirtschaftslehre. München.

Kushmerick, N., D. Weld, et al. (1997). Wrapper Induction for Information Extraction. 10th International Conference on Artificial Intelligence (IJCAI).

Landsberger, M. and D. Peled (1977). "Duration of offers, price structure and the gain from search." *Journal of Economic Theory* **16**: 17-37.

Laux, H. (1995). Entscheidungstheorie. Berlin, Springer.

Lazerson, M. H. (1988). "Organizational growth of small firms: An outcome of markets and hierarchies?" *American Sociological Review* **53**: 330-342.

Lee, L. and D. W. Dobler (1971). Purchasing and Materials Management: Text and Cases. New York, McGraw-Hill.

Lee, R. M. (1998). "Towards Open Electronic Contracting." *Electronic Markets* **8**: 3-8.

Lee, R. M. (1999). InterProcs Designer: A CASE Tool for Designing Electronic Trade Procedures.

Macneil, I. R. (1978). "Contracts: Adjustment of Long-Term Economic Relations under Classical, Neoclassical and Relational Contract Law." *Northwestern University Law Review* **72**: 854-905.

MacQueen, J. B. (1964). "Optimal Policies for a Class of Search and Evaluation Problems." *Management Science* **10**: 746-759.

Mahajan, V. and R. A. Peterson (1985). Models for Innovation Diffusion. Newbury Park.

Malone, T. W., J. Yates, et al. (1987). "Electronic Markets and Electronic Hierarchies." *Communications of the ACM* **30**: 484-497.

Mardesich, J. (1996). Onsale takes auction gavel electronic. Computer Reseller News. http://www.crn.com/print-archive/19960708/691news008.asp.

Mattes, F. (1999). Electronic Business-to-Business: E-Commerce mit Internet und EDI. Stuttgart, Schaeffer-Poeschel.

McAfee, R. P. and J. McMillan (1987). "Auctions and Bidding." *Journal of Economic Literature* **25**: 699-738.

McCall, J. J. (1965). "The Economics of Information and Optimal Stopping Rules." *Journal of Business* **38**: 300-317.

McKenna, C. J. (1987). Theories of Individual Search Behaviour. Surveys in the Economics of Uncertainty. J. D. Hey and P. J. Lambert. New York, Basil Blackwell Inc.: 91-109.

Mendenhall, W., R. L. Schaeffer, et al. (1981). Mathematical Statistics with Applications. Boston, MA, Duxbury Press.

Merrick, P. and C. Allen (1997). Web Interface Definition Language (WIDL), webMethods. 1999. http://www.w3.org/TR/NOTE-widl-970922.html.

Mertens, P. (1988). Industrielle Datenverarbeitung. Wiesbaden.

Mertens, P., F. Bodendorf, et al. (1998). Grundzüge der Wirtschaftsinformatik. Berlin.

Mertens, P. and J. Griese (1991). Integrierte Informationsverarbeitung. Wiesbaden.

Michaelis, E. (1985). Organisation unternehmerischer Aufgaben - Transaktionskosten als Beurteilungskriterium. Frankfurt, Bern, New York.

Milgrom, P. (1989). "Auctions and Bidding: A Primer." *Journal of Economic Perspectives* **3**: 3-22.

Milgrom, P. and J. Roberts (1992). Economics, Organization, and Management. Englewood Cliffs, NJ, Prentice-Hall.

Minahan, T. A. (1999). Intelisys Model Leverages Open Standards to Broaden Participation in Internet Procurement Communities, Aberdeen Group. 1999. http://www.aberdeen.com/cgi-bin/rf.cgi?doc_id=07991540.

Monteverde, K. and D. J. Teece (1982). "Supplier switching costs and vertical integration in the automobile industry." *Bell Journal of Economics* **12**: 206-213.

Moukas, A., R. Guttman, et al. (1998). Agent-mediated Electronic Commerce: An MIT Media Laboratory Perspective. International Conference on Electronic Commerce (ICEC '98), Seoul.

Nash, J. F. (1950). "The Bargaining Problem." *Econometrica* **19**: 155-162.

Nash, J. F. (1953). "Two-Person Cooperative Games." *Econometrica* **21**: 128-140.

Nelson, P. (1970). "Information and Consumer Behaviour." *Journal of Political Economy* **78**: 311-329.

Nenninger, M. and M. H. Gerst (1999). Wettbewerbsvorteile durch Electronic Procurement - Strategien, Konzeption und Realisierung. Management-Handbuch Electronic Commerce. S. Hermanns and M. Sauter. Munich.

Neo, B. S. (1992). "The Implementation of an Electronic Market for Pig Trading in Singapore." *Journal of Strategic Information systems* **1**: 278-288.

Neuburger, R. (1994). Electronic Data Interchange: Einsatzmöglichkeiten und ökonomische Auswirkungen. Wiesbaden, Gabler.

Niggl, J. (1994). Die Entstehung von Electronic Data Interchange Standards. Wiesbaden, Germany.

Noordewier, T. G. (1989). "A Comparison of Blanket and Systems Contracts." *Journal of Purchasing and Materials Management*: 35-40.

OAG (1998). OAGIS: Open Applications Group Integration Specification, release 6.1, Open Applications Group (OAG).

Oberlack, H. G. (1989). Handelshemmnisse durch Produktstandards: Ökonomische Aspekte ihrer Beseitigung. Hamburg.

OBI-Consortium (1999). Open Buying on the Internet (OBI): Technical Specifications: Release V2.0, OBI-Consortium. http://www.openbuy.org.

O'Neal, C. R. (1989). "JIT procurement and relationship marketing." *Industrial Marketing Management* 18: 55-63.

Onsale (1999). Auction Process, Onsale. **1999**. http://www.onsale.com/howto/process.htm.

Orlov, L. M. (1999). Oracle Leads SAP To Procurement Apps. Cambridge, MA, Forrester Research, Inc. http://www.oracle.com/applications/internetprocurement/forrester.pdf.

OTP-Consortium (1998). Internet Open Trading Protocol. http://www.otp.org.

Parsons, S., C. Sierra, et al. (1998). "Agents that reason and negotiate by arguing." *Journal of Logic and Computation* 8: 261-292.

Perlman, K. I. (1990). Handbook of Purchasing and Materials Management. Chicago, Probus Publishing.

Pfeffer, J. and G. R. Salincik (1978). The External Control of Organizations: A Resource Dependence Perspective. New York.

Picot, A. (1982). "Transaktionskostenansatz in der Organisationstheorie: Stand der Diskussion und Aussagenwert." *Die Betriebswirtschaft* 42: 267-284.

Picot, A. (1991). "Ein neuer Ansatz zur Gestaltung der Leistungstiefe." *Zeitschrift für betriebswirtschaftliche Forschung* 43: 336-357.

Picot, A. and H. Dietl (1990). "Transaktionskostentheorie." *Wirtschaftswissenschaftliches Studium* 19: 178-184.

Picot, A., R. Reichwald, et al. (1996). Die grenzenlose Unternehmung. Wiesbaden.

Porter, M. E. (1980). Competitive Strategy: Techniques for Analyzing Industries and Competitors. New York, The Free Press.

Porter, M. E. (1985). Competitive Advantage: Creating and Sustaining Superior Performance. New York, The Free Press.

Pruitt, D. G. (1983). Achieving Integrative Agreements. Negotiating in Organizations. M. H. Bazerman and R. J. Lewicki. Beverly Hills, CA, Sage Publications.

Purchasing (1999). Buyers' guide to software for purchasing, Purchasing Online. **1999**. http://www.manufacturing.net/magazine/purchasing/archives/1999/pur0715.99/071comp.htm.

Rawlins, M. C. (1998). Future EDI: An Overview of Emerging Technologies Which Might Replace X12 and EDIFACT. **1998**. http://www.metro-net.com/~rawlins/future.html.

Reck, M. (1997). "Trading-Process Characteristics of Electronic Auctions." *EM - Electronic Markets* 7: 17-23.

Reekers, N. and S. Smithson (1994). The Impact of Electronic Data Interchange on Interorganizational Relationships: Integrating Theoretical Perspectives. Hawaii International Conference on System Sciences (HICCS), Wailea, Maui, Hawaii.

Rennings, K., M. Fonger, et al. (1992). Make or Buy: Transaktionskostentheorie als Entscheidungshilfe für die Verkehrswirtschaft. Göttingen.

Resnick, P., N. Iacovou, et al. (1994). GroupLens: An open architecture for collaborative filtering of netnews. Computer Supported Collaborative Work Conference.

Rose, F. (1999). The Economics, Concept, and Design of Information Intermediaries. Heidelberg, Germany, Physica-Verlag.

Rothschild, M. (1974). "Searching for the lowest price when the distribution of prices is unknown." *Journal of Political Economy* 82: 689-711.

Rothschild, M. and J. E. Stiglitz (1970). "Increasing risk: 1. A definition." *Journal of Economic Theory* 2: 225-243.

Rowley, J. E. (1992). Organizing Knowledge. Aldershot, England, Ashgate.

Scheer, A.-W. (1990). CIM: der computergestützte Industriebetrieb. Würzburg.

Schmid, B. (1993). "Elektronische Märkte." *Wirtschaftsinformatik* 35: 465-480.

Schneeweiß, H. (1966). "Das Grundmodell der Entscheidungstheorie." *Statistische Hefte* 7: 125-137.

Segev, A., J. Gebauer, et al. (1998). Procurement in the Internet Age - Current Practices and Emerging Trends (Results From a Field Study). Berkeley, CA., USA, Fisher Center for Management and Information Technology, Haas School of Business, University of California, Berkeley.

Segev, A., J. Porra, et al. (1999). "Internet-Based EDI Strategy." *Forthcoming in Decision Support Systems*.

Shapiro, C. (1983). "Premiums for High Quality Products as Rents to Reputation." *Quarterly Journal of Economics*.

Shepard, A. (1987). "Licencing to Enhance Demand for New Technologies." *Rand Journal of Economics* 18: 360-368.

Simon, H. A. (1976). Administrative Behavior: A Study of Decision-Making Processes in Administrative Organization. New York, London.

Stair, R. M. and G. W. Reynolds (1998). Principles of Information Systems: A Managerial Approach. Cambridge, Mass., Course Technology.

Stigler, G. J. (1961). "The Economics of Information." *The Journal of Political Economy* 69: 213-225.

Swann, G. (1987). Industry Standard Microprcessors and the Strategy of Second-Source Production. Product Standardization and Competitive Strategy. L. Gabel. Amsterdam: 239-262.

Sydow, J. (1992). Strategische Netzwerke: Evolution und Organisation. Wiesbaden, Gabler.

Telser, L. G. (1973). "Searching for the Lowest Price." *Economics of Information* **63**: 40-49.

Thum, M. (1995). Netzwerkeffekte, Standardisierung und staatlicher Regelungsbedarf. Tübingen, J. C. B. Mohr (Paul Siebeck).

Tietzel, M. (1981). "Die Ökonomie der Property Rights: Ein Überblick." *Zeitschrift für Wirtschaftspolitik* **30**: 207-243.

Tucker, M. J. (1997). EDI and the Net: A profitable partnering, Datamation. **1999**. http://www.datamation.com/PlugIn/issues/1997/april/04ecom.html.

Turban, E. (1997). "Auctions and Bidding on the Internet: An Assessment." *International Journal of Electronic Markets* **7**: 7-11.

Tversky, A. and D. Kahneman (1981). "The Framing of Decisions and the Psychology of Choice." *Science* **211**: 453-458.

Valente, T. W. (1995). Network models of the diffusion of innovations. Cresskill, NJ, Hampton Press.

van Heck, E., E. van Damme, et al. (1997). New Entrants and the Role of Information Technology: A Case Study of the Tele-Flower Auction in the Netherlands. 30th Annual Hawaii International Conference on System Sciences (HICCS), Hawaii.

Varian, H. (1995). Economic Mechanism Design for Computerized Agents. USENIX Workshop on Electronic Commerce, New York.

Vickrey, W. (1961). "Counterspeculation, Auctions, and Competitive Sealed Tenders." *Journal of Finance* **16**: 8-37.

Vogelmann, H. (1997). Konzeption und Implementierung eines wissensbasierten Systems zur Akquisitionsunterstützung für den Outsourcing-Markt. Regensburg.

Vries, H. d. (1996). Standardization - What's in a name? EURAS-Conference: Standards and Society, Stockholm.

W3C (1998a). Extensible Style Language (XSL), World Wide Web Consortium. http://www.w3.org/Style/XSL/.

W3C (1998b). The Extensible Markup Language (XML) 1.0, World Wide Web Consortium. http://www.w3.org/TR/1998/REC-xml-19980210.html.

W3C (1998c). Web Style Sheets, World Wide Web Consortium. http://www.w3.org/Style/.

Wagner, R. (1994). Die Grenzen der Unternehmung - Beiträge zur ökonomischen Theorie der Unternehmung. Darmstadt.

Wales, M. G. (1999). "WIDL: Interface Definition for the Web." *IEEE Internet Computing* 3.

Walker, G. and D. Weber (1984). "A Transaction Cost Approach to Make-or-Buy Decisions." *Administrative Science Quarterly* 29: 373-391.

Weber, S. (2000). Decisions on Information Technology Standards Considering Technological Dependencies. Frankfurt am Main, Sonderforschungsbereich 403.

Webopaedia (1996c). ISO 9000, Webopaedia. 1999. http://webopedia.internet.com/TERM/I/ISO_9000.html.

Webopaedia (1999a). Moore's Law, Webopaedia. 1999. http://webopaedia.internet.com/TERM/M/Moores_Law.html.

Webopaedia (1999b). ATM, Webopaedia. 1999. http://webopedia.internet.com/TERM/A/ATM.html.

Wedekind, H. (1975). Datenorganisation. Berlin.

Wegehenkel, L. (1981). Gleichgewicht, Transaktionskosten und Evolution. Tübingen.

Weitzel, T., P. Buxmann, et al. (1998). XML: Konzept und Anwendung der Extensible Markup Language. Frankfurt am Main, Sonderforschungsbereich 403. http://caladan.wiwi.uni-frankfurt.de/iwi/projectb3/deu/publikat/xml/.

Weizsäcker, C. C. v. (1984). "The Costs of Substitution." *Econometrica* 52: 1085-1116.

Westarp, F. and O. Wendt (2000). Diffusion Follows Structure - A Network Model of the Software Market. 33rd Hawaii International Conference on System Sciences (HICSS), Hawaii.

Westarp, F. v., S. Weber, et al. (1997). Communication Services Supplied by Intermediaries in Information Networks: The EDI Example. Frankfurt am Main, Sonderforschungsbereich 403.

Westarp, F. v., T. Weitzel, et al. (1999). The Status Quo and the Future of EDI - Results of an Empirical Study. European Conference on Information Systems (ECIS), Copenhagen.

Wilde, L. L. (1980). "On the Optimal Theory of Inspection and Evaluation in Product Markets." *Econometrica* 48: 1265-1279.

Williamson (1985). The Economic Institutions of Capitalism: Firms, Markets, Relational Contracting. London, Free Press.

Williamson, O. E. (1975). Markets and Hierarchies: Analysis and Antitrust Implications. A Study in the Economics of Internal Organization. London.

Williamson, O. E. (1991). The Logic of Economic Organization. The Nature of the Firm. O. E. Williamson. New York, Oxford: 90-116.

Williamson, O. E. and S. E. Masten, Eds. (1995). Transaction Cost Economics. Aldershot, Hants, Edgar Elgar Publishing Ltd.

Windsperger, J. (1983). "Transaktionskosten in der Theorie der Firma." *Zeitschrift für Betriebswirtschaft*: 889-903.

Windsperger, J. (1996). Transaktionskostenansatz der Entstehung der Unternehmensorganisation. Heidelberg.

Wolff, B. (1994). Organisation durch Verträge. Wiesbaden.

Wolfram, S. (1999). The Mathematica Book. Cambridge.

Wurman, P. R., W. E. Walsh, et al. (1998). "Flexible Double Auctions for Electronic Commerce: Theory and Implementation." *Decision Support Systems* **24**: 17-27.

Wurman, P. R., M. P. Wellman, et al. (1998). The Michigan Internet AuctionBot: A Configurable Auction Server for Human and Software Agents. Second International Conference on Autonomous Agents (Agents-98), Minneapolis, MN.

Zenz, G. J. (1994). Purchasing and the Management of Materials. New York, John Wiley & Sons.

7 Appendices

7.1 Appendix A: proof of (eq. 35)

Applying integration by parts to (eq. 35) we obtain

$$\text{(eq. 152)} \quad R(p^*) = \frac{vol\left[p^* F(p^*) - \int_0^{p^*} F(p)dp \right] + c}{F(p^*)}$$

which can be transformed to receive

$$\text{(eq. 153)} \quad R(p^*) = \frac{vol\, p^* F(p^*) - vol \int_0^{p^*} F(p)dp + c}{F(p^*)}.$$

Since the term $-vol \int_0^{p^*} F(p)dp + c$ is equivalent to our indifference condition

(eq. 24) it evaluates to zero and we receive

$$\text{(eq. 154)} \quad R(p^*) = \frac{vol\, p^* F(p^*)}{F(p^*)} = vol\, p^*.$$

7.2 Appendix B: proof of non-negative values of (eq. 63)

To verify whether (eq. 63) can be negative it is sufficient to show that the sum of the first two terms on the right-hand side of (eq. 63) is at least zero, i.e.

$$(eq.\ 155)\quad p^* - \frac{c}{vol\ F(p^*)} \geq 0.$$

Transforming (eq. 155) yields

$$(eq.\ 156)\quad vol\ p^* \geq \frac{c}{F(p^*)}.$$

The resulting formulation is familiar from (eq. 35) and (eq. 30). Substitution leads to

$$(eq.\ 157)\quad AC + EC \geq EC$$

from which it is obvious that it is always fulfilled.

7.3 Appendix C: proof of (eq. 80)

If a simultaneous change in vol and c lets the indifference price p_k^* unchanged, then the total differential

$$(eq.\ 158)\quad dp_k^* = \frac{\partial p_k^*}{\partial vol} dvol + \frac{\partial p_k^*}{\partial c} dc = 0$$

must solve for zero. Solving for $\dfrac{dc}{dvol}$ leads to the marginal rate of substitution for c and vol

$$(eq.\ 159)\quad \frac{dc}{dvol} = -\frac{\dfrac{\partial p_k^*}{\partial vol}}{\dfrac{\partial p_k^*}{\partial c}} = \frac{\dfrac{1}{vol^2}\left(\dfrac{c}{F(p^*)} + inc\right)}{\dfrac{1}{vol\ F(p^*)}}$$

where the numerator and denominator of the third term are taken from (eq. 78) and (eq. 73) respectively. Simplifying this term leads to (eq. 80).

7.4 Appendix D: proof of (eq. 108)

Reducing (eq. 104) to higher terms and forming the sum of (eq. 104) and (eq. 107) while neglecting implementation costs leads to

$$(eq.\ 160)\quad R(p^*_{i,j}) = \frac{\alpha_i \beta_j vol\left[p^*_{i,j}F(p^*_{i,j}) - \int\limits_0^{p^*_{i,j}} F(p)dp \right] + c_i}{\alpha_i \beta_j F(p^*_{i,j})}.$$

which can be transformed to receive

$$(eq.\ 161)\quad R(p^*_{i,j}) = \frac{\alpha_i \beta_j vol\, p^*_{i,j}F(p^*_{i,j}) - \alpha_i \beta_j vol \int\limits_0^{p^*_{i,j}} F(p)dp + c_i}{\alpha_i \beta_j F(p^*_{i,j})}.$$

The term $\alpha_i \beta_j volume \int\limits_0^{p^*_{i,j}} F(p)dp - c_i$ is equivalent to our modified indifference condition (eq. 105) and evaluates to zero. Additional transformation results in

$$(eq.\ 162)\quad R(p^*_{i,j}) = \frac{\alpha_i \beta_j vol\, p^*_{i,j}F(p^*_{i,j})}{\alpha_i \beta_j F(p^*_{i,j})} = vol\, p^*_{i,j}.$$

7.5 Appendix E: proof of (eq. 130)

From (eq. 124) and (eq. 108) while abstaining from implementation costs we can formulate p_c as

$$(eq.\ 163)\quad p_c = \frac{AC_{i,j}}{vol(t)} = p^*_{i,j} - \frac{c_i}{vol(t)\alpha_i(t)\beta_j F(p^*_{i,j})}.$$

To form the derivation of (eq. 163) in respect of t the result from (eq. 128) can be used to determine the partial derivation of $p_{i,j}{}^*$. After deriving the last term of (eq. 163) and factoring out we receive

(eq. 164)

$$\frac{\partial p_c}{\partial t} = \frac{c_i^2 f(p_{i,j}^*)\left(1 + \frac{1-\alpha_{i,0}}{\alpha_{i,0}} e^{-b_i t}\left[1 - b_i(T-t)\right]\right)\left(1 + \frac{1-\alpha_{i,0}}{\alpha_{i,0}} e^{-b_i t}\right)}{frq^2 (T-t)^3 \beta_j F(p_{i,j}^*)^3}.$$

Since the first factor in brackets in the numerator of (eq. 164) equals the expression of (eq. 128) which we used to determine t^*, the first-order conditions based on (eq. 164) and (eq. 128) solve for the same value of t.

8 List of Figures

Figure 1: The value chain of an organization.. Source: (Porter 1985, p. 37) 13

Figure 2: Phases of a supplier relationship. 25

Figure 3: Phases of a supplier relationship – detailed view. 26

Figure 4: Search strategy when observing the single attribute X. 29

Figure 5: Graphic determination of the optimal reservation value, following (Hey 1981, p. 63, Figure 5.1). 29

Figure 6: Graphic determination of the optimal reservation price, following (Hey 1981, p. 114, Figure 7.1). 30

Figure 7: Sampling in a two-stage search process for quality and price, following (Rose 1999, p. 93, Figure 12). 35

Figure 8: Efficient frontier of contracts between two parties, following (Jelassi and Jones 1988). 37

Figure 9: Different notions of "frequency". 49

Figure 10: Efficient governance. Source: (Williamson 1985, p. 79, Figure 3-2) 56

Figure 11: The importance of selected factors for decisions on software. Source: (Westarp and Wendt 2000, Figure 2) 65

Figure 12: Static communication network environment of consumer A, following (Westarp and Wendt 2000, Figure 3). 67

Figure 13: Dynamic communication network environment of consumer A. 68

Figure 14: Application software based on EDI-system, following (Mattes 1999, p. 98). 75

Figure 15: Communication standards used in procurement applications and supporting services. 76

Figure 16: Product page for an Onsale auction of a computer mass storage device. Source: http://www.onsale.com 90

Figure 17: Product page (continued) with the current high bidders. Source: http://www.onsale.com 91

Figure 18:   Types and directions of auction messages, following (Reck 1997, Figure 1). 92

Figure 19:   Agents' strategies in Kasbah, following (Moukas, Guttman et al. 1998, Figure 1). 97

Figure 20:   The creation of BOV and FSV related standards. Source: (ISO/IEC 1997, Figure 2)....................................... 101

Figure 21:   Documentary Petri Nets for the exchange of a purchase order and purchase order acknowledgement between buyer and seller.Source: (Lee 1999, p. 4)....................................... 103

Figure 22:   Integration scenario "purchasing ordering process". Source: (OAG 1998, Section 2, p. 12)..................................... 105

Figure 23:   Structure of a business object document. Source: (OAG 1998, p. 2-2) 105

Figure 24:   Trading roles in OTP. Source: (OTP-Consortium 1998, p. 2, Figure 1) 108

Figure 25:   Structure of an OTP purchase transaction. 109

Figure 26:   Structure of an OTP message. Source: (OTP-Consortium 1998, p. 13)....................................... 110

Figure 27:   OBI system entities and (simplified) information flows, following (OBI-Consortium 1999, p. 10, Figure 2-2). 112

Figure 28:   Overview of selected EDI standards, following (Neuburger 1994, p. 22, Figure 5). 116

Figure 29:   The use of EDI standards in Germany. Source: (Westarp, Weitzel et al. 1999, Figure 1) 117

Figure 30:   The use of EDI standards in the U.S. Source: (Westarp, Weitzel et al. 1999, Figure 2) 118

Figure 31:   Hierarchy of an EDIFACT document exchange from interchange level to data element level. Source: (Berge 1989, p. 71, Figure 5.6) 121

Figure 32:   EDIFACT enveloping structure, following (Emmelhainz 1993, p. 71, Figure 5-2). 122

Figure 33:   Purchase order segment table. Source: (Emmelhainz 1993, p. 73, Figure 5-4) 123

Figure 34:   Simplified LIN segment directory, following (Emmelhainz 1993, p. 74, Table 5-1). 124

Figure 35:   Line item segment with explanation of the data elements, following (Emmelhainz 1993, p. 76)........................... 125

Figure 36:   Product attributes affect forms of organization. Source: (Malone, Yates et al. 1987, p. 487, Figure 1).................. 144

Figure 37:   Matrix of prospective decision results in a risky situation. Source: (Laux 1995, p. 32)... 151

Figure 38: PDF and CDF of a lognormally distributed random variable........ 156

Figure 39: Plots of PDFs in dependence on the parameters μ_p (plot on the left, given σ_p and $\mu_1<\mu_2<\mu_3$) and σ_p (plot on the right, given μ_p and $\sigma_1<\sigma_2<\sigma_3$). 157

Figure 40: Plots of CDFs in dependence on the parameters μ_p (plot on the left, given σ_p and $\mu_1<\mu_2<\mu_3$) and σ_p (plot on the right, given μ_p and $\sigma_1<\sigma_2<\sigma_3$). 157

Figure 41: Graphic representation of the indifference condition. 159

Figure 42: Reservation value as a function of the marginal evaluation costs. 165

Figure 43: Reservation value as a function of the transaction volume. 166

Figure 44: CDFs with different standard deviations of supplier prices and the determination of the reservation value. 168

Figure 45: Moving the PDF and CDF of the lognormally distributed variable p to the right. 169

Figure 46: CDFs when changing the mean price from μ_p to μ_p', holding the standard deviation constant. 170

Figure 47: Reservation value as a function of the mean price. 171

Figure 48: Cost curves and point of indifference. 175

Figure 49: Indifference price as a function of the marginal evaluation costs (left) and in dependence on the complexity of the good/transaction (right). 177

Figure 50: Indifference price as a function of the adaptation costs (left) and in dependence on the complexity of the good/transaction (right). 177

Figure 51: Surface graphics of the indifference price as a function of the adaptation costs and the marginal evaluation costs (left) and contour plot of the indifference price (right). 178

Figure 52: Indifference price as a function of the transaction volume. 180

Figure 53: Surface graphics of the indifference price as a function of the marginal evaluation costs and the transaction volume (left) and contour plot of the indifference price (right). 182

Figure 54: Surface graphics of the indifference price as a function of the initialization costs and the transaction volume (left) and contour plot of the indifference price (right). 183

Figure 55: Paths of development of C_{change} and C_{keep} in scenario 1 188

Figure 56: Paths of development of C_{change} and C_{keep} in scenario 2 189

Figure 57: Marginal evaluation costs as a function of time. 192

Figure 58: Point in time of minimum reservation value as a function of g (left) and T (right). 194

264

Figure 59: Contracting sequence when marginal evaluation costs decrease
over time.. 195

Figure 60: General case of an s-shaped diffusion curve.
Source: (Mahajan and Peterson 1985, Figure 2.2, p.19) 207

Figure 61: System of diffusion curves of information technology i for
varying b_i. 208

Figure 62: Reservation value and expected supplier prices as functions of
time... 210

Figure 63: Point in time of minimum reservation value as a function of T. ... 212

Figure 64: Point in time of minimum reservation value as a function of
$\alpha_{i,0}$.. 212

Figure 65: Point in time of minimum reservation value as a function of b_i. ... 213

Figure 66: The impact of decreasing marginal evaluation costs,
initialization costs, and increasing frequency on the stability of
supplier relationships and expected contract duration.................. 215

Figure 67: Stability of supplier relationship and expected contract duration
as a function of T. 215

Figure 68: Stability of supplier relationship and expected contract duration
as a function of $\alpha_{i,0}$ and T where $T<T'$.. 216

Figure 69: Stability of supplier relationship and expected contract duration
as a function of b_i where $T<T'$. 217

Figure 70: Reservation value and expected supplier prices as functions of
time... 218

Figure 71: Graphic determination of the critical values y_1^* and ime_1^*. 222

Figure 72: Critical implementation costs of information technology 1 as a
function of the diffusion (left) and the marginal evaluation
costs of information technology 0 (right). 223

Figure 73: Critical diffusion of information technology 1 as a function of
the diffusion of information technology 0. 224

Figure 74: Critical marginal evaluation costs of information technology 1
as a function of the marginal evaluation costs of information
technology 0. 225

Figure 75: Graphic representation of the market shares of information
technology 0 (A) and 1 (B). 226

9 List of Tables

Table 1: Practical examples of classical, neoclassical, and relational contracts. 24

Table 2: Synopsis of transaction determinants and their influence on transaction costs. 54

Table 3: Relative costs of markets and hierarchies, following (Malone, Yates et al. 1987, p. 485, Table I). 143

Table 4: Transaction determinants, respective model parameters, and analysis results. 185

Table 5: Determining the stability of a supplier relationship and contract duration by values of T, t^*, and $p_{i,j}{}^*(t=0)$-$p_{i,j}{}^*(t=t^*)$. 214

10 List of Used Symbols

Symbols used in chapter 2

A	Combination of the utilities of two parties in a two-person bargaining game.
B	Combination of the utilities of two parties in a two-person bargaining game.
c	Marginal evaluation costs in the basic model of search theory.
C	Production costs (in the section on transaction cost theory); combination of the utilities of two parties in a two-person bargaining game (in the section on negotiations).
C_a	Average production costs.
c_f	Fixed costs.
c_v	Variable costs.
E	Expected price resulting from search.
F	Cumulative distribution function.
m	Lower bound of the price of the product sought in the determination of the optimal sample size.
N	Number of search steps before search is stopped.
N^*	Optimal sample size.
p	Observation of the random variable P.
P	Random variable of the product price.
p^*	Reservation value of the optimal search strategy when product prices are sought.
p_1^*	Reservation value of the optimal search strategy in a multi-stage search process.
p_2^*	Reservation value of the optimal search strategy in a multi-stage search process.

u	Upper bound of the price of the product sought in the determination of the optimal sample size.
x	Observation of the random variable X (in the section on search theory); number of produced goods (in the section on transaction cost theory).
X	Random variable of the product attribute.
x^*	Reservation value of the optimal search strategy.

Symbols used in chapter 3

p_i	Price charged for the consumption of good i.
r	Basic willingness to pay.
v	Externality function.
y_i^e	Installed base.

Symbols used in chapter 4

ad	Adaptation costs.
α_i	Dissemination of information technology i.
α_i^*	Critical dissemination of information technology i.
$\alpha_{i,0}$	Initial diffusion of information technology i.
$\alpha_{i,0,0}$	Value of $\alpha_{i,0}$ for which t^* evaluates to zero.
A_a	Alternative of action a.
AC	Expected acquisition costs.
$AC_{i,j}$	Expected acquisition costs when using information technology i for the support of the evaluation phase and information technology j for the support of the settlement phase of a supplier relationship.
b	Point of intersection of C_{keep} and the axis of ordinates (in the section on outsourcing decisions); index of imitation in the internal-influence diffusion model (in the section on the diffusion of technology).
b_c	Intersection of the costs of changing transaction partner and the axis of ordinates.
b_i	Index of imitation of the diffusion curve of information technology i.
$b_{i,0}$	Value of b_i for which t^* evaluates to zero.
b_j	Index of imitation of the diffusion curve of information technology j.
b_k	Intersection of the costs of keeping transaction partner and the axis of ordinates.

b_{max}	Value of b_i for which t^* reaches a maximum.
β_j	Dissemination of information technology j.
$\beta_{j,0}$	Initial diffusion of information technology j.
$\beta_{j,0,0}$	Value of $\beta_{j,0}$ for which t^* evaluates to zero.
c	Marginal evaluation costs in the basic model of decisions about supplier relationships.
c_0	Starting value for the marginal evaluation costs when the marginal evaluation costs are a function of time.
c_i	Marginal evaluation costs when using information technology i.
c_i^*	Critical marginal evaluation costs when using information technology i.
C_{change}	Total cost of a supplier relationship when changing transaction partner.
$C_{change,i,j}$	Total cost of a supplier relationship when changing transaction partner using information technology i for the support of the evaluation phase and information technology j for the support of the settlement phase of a supplier relationship.
C_{keep}	Total cost of a supplier relationship when retaining transaction partner.
$C_{keep,i,j}$	Total cost of a supplier relationship when retaining transaction partner using information technology i for the support of the evaluation phase and information technology j for the support of the settlement phase of a supplier relationship.
ΔE_n	Additional return of search step n.
EC	Expected evaluation costs.
$EC_{i,j}$	Expected evaluation costs when using information technology i for the support of the evaluation phase and information technology j for the support of the settlement phase of a supplier relationship.
ex	Costs of exchanging goods.
f	Probability density function.
E	Expected price.
F	Cumulative distribution function.
fre	Frequency.
g	Rate of progress in information technology.
G	Cumulative distribution function.
I	Set of available information technology solutions which can be used to support the evaluation phase of a supplier relationship.
i	Element of I.

ime_i	Implementation costs of information technology i for the support of the evaluation phase of a supplier relationship.
ime_i^*	Critical implementation costs of information technology i.
ims_j	Implementation costs of information technology j for the support of the settlement phase of a supplier relationship.
in	Initialization costs.
in_j	Initialization costs when using information technology j.
J	Set of available information technology solutions which can be used to support the settlement phase of a supplier relationship.
j	Element of J.
l	Lower bound of the marginal evaluation costs.
μ_L	Parameter of a lognormal distribution.
μ_p	Mean value of P.
N_0	Cumulative number of adopters at time t_0.
$\overline{N}$	Total number of adopters of an innovation in a social system.
p	Observation of P.
P	Random variable of supplier prices.
p^*	Reservation price of the optimal search strategy when supplier prices are sought.
p_0	Current supplier price.
p_c	Expected acquisition price when supplier is changed.
p_F^*	Reservation value of the optimal search strategy when prices are distributed according to F.
p_G^*	Reservation value of the optimal search strategy when prices are distributed according to G.
$p_{i,j}^*$	Reservation price of the optimal search strategy when using information technology i for the support of the evaluation phase and information technology j for the support of the settlement phase of a supplier relationship.
p_n	Lowest price after n search steps.
p_k	Calculated price when retaining transaction partner.
p_k^*	Calculated price at which the decision-maker is indifferent concerning the alternatives of changing and keeping transaction partner.
$p(S_s)$	Probability of the occurrence of state s.
rad_j	Adaptation cost reductions when using information technology j.
r_{as}	Decision result of alternative a when state s occurs.

rex_j	Reduction of costs of exchanging goods when using information technology j.
rin_j	Reduction of initialization costs when using information technology j.
s_c	Gradient of the straight line which represents the costs of changing transaction partner.
s_k	Gradient of the straight line which represents the costs of keeping transaction partner.
S_s	State s of the environment.
SC	Settlement costs.
$SC_{i,j}$	Settlement costs when using information technology i for the support of the evaluation phase and information technology j for the support of the settlement phase of a supplier relationship.
σ_L	Dispersion parameter of a lognormal distribution.
σ_F	Standard deviation of F.
σ_G	Standard deviation of G.
σ_p	Standard deviation of supplier prices.
t	Point in time.
t_0	Initial point in time.
T	Final point in time at which a product is purchased.
T_0	Value of T for which t^* evaluates to zero.
$\vec{v}$	Vector of changes in the marginal evaluation costs and transaction volume.
vol	Transaction volume.
vol_u	Upper bound of the transaction volume.
W	Product log function.
y	Unit marginal evaluation costs.
y_i	Marginal evaluation costs per dissemination of information technology i.

11 List of Abbreviations

ANSI	American National Standards Institute
API	Application Programming Interface
BOD	Business Object Document
BOV	Business Operational View
CDF	cumulative distribution function
CEFIC	Conseil Européen des Fédérations de l'Industrie Chemique
CORBA	Common Object Request Broker Architecture
DAKOSY	Datenkommunikationssystem
DPN	Documentary Petri Net
DPS	Desktop Purchasing System
DTAM	Document Transfer, Access and Manipulation-standard
EDI	Electronic Data Interchange
EDIFACT	Electronic Data Interchange for Administration, Commerce and Transport
EDIFICE	Electronic Data Interchange Forum for Companies with Interests in Computing and Electronics
ERP	Enterprise Resource Planning
EURIDIS	Erasmus University Research Institute for Decision and Information Systems
FSV	Functional Service View
HTML	Hypertext Markup Language
HTTP	Hypertext Transfer Protocol
IETF	Internet Engineering Task Force
IGES	Initial Graphics Exchange Specification
IOTP	Internet Open Trading Protocol
ISO	International Standards Organization

ISO/IEC	Organization for Standardization/International Electrotechnical Commission
ISO/OSI	International Standards Organization/Open System Interconnection
JTC1/SC30	Joint Technical Committee 1/Subcommittee 30
NSS	Negotiation Support System
OAG	Open Applications Group
OAGIS	Open Applications Group Integration Specifications
OBI	Open Buying on the Internet
ODA/ODIF	Office Document Architecture/ Office Document Interchange Format
ODETTE	Organization for Data Exchange by Teletransmission in Europe
OSD	Open Software Description
OTP	Open Trading Protocol
PCG	Procedure Constraint Grammar
PDF	probability density function
RINET	Reinsurance and Insurance Network
SEDAS	Standardregeln einheitlicher Datenaustauschsysteme
SET	Standard d'Exchange et de Transfert
STEP	Standard for the Exchange of Product Model Data
SWIFT	Society for Worldwide Interbank Financial Telecommunications
TCP/IP	Transport Control Protocol/Internet Protocol
TRADACOMS	Trade Data Communications Standard
UCC	Uniform Code Council
UPC	Universal Product Code
VAN	Value Added Network
VDA	Verband der Automobilindustrie
VDA-FS	Flächenschnittstelle des Verbands der Automobilindustrie
WAN	Wide Area Network
WIDL	Web Interface Definition Language
XML	Extensible Markup Language